VONNEGUT IN AMERICA

VONNEGUT IN AMERICA

an introduction to the life and work of Kurt Vonnegut

Original Essays Edited by
JEROME KLINKOWITZ *and*
DONALD L. LAWLER

DELACORTE PRESS/SEYMOUR LAWRENCE

Published by
Delacorte Press/Seymour Lawrence
1 Dag Hammarskjold Plaza
New York, New York 10017

"Kurt Vonnegut as an American Dissident" by Donald M. Fiene was developed from essays that have appeared in the *New York Times Book Review* and the *Russian Literature Triquarterly*.

Manufactured in the United States of America

First Delacorte printing

Designed by Leonard Telesca

Library of Congress Cataloging in Publication Data

Main entry under title:

Vonnegut in America.

The Vonnegut bibliography: p.
Includes index.
1. Vonnegut, Kurt—Criticism and interpretation—Addresses, essays, lectures. I. Klinkowitz, Jerome. II. Lawler, Donald L.
PS3572.05Z9 813'.5'4 77-9939

ISBN 0-440-09343-0

158-169

Contents

Acknowledgments ix

Preface xi

PART ONE:—VONNEGUT IN AMERICA

Kurt Vonnegut: A Chronology
JEROME KLINKOWITZ 3

Vonnegut in America
JEROME KLINKOWITZ 7

A Vonnegut Album
(*photographs between pages 37 and 48*) 37

PART TWO:—ASPECTS OF VONNEGUT

Vonnegut in Academe (I)
DONALD L. LAWLER 51
A Do-It-Yourself Story Collection by Kurt Vonnegut
JEROME KLINKOWITZ 53
The Sirens of Titan: Vonnegut's Metaphysical Shaggy-Dog Story
DONALD L. LAWLER 61
Kurt Vonnegut as Science-Fiction Writer
WILLIS E. MCNELLY 87
Technique as Recovery: *Lolita* and *Mother Night*
WILLIAM VEEDER 97
Vonnegut's Satire
CONRAD FESTA 133
The Later Vonnegut
PETER J. REED 150
Vonnegut in Academe (II)
DONALD L. LAWLER 187

PART THREE:—THE VONNEGUT BIBLIOGRAPHY

The Vonnegut Bibliography
JEROME KLINKOWITZ 217

APPENDIX:—VONNEGUT ABROAD

A Note on Vonnegut in Europe
JEROME KLINKOWITZ 255

Kurt Vonnegut as an American Dissident: His Popularity in the Soviet Union and His Affinities with Russian Literature
DONALD M. FIENE 258

Contributors 294

Index 297

Acknowledgments

All quotations from the works of Kurt Vonnegut are © 1952, 1959, 1961, 1963, 1965, 1968, 1969, 1970, 1971, 1973, 1974, 1976 Kurt Vonnegut, Jr., and are used with the permission of Mr. Vonnegut and his publisher, Delacorte Press/Seymour Lawrence. Page numbers, included parenthetically, refer to the standard editions of *Player Piano, The Sirens of Titan, Mother Night, Cat's Cradle,* and *God Bless You, Mr. Rosewater,* as published by Mr. Lawrence in 1971 (pagination in these volumes conforms to their first editions and to the Delta editions published by the Dell Publishing Co., Inc.); quotations from *Slaughterhouse-Five* and after come from the first editions published by Delacorte Press/Seymour Lawrence, which have been photographically reproduced as Delta editions.

The Vonnegut Bibliography which concludes this volume was enriched by contributions from Don Fiene (who researched material published in the Soviet Union), Asa Pieratt, and John Somer, and from the international community of Vonnegut scholars, which includes Andrew Mylett (England), André LeVot (France), Manfred Puetz (West Germany), Zoltán Abádi-Nagy (Hungary), and Jerzy Kutnik (Poland).

Julie Huffman and Elaine Klinkowitz organized the manuscript and supplied editorial help. Our universities offered support and encouragement for our project. We extend special thanks to Dr. Bernard Vonnegut, Loree Rackstraw, and Ms. Jill Krementz for supplying photographs. Mr. Kurt Vonnegut was especially generous in supplying historical and bibliographical information, and deserves our most sincere thanks.

—J.K.
—D.L.L.

Preface

Each generation of Americans seems to produce a writer whose voice is modulated in tones both unmistakably American and unmistakably appropriate to the times. One cannot really say that the writer defines the style of an era, any more than one can assert that an age determines the manner in which, say, a Twain or a Vonnegut speaks to his generation through his fiction. It is something Americans recognize as having an uncanny and unpredictable sense of fitness, like the bits of contemporary history reported each evening with the reassuring authority of Walter Cronkite's voice. Even when the news is bad, it is comforting to know that Cronkite will get it straight and make it both understandable and bearable, just because he talks about it. In the twenties and thirties, it was Gershwin's music, Hemingway's prose, and Norman Rockwell's graphics. Today, the personalities and styles have changed to serve the perceptions, express the values, and strike the accents of a new generation.

Vonnegut and America are two subjects which for the past decade can hardly be considered apart from each other. Few writers have risen to such stature as Vonnegut's without being very close to the life of their generation and their country, and for Kurt Vonnegut, there is a deep affinity with American life. His rise to popularity during the sixties was an event itself, taking its place alongside other milestones of popular history during those tumultuous times. Cultural historians already perceive those events as important episodes in the evolution of American culture. But Vonnegut's importance is something more than as the spokesman of a counterculture. It is more like the authentic idiom of a whole culture, with its contradictions, dissonances, and dreams as parts of the full orchestration. There has never been another writer quite like Vonnegut, just as there has never been another decade in America quite like the sixties. And yet, we can see even now that neither is unique, that each is already part of the continuous history and culture of modern times and thought. Nevertheless, it was with such novels as *Cat's Cradle* and *Slaughterhouse-Five* that contemporary culture came of age.

One purpose of this book is to show how Vonnegut's posture as a writer seems to grow out of his realization of the possibilities of our common American culture with its disparate energies and its eclectic forms. Through his novels, stories, and even his essays (as collected in *Wampeters, Foma & Granfalloons*), we see that Vonnegut has constructed his own personal mythology for dealing with the world. But unlike other modern writers whose system of values derives from an esoteric mix of philosophies and psychologies, Vonnegut never lets us forget that he is a familiar type, indigenous to our culture. He is a middle-class American, content with himself to remain so, given to practical jokes and even, occasionally, to crying in his beer. He has steadfastly refused to become an aloof, alienated intellectual. He is the fellow we are more likely to meet at the hardware store on Saturday morning than at the University Club on Friday afternoon. The materials of Vonnegut's vision are as common as his Indiana childhood, his fraternity days at Cornell, his experiences as a soldier in World War II, his job as a PR man for a large corporation, and finally as a writer hacking out stories for the *Saturday Evening Post*—earning, he once reported, "about as much as the manager of a junior high school cafeteria." When Vonnegut was brought to prominence in the sixties by a wave of young people disaffected with the older generation, the image they were really celebrating in Vonnegut was that of their own fathers (with tie off and collar unbuttoned), whom they had chosen to reject in real life for other reasons.

Vonnegut's rise to fame is one of the themes of this book. It happened mainly in the colleges and universities of America. But, unlike earlier student fads, this special excitement over the appearance of a new writer was shared by many of their instructors and professors as well. Faulkner, Fitzgerald, and even Hemingway had to wait until their declining years to receive serious academic study, but Vonnegut has been given careful and considered attention during the years of his ascendancy and greatest activity. Perhaps because of this balanced assessment, his reputation has been stabilized. While other student causes have been lost or abandoned, Vonnegut remains a major contributor to our national culture.

The chapters forming the second part of this book were written for what has become a recurrent seminar of the Modern Language Association of America on the work of Kurt

Vonnegut. The 1975 meeting, held in San Francisco, was chaired by Donald Lawler of East Carolina University, who assembled as panelists Jerome Klinkowitz of the University of Northern Iowa, Willis McNelly of California State University at Fullerton, William Veeder of the University of Chicago, Conrad Festa of Old Dominion University, and Peter Reed of the University of Minnesota. Each panelist prepared a paper on an aspect of Vonnegut's achievement as a writer. The aim was to produce a body of critical opinion in which Vonnegut's work would be seen in a contemporary critical perspective. The panelists represented different regions of the country and have different critical interests in Vonnegut's fiction. They range from a science-fiction specialist to scholars of Victorian literature. Taken as a whole, their work represents a current sampling of the academic response which Vonnegut's work has evoked from those critics and scholars whose job it is to teach his books. Not everyone who reads Vonnegut or even teaches him is convinced of his worth or durability as a writer. Their views will also become a part of the ongoing dialogue which will lead eventually to some kind of consensus about where Vonnegut will take his place, once the literary history of these times has achieved the status of received opinion.

In the meantime, the editors hope that this book will serve to place Vonnegut in relation to his times and to the culture from which he has arisen and which he has been instrumental in shaping. We believe that the materials collected here will help establish the context of a more serious but, we hope, not necessarily more solemn dialogue on Vonnegut, the American writer of the sixties and seventies. In the repeated echoes of his famous tag lines, each a carefully selected cliché, in the irreverent humor of his characters, in the implausible plots, and in the personal involvement of the author in his fictive world (felt as a distorted but recognizable image of our common experience), we catch glimpses of a moralist whose sympathy with human suffering, even with human folly, seems genuine. We can take it to the bank. Vonnegut is the compassionate satirist who does not have to make us seem worse than we are to make us laugh at ourselves, and who, understanding us, reminds us that the proper study of mankind is still man. Vonnegut seems to be there in his fiction with a tolerant and reassuring irony to tell us that it is somehow all right, that humanity remains most worth caring about. No matter how evil, stupid, or inept we become as a culture or as a people, Vonnegut is there in his fiction reminding us not to give up on the human race. He is forever prompting us to recall that common humanity, a sense of decency, and good manners are the basis of civilized behavior, and civilized behavior is within almost everybody's capabilities. At heart, therefore, to see Vonnegut as a humanist as well as a humorist is to see him in true relation to his times and his culture.

PART 1

VONNEGUT IN AMERICA

Jerome Klinkowitz

Kurt Vonnegut: A Chronology

1922 Born November 11, 1922, in Indianapolis, Indiana, son of Kurt, Sr., and Edith Lieber Vonnegut. Older siblings: Bernard and Alice.

1936–1940 Student at Shortridge High School, Indianapolis, where during his junior and senior years he was one of the editors of its daily paper, the *Echo*.

1940–1943 Student at Cornell University, Ithaca, New York, majoring in chemistry and biology. Managing editor and columnist for its daily paper, the *Sun*.

1943 Enlisted in the United States Army; sent to Carnegie Institute of Technology and the University of Tennessee to study mechanical engineering.

1944 Death of his mother, May 14, 1944. Interned as a prisoner of war in Dresden, Germany, after his capture by the Germans at the Battle of the Bulge, December 22, 1944.

1945 Experienced the Allied firebombing of Dresden, February 13, 1945; repatriated May 22, 1945. Marriage to Jane Marie Cox, September 1, 1945. Moved to Chicago, Illinois, in December.

1946–1947 Worked for Chicago City News Bureau. Graduate student in anthropology, University of Chicago.

1947 Moved to Schenectady, New York, where he worked as a publicist for the General Electric Corporation and its Research Laboratory.

1950 Published his first story, "Report on the Barnhouse Effect," in *Collier's* magazine, February 11, 1950.

1951 Quit his job at General Electric and moved with his family to Provincetown, Massachusetts (later to West Barnstable, Massachusetts), to write full time.

1952 His first novel, *Player Piano*, published by Charles Scribner's Sons (New York).

1953 *Player Piano* published by Macmillan in London and issued as a Science Fiction Book Club selection by Doubleday.

1954 First paperback publication: *Utopia-14* (Bantam, New York), a retitled edition of *Player Piano*.

1954–1956 Taught English at the Hopefield School (for emotionally disturbed children) on Cape Cod; worked for an industrial advertising agency; began his own automobile-sales agency.

1957 Death of his father, October 1, 1957.

1958–1959 Death of his sister and brother-in-law; adopted their three oldest children.

1959 *The Sirens of Titan* published as a paperback original.

1961 *Canary in a Cat House*, a collection of short stories, published as a paperback original. *Sirens* reissued in hardcover.

1962 *Mother Night* published as a paperback original.

1963 *Cat's Cradle* published as a hardcover original.

1965 *God Bless You, Mr. Rosewater* published as a hardcover original. First reviews and personal journalism for large-circulation magazines. Began two-year residency at the University of Iowa Writers Workshop.

1966–1967 Hardcover reissue of *Player Piano* and *Mother Night;* paperback reissue of these and his other novels.

1967 Offer of a three-book contract from Delacorte Press/Seymour Lawrence, who later reprinted all of his works in hardcover. Guggenheim Fellowship, including travel to Dresden, East Germany.

1968 *Welcome to the Monkey House* published by Delacorte Press/Seymour Lawrence.

1969 *Slaughterhouse-Five* published by Delacorte Press/Seymour Lawrence.

1970 Taught creative writing at Harvard University. Wrote *Happy Birthday, Wanda June* for the Broadway stage (and later for the cinema). Visited Biafra as it fell to Nigerian army.

1971 Awarded a Master's degree in anthropology by the University of Chicago after their decision that *Cat's Cradle* could serve as a thesis. Moved, alone, to New York City.

1972 *Between Time and Timbuktu* produced as a television special by National Educational Television, and as a book by Delacorte Press/Seymour Lawrence. His son Mark suffered a schizophrenic breakdown, which later supplied the basis for a book, *The Eden Express. Slaughterhouse-Five* produced as a film. Elected vice-president of the P.E.N. American Center. Elected to membership in the National Institute of Arts and Letters.

1973 *Breakfast of Champions* published in a first edition of 100,000 copies by Delacorte Press/Seymour Lawrence. Appointed Distinguished Professor of English Prose by the

City University of New York, replacing Anthony Burgess.

1974 *Wampeters, Foma & Granfalloons* published by Delacorte Press/Seymour Lawrence.

1976 *Slapstick; Or, Lonesome No More* published in a first edition of 150,000 copies by Delacorte Press/Seymour Lawrence.

1977 Birth of a first grandchild, Zachary (Mark's son).

Jerome Klinkowitz

Vonnegut in America

Two constant threads run through the writing of Kurt Vonnegut. The first is Vonnegut himself, and second is the America he has lived in. He did not achieve recognition until the late 1960s, when both his writing style and the style of American life were bordering on the extreme; but for the most part, his thinking grew out of the solid, middle-class heritage most of his countrymen share. In both his fiction and his journalistic writing, Vonnegut found a way of taking events—even the fantasies of science fiction and the calamities of our recent national history—and measuring them against the mundane, stable facts of his own American life. His happy childhood in a large family in the Midwest, his study of science in college, his fraternity life, his service in World War II, his study under the GI Bill after the war, his public-relations work for a giant corporation, and his own large and growing family—these experiences, which can easily be duplicated in the lives of perhaps a million American men his age, have been fashioned by Kurt Vonnegut into a personal mythology by which he judges the world. Because its sources are so common, it becomes a mythology for America itself, which is the principal reason why Vonnegut is so popular.

Vonnegut grew up during the Great Depression, an experience which shaped both his life and his fictional style. When he was still young enough to modify his notions of reality, young Kurt saw his entire world transformed. His father, who was a second-generation architect, went ten years without a commission, because of the depressed conditions in the building trades. His mother, who had grown up in the comfortable wealth of the Lieber brewing fortune, was subjected to the humiliation of selling her family crystal and china. The Vonnegut family moved from their beautiful Illinois Street home in Indianapolis to a modest house two blocks away, while they gathered resources to build a more economical home in the suburb of Williams Creek. Twenty years later, when his father died, Vonnegut turned to the Depression in an unfinished novel titled *Upstairs and Downstairs*. Its plot centers on the economic hardships of the narrator's family, which force them to rent the upstairs of their home to an eccentric businessman named Fred Barry (who would appear many years later in *Breakfast of Champions*). One of Fred's quirks is to give the young narrator a wallet with six hundred dollars, "And in those days you could have bought the moon for six hundred dollars. That was in nineteen thirty-six." Fred makes him keep the money "for a whole day, just to see what having that much money felt like." Money, of course, can transform one's world, just as the lack of it had changed the boy's world in this story. How money, or other things, can absolutely change one's idea of reality was a theme that Vonnegut would explore in every one of his novels from *Player Piano* through *Slapstick*.

The Depression also served to move Vonnegut out of Indianapolis, to begin the migration that would eventually carry him far from his Indiana roots. "My father told me that I was absolutely not to become the third-generation architect in Indianapolis with the name Vonnegut."[1] Instead, the young man was told to study something useful. With his older brother, Bernard, well on his way to a brilliant career in atmospheric physics, Kurt chose to study chemistry at Cornell University. In 1940 he left Indianapolis, never to live there again.

But from his Indiana years Vonnegut took two precious gifts: the ideals of his parents and his family, and the humor of the radio and film comedians of the Depression era, which helped him through each day when economic hardships threatened their happy family life. "When people ask me who my culture heroes are," Vonnegut wrote in the preface to *Between Time and Timbuktu*, "I express pious gratitude for Mark Twain and James Joyce and so on. But the truth is that I am a barbarian, whose deepest cultural debts are to Laurel and Hardy, Stoopnagel and Bud, Buster Keaton, Fred Allen, Jack Benny, Charlie Chaplin, Easy Aces, Henry Morgan, and so on. They made me hilarious during the Great Depression, and all the lesser depressions after that" (page xvii). His novel *Breakfast of Champions* is dedicated to "Phoebe Hurty, who comforted me in Indianapolis—during the Great Depression"; Mrs. Hurty, a forty-year-old widow, was the inspiration for Vonnegut's bawdiness and lack of respect for sacred cows of our culture, an attitude which she believed would shape a new American prosperity and which Vonnegut uses as the stylistic base for his self-created world.

Although the firebombing of Dresden is usually considered

the most traumatic event in Vonnegut's life, both as a writer and as a person, he himself describes the Depression as "a very bad time in the history of the country, far more unbearable than the First or Second World Wars, I think." In his conversation with Robert Scholes, reprinted in *The Vonnegut Statement*, Vonnegut argues that "The Depression did break people's spirits. And from the comedians—there was one each day, at least, as Fred Allen, Jack Benny, and so forth, you got your little dose of humor every day, and the people did cluster around radios to pick up an amount of encouragement, an amount of relief." During their interview, which was broadcast on the University of Iowa's educational station, Vonnegut and Scholes became radio comedians themselves, exchanging favorite jokes from the period. Vonnegut chose one by Henry Morgan, who followed Benny and Allen each Sunday night: "You know that cat that inherited five million dollars last year? Well, he died. Left his money to another cat."[2] In the foreword to a collection of Bob and Ray's radio scripts, Vonnegut cites the affinity of their work with the comedians of the Depression:

> They aren't like most other comedians' jokes these days, aren't rooted in show business and the world of celebrities and news of the day. They feature Americans who are almost always fourth-rate or below, engaged in enterprises which, if not contemptible, are at least insane.
>
> And while other comedians show us persons tormented by bad luck and enemies and so on, Bob and Ray's characters threaten to wreck themselves and their surroundings with their own stupidity. There is a refreshing and beautiful innocence in Bob's and Ray's humor.
>
> Man is not evil, they seem to say. He is simply too hilariously stupid to survive.
>
> And this I believe.[3]

Vonnegut's own novel *Slapstick*, which the author describes as an autobiography and which contains a compendium of his personal beliefs, is dedicated to the film comedians Laurel and Hardy. His life, Vonnegut says, "is grotesque, situational poetry—like the slapstick film comedies, especially those of Laurel and Hardy, of long ago." This is what life feels like to him, Vonnegut insists, with all its "tests of my limited agility and intelligence. They go on and on." What Vonnegut admires in Laurel and Hardy is "that they did their best with every test. They never failed to bargain in good faith with their destinies, and were screamingly adorable and funny on that account" (page 1).

The great popular comedians of the American 1930s gave Vonnegut the basis for his artistic style, and his central beliefs can be seen as coming from an equally humble source: the lessons of his parents and schoolteachers from the same period. He disagreed with a *Playboy* interviewer (who thought he was a radical), claiming that "Everything I believe I was taught in junior civics during the Great Depression—at School 43 in Indianapolis, with full approval of the school board."[4] As for his seemingly contemporary antiwar notions, Vonnegut recalls that "My generation was a pacifistic one. We had contempt for large standing armies. We were glad that the military man never held a high job. The soldiers were like Indians: They stayed on the reservations. The poems of the class of 1940 were pacifistic."[5] When Wilfrid Sheed asked him where he got his youth-minded notions, he replied, "I got them from my parents. I thought about it and decided they were right."[6] More specifically, "My parents were gentle, cultivated people—pacifists who taught me an irreverence toward all sacred cows."[7]

According to his father's wishes, Vonnegut left for Cornell University to study chemistry and biology, in the hope of becoming either a biochemist or a chemical engineer. But he soon found an extracurricular interest: writing for the Cornell *Sun*, a student-owned daily which competed professionally with the other Ithaca newspapers. During his high-school days Vonnegut had written for the Shortridge *Echo*, the only high-school daily of its time; by his junior and senior years he had become the Tuesday-edition editor, getting regular experience writing for an audience he would have to face later that day. At Cornell Vonnegut became managing editor of the *Sun* and wrote a regular column. Among the usual collegiate concerns for fraternity pranks Vonnegut interjected serious editorials against American participation in World War II, a stand which led his fellow editors to publish disclaimers from Vonnegut's views. But by January 1943, Vonnegut had decided to enlist. At first he was turned down, because of an unnoticed case of viral pneumonia and later because the aftermath of the sickness was diagnosed as tuberculosis. But in March he was accepted. Mrs. Vonnegut was distressed by her son's participation in a war she abhorred, and her health began to fail. She died in May 1944, when her son was home on leave.

The Army sent Vonnegut back to school—Carnegie Institute of Technology and the University of Tennessee—where he studied mechanical engineering for eighteen months. But on November 10, 1944, when he arrived in England with the 106th Infantry Division, Vonnegut was assigned as an advance infantry scout. In early December, the Green Division landed at Le Havre to replace the 2nd Division, which had suffered heavy losses in its six-month drive from the Normandy beaches. There was at first no hostile action—the 106th merely took over the 2nd's emplacements. But with the Battle of the Bulge, Vonnegut's outfit—2nd Battalion, 423rd Regiment—was shattered, and he wandered between the lines for several days until December 22, when he was captured by the Germans. Private Vonnegut was sent as conscript labor to Dresden, Germany, an artistic treasure and an open city with no large war industries, where he worked in a factory that produced vitamin-enriched malt syrup for pregnant women. Because he was quartered with other American prisoners several stories below ground in a meat locker, Vonnegut was one of a very small group that survived the Allied firebombing of Dresden on the night of February 13, 1945. American and British warplanes used modern science and technology to create a literal firestorm, conceived as an act of terror to break the German spirit. It incinerated the architectural treasures of Dresden ("A terrible thing for the son of an architect to see," Vonnegut recalls) and slaughtered 135,000 civilian inhabitants—the largest massacre in European history, twice the number of casualties at Hiroshima. Vonnegut and his fellow prisoners were drafted as corpse-miners, taking the dead Germans from their shelters and stacking them in funeral pyres across the ravaged city. His final experiences in the war came in May, when, after the general surrender, his guards simply disappeared. Vonnegut again wandered between lines for several days, until he was repatriated by the Russians on May 22.

Kurt Vonnegut married his childhood sweetheart, Jane Cox, in September of 1945, and began work on a Master's degree in anthropology at the University of Chicago. Years later he said: "A first-grader should understand that his culture isn't a rational invention; that there are thousands of other cultures and they all work pretty well; that all cultures function on faith rather than truth; that there are lots of alternatives to our own society. I didn't find that out for sure until I was in the graduate school of the University of Chicago. It was terribly exciting."[8] Vonnegut took well to anthropological study, but his plans for a thesis were rejected, perhaps because they were too artistically conceived. He first hoped to study exactly what it took to form a revolutionary group; his two samples were the Cubist painters in France and the Ghost Dance movement among American Plains Indians of the 1890s. Vonnegut's faculty committee rejected this thesis, as they did his next, which he submitted years later: "Fluctuations Between Good and Evil in Simple Tales." This study took Russian folktales, Kentucky mountain ballads, and stories from a wide variety of magazines and demonstrated that each had a definite and identifiable structure. Although his work was rejected, it provided Vonnegut with a firm understanding of popular-magazine formulas, which in coming years he would exploit as a regular contributor to *Collier's*, *Cosmopolitan*, the *Saturday Evening Post*, and other family journals of the period.

Vonnegut left Chicago without his Master's degree. Because he had never taken a Bachelor's degree at Cornell or during his Army training, he had nothing but a high-school diploma to qualify him for work in the tight postwar economy. While studying in Chicago he had spent some time as a cub reporter for the Chicago News Bureau, a pool which supplied the basic local stories to all four newspapers. For twenty-eight dollars a week, Vonnegut filed stories of robberies, assaults, fires, accidents, and other middle-class tragedies. He recalls one in the opening pages of *Slaughterhouse-Five:*

> It was about a young veteran who had taken a job running an old-fashioned elevator in an office building. The elevator door on the first floor was ornamental iron lace. Iron ivy snaked in and out of the holes. There was an iron twig with two iron lovebirds perched upon it.
>
> This veteran decided to take his car into the basement, and he closed the door and started down, but his wedding ring was caught in all the ornaments. So he was hoisted into the air

and the floor of the car went down, dropped out from under him, and the top of the car squashed him. So it goes.

So I phoned this in, and the woman who was going to [write the story] asked me, "What did his wife say?"

"She doesn't know yet," I said. "It just happened."

"Call her up and get a statement."

"What?"

"Tell her you're Captain Finn of the Police Department. Say you have some sad news. Give her the news, and see what she says."

So I did. She said about what you would expect her to say. There was a baby. And so on. [page 8]

In 1947 Vonnegut moved to a better job, less concerned with the traumas of life, which offered him a better chance to build himself a family membership in the American middle class. For ninety-two dollars a week, he wrote public-relations copy for the Research Laboratory at the General Electric Corporation in Schenectady, where his brother, Bernard, was at work in atmospheric physics. Here Vonnegut complemented his knowledge of science with first-hand experiences among the G.E. researchers. During the day he would study their innovations, seeking ways to place double-page photo spreads of this work in *Life* magazine. Evenings he and Jane would socialize with the scientists and their wives. But again Vonnegut's disposition was to be artistic, and what he absorbed from General Electric, day and evening, was fashioned into his first finished novel, *Player Piano.* Although set in the future, following a Third World War, Vonnegut was in fact writing a novel about his current life, "about things I could not avoid seeing and hearing in Schenectady, a very real town, awkwardly set in the gruesome now."[9] His subject was not only the implications of advancing technology for human life, but also the ways and means by which a giant corporation controls its employees. Both worked against the meaning of simple human worth—a value which Vonnegut identified from his own experiences in American middle-class life. During the late 1940s he was also writing short stories that extolled the virtues of plain, simple Americans when tested against the pretenses of progress, wealth, and power. However, his own public-relations department had written the slogan "At General Electric, Progress Is Our Most Important Product," and so Schenectady became an uncomfortable home for the writer of such fiction. In 1951, with his novel accepted by Scribner's and half a dozen stories sold to *Collier's* and the *Post*, Kurt Vonnegut quit his job at G.E. and set out on his professional writing career.

The first story, "Report on the Barnhouse Effect," had been sold to *Collier's* for $750—a lot for a worker earning only $92 a week, but hardly enough to support a growing family. With one rejected story came a note from *Collier's* editor Knox Burger, asking "Are you the Vonnegut who was at Cornell?" Burger soon became a friend, directing the fledgling writer to the literary agency of Kenneth Littauer and Max Wilkinson, where Vonnegut learned how to earn the most from the magazine market. Littauer, a colonel from the World War I Lafayette Escadrille, was a colorful figure; Vonnegut recalls him as "the first man to strafe a trench from an airplane." As a working literary agent, Littauer knew that the most important element for the weekly magazines was that of *story*. "Colonel Littauer was the man who taught me how to tell a story," Vonnegut insists today, although Littauer was in fact tapping a strength reaching back to Vonnegut's childhood. "As a boy," Vonnegut recounted shortly after the publication of *Breakfast of Champions*, "I read an awful lot of Robert Louis Stevenson and was excited by stories which were well-made. Real 'story' stories . . . with a beginning, middle, and end. Because of the early admiration for him I still try to be a storyteller, to tell a story with some shape to it."[10] Vonnegut's method throughout the 1950s was to search out stories, hunting for subjects "the way a cartoonist would make up cartoons"[11] for the same magazines, and then give them the shape necessary for a sale to *Collier's* or the *Post*. His field of experience was the middle-class life he was leading on Cape Cod: raising his family, repairing his house, socializing with neighbors, and taking up such occasional odd jobs as writing ad copy and selling the first Saab automobiles in the area. Before long, Vonnegut had found the necessary formula for shaping these experiences into saleable fiction; in the mid-'50s his stories for the *Post* earned upward of $2,700 apiece, and as a *Post* and *Collier's* regular he could count on a modest but dependable income, about what one would make "being in charge of a cafeteria at a pretty good junior high school."[12]

Many of these stories, later collected in *Canary in a Cat House* and *Welcome to the Monkey House*, featured small business and tradesmen from New England, a group to which Vonnegut believed he himself belonged. "My career grew just the way a well-managed business is supposed to grow," he recalled for a *Playboy* interviewer in 1973. "After 20 years at a greasy grind, I find that all my books are in print and selling steadily. They will go on selling for a little while."[13] But all these years Vonnegut was living a special variety of middle-class life—living it, and also studying it artistically. Most of his jokes in such novels as *The Sirens of Titan* and *Mother Night* are plays on middle-class manners, or the inserting of common bourgeois reactions into the absurdities of Nazi Germany or outer-space technology. A comment from a session with students at the University of Iowa reveals how he was shaping his life, too, according to his particular brand of humorous pessimism:

> When I became a writer, I quit General Electric, had a family, and moved to Cape Cod, which was an alarming thing to do. It frightened me so much about what might happen to my family that I bought a perfect bruiser of a life insurance policy. Every nickel I made went into this until it was obvious I could make a hell of a lot of money by merely dying. I became obsessed with this idea. I talked to a scientist I knew about life insurance (you should have some scientists among your friends—they think straight); this guy (his name is Dr. John Fisher) was a well-known metallurgist (and his wife's name is Josephine). I said, "John, how much life insurance have you got?" He said, "None." And I said, "What, you don't have *any* insurance?" and he said, "Hell, no, what do I care what happens to Jo after I'm dead? I won't feel anything." It was release. I let my policy lapse.[14]

Selling stories to *Collier's* and the *Post*, and even occasionally to *Argosy*, *Redbook*, and the *Ladies' Home Journal*, provided Vonnegut and his family with an income during the 1950s. There were problems now and then, such as periods when nothing would sell or the year-long writer's block Vonnegut suffered when his father died in 1957, but the author chose to view them as occupational hazards. At other times several stories would sell simultaneously, and the Vonneguts would seemingly be deluged with money. All in all, it was an exaggerated version of the lives most Americans were leading at the time: buying homes with expansion attics, adding rooms for more and more children, and dreaming the American dream, which according to the magazines Vonnegut wrote for consisted of a Buick Roadmaster and an all-electric home.

But by the end of the decade Kurt Vonnegut's business was in trouble. Other small-business men suffered during the financial recessions of 1957 and 1959, but Vonnegut faced a catastrophe when the weekly family magazines began to go out of business. Even before the death of *Collier's* and the monumental collapse of the *Saturday Evening Post*, the economic shake-ups in these publishing corporations cost Vonnegut the editorial contacts he had so carefully established when he left G.E. Stories that might be rejected by the better-paying markets were now submitted to the science-fiction journals; Littauer and Wilkinson found a home for Vonnegut stories in such far-ranging magazines as *Venture: Traveller's World* and *Worlds of If*.

Vonnegut's own enterprising nature opened up a new field: paperback originals. By the decade's end he had not written a novel for seven years, and he might have stayed with short fiction entirely had not circumstances destroyed his market. These same circumstances took his friend Knox Burger into paperback publishing, where he was able to find Vonnegut a contract. As Vonnegut described it for Richard Todd in the *New York Times Magazine*, Knox Burger met Vonnegut at a party and asked him if he had any ideas for a novel. "I had no idea at all for a book," Vonnegut later admitted, "but I started talking and told him the story of *The Sirens of Titan*. Every mother's favorite child is the one that's delivered by natural childbirth. *Sirens of Titan* was that kind of book."[15]

The advantage of paperback writing was that the author needed only one chapter and an outline to be paid what he had received for a first-class *Post* story. Since, Vonnegut recalls, he was always needing money right away, he had no choice but to write for this market. *The Sirens of Titan* and *Mother Night* appeared as paperback originals, getting no reviews and being sold largely in drugstores and bus stations. To this day Vonnegut, almost like his mythical science-fiction writer Kilgore Trout, does not have a copy of his paperback collection *Canary in a Cat House*. Such editions were ephemeral when published, were not saved, and today copies are so rare that even rare-book dealers cannot obtain them. As he later confessed to the Sunday readers of *Family Week* magazine, "Kilgore Trout is the lonesome and unappreciated writer I thought I might become."[16] Between 1959 and 1963 Vonnegut came the closest ever to being Trout himself.

In 1962 Samuel Stewart, who had worked for the Western Printing Company when it produced *The Sirens of Titan* for Dell, moved to a hardcover publisher: Holt, Rinehart & Winston. Vonnegut had completed his next novel, *Cat's Cradle*, with an eye to the same paperback market that had accepted his three previous books, but Stewart helped him acquire a hardcover contract for the new work. And so, by 1963—thirteen years after he had written *Player Piano* and left G.E.—Vonnegut had begun to receive attention for his novels. But he was labeled as a science-fictionist. He had never written *for* the science-fiction journals, but merely sent them his regular stories after they had been rejected by the better-paying markets. "Unready to Wear," from *Galaxy Science Fiction* of April 1953, is a companion piece to "The Euphio Question," which *Collier's* had printed as a family story two years before. Up until the early 1960s—when he could no longer submit his stories to *Collier's* and the *Post*—Vonnegut published only one other story in a science-fiction journal ("The Big Trip Up Yonder," another family-oriented piece). His publishers chose to market his work as science fiction. Bantam decided to retitle his first novel *Utopia-14* and issue it with a garish cover, and Dell packaged *The Sirens of Titan* as pure space opera. When his complete works were reissued by Dell in 1970, Vonnegut insisted that they be catalogued as straight mass-market paperbacks, not as science fiction.

"Critics all come out of the English departments," Vonnegut said in 1970, recalling that his own background was more common. "They believe that in order for a person to be sensitive and creative he can't understand how a refrigerator works. I know how my refrigerator works. Mark Twain knew how to pilot a boat up the Mississippi. Joseph Conrad could fix an engine. H. G. Wells, who should have gotten the Nobel Prize, was considered a lowbrow."[17] It has always been a ground rule "that you can't be a serious writer and include technology," he complained the next year. "The serious-minded writers ignore technology because they don't know much about it. But you can't leave machinery out anymore."[18] Quite simply, "Any twentieth-century novel reflecting life as it is lived now must have an awful lot of machinery."[19] People who thought he was writing about the distant future in *Player Piano*, Vonnegut insists, had not been around modern factories such as the G.E. plant in Schenectady—which, seen in person, conforms closely to the installation described in that novel. As for the devices of science fiction themselves, Vonnegut told another interviewer that "An imaginary planet has a role like a clown in a Shakespeare play. Every so often an audience needs a breather, a fresh view. Other planets provide that." But Vonnegut is careful not to invest his alien planets with too much believability, as a stock science-fiction writer might. "One thing which distresses me about space progress is that we are heading for other planets. This gives us a wrong idea that this one is disposable and that when we use it up we'll go on to others."[20]

Vonnegut is emphatic about the writer's responsibility. Invited to comment on the Apollo 11 Moon Launch because of his science-fiction reputation, Vonnegut responded by telling CBS News that "I am really not a science-fiction writer and I'm not well educated in science. The sort of dreams that I would have would be a habitable New York City, for instance. It would seem to me that that would be a reasonable thing to do with the money, to get this colony in class A shape." When challenged by Harry Reasoner as to whether such things had ever happened in the history of human governments, Vonnegut answered, "Well, I thought Napoleon III did very well with Paris. I admired that."[21] As a practicing writer, he has always been adamant about readability and even personal responsibility to his audience. That was the advantage of writing for student dailies at Shortridge High School and Cornell University, where he had to face his readers in person, encountering firsthand the reactions to what he wrote. As an innovative novelist in the 1960s and 1970s, with his contemporaries the sometimes puzzling Donald Barthelme, Thomas Pynchon, and John Barth, Vonnegut was aware of his own special limitations. Just as a composer depends upon the ability of musicians to play his works, so too a writer has to rely on the talent of his readers to perform his writing in their heads. And again, as a responsible middle-class craftsman, Vonnegut appreciates the tools of his trade. He returned to the printed page after brief flirtations with cinema, television, and the stage for two reasons: because only in fiction could he include himself as a character, and because mistakes in film were egregiously expensive to correct. His typewriter allows him to reach his audience economically.

The writer's function in society, Vonnegut insists, is to respond to life. This principle brought science and technology into his writings, but it also kept him from being defined simply as a science-fictionist. He goes so far as to "agree with dictators" that "an artist should serve his society, and I would not be interested in writing if I didn't feel that what I wrote was an act of good citizenship or an attempt, at any rate, to be a good citizen." The way Vonnegut works is to let his brain be "sensitive to what people are thinking around me, what is on the mind of society. I would like that very much—if I were a useful, specialized sort of organism."[22]

Addressing the American Physical Society, this sometime teacher of creative writing sought to justify his occupation to his fellow teachers of physics. Reprinted in *Wampeters, Foma & Granfalloons,* Vonnegut's answer began with his own self-questioning:

> I often wondered what I was doing, teaching creative writing, since the demand for creative writers is very small in this vale of tears. I was perplexed as to what the usefulness of any of the arts might be, with the possible exception of interior decoration. The most positive notion I could come up with was what I call the canary-in-the-coal-mine theory of the arts. This theory argues that artists are useful to society because they are so sensitive. They are supersensitive. They keel over like canaries in coal mines filled with poison gas, long before more robust types realize that any danger is there. [page 92]

Writers are "agents of change . . . a means of introducing new ideas into society, and also a means of responding to life," Vonnegut said in 1973.[23] His defensive role can be as simple as paranoia. "You can't write novels without a touch of paranoia," Vonnegut told Israel Shenker; "I'm paranoid as an act of good citizenship, concerned about what the powerful people are up to."[24] As the basis of it all is his own person, the therapeutic reason for being a writer in the first place. "It is for my own sanity," he acknowledged during his tenure at the University of Iowa's Writers Workshop, "that I try to write a good book."[25] His role as a teacher at Iowa coincided with his mission as a writer: "You catch people before they become generals and senators and presidents, and you poison their minds with humanity."[26]

As the 1960s progressed, Vonnegut moved closer to achieving the public stature he now enjoys. But first came a point of deep crisis. By 1965 he had published another hardcover novel, the bitterly satirical *God Bless You, Mr. Rosewa-*

ter. But, like its predecessor *Cat's Cradle*, fewer than seven thousand copies were printed, and it is doubtful that even half of these sold. His science-fiction reputation was keeping Vonnegut out of the serious review columns and off the best shelves of bookstores and libraries. Moreover, his subject—the technological destruction of the world (or, more hopefully, the ideological reorganization of society)—was uncomfortably close to the realities Americans were living with day to day. Vietnam, student disorders, and the other great national calamities were still a year or two away, and Americans needed to be reminded about the benevolent effects of satire.

With no publicity or distribution for his novels and no market for his short stories, Vonnegut could turn only to teaching, and for a relatively low salary he moved back to the Midwest, to Iowa City, Iowa, where he joined the faculty of the University of Iowa's creative-writing department, the Writers Workshop.

When he arrived in Iowa City for the fall semester of 1965, Vonnegut's career could not have been in worse shape. Except for *God Bless You, Mr. Rosewater*, his novels were out of print, and *Rosewater* was fast on its way to the remainder bins. He hadn't published a story in the well-paying slick magazines since 1963, and that year there had been only one, the year before that two, and the year before that just three. His career as a short-fictionist was over. His intention at Iowa City was to write his war novel, *Slaughterhouse-Five*. But the Dresden experience had been blocked for years; each time he tried to write about it, he hit a blank wall. Finally, his chances for academic advancement were slim: He had left Chicago without a degree, and university politicians are prone to look at a high-school diploma with dismay, if not outright scorn. In 1965 Vonnegut's prospects were as ragged and dilapidated as the broken-down Volkswagen which barely got him into town.

That Vonnegut's career took its ultimate turn for the better in Iowa City is undebatable. Iowa City was a totally new environment, almost made to order for his current needs. As he faced the problem of trying to write his seemingly unwritable novel, Vonnegut found himself for the first time in the company of other writers and critics, professionals in the art of talking about literature. For years Vonnegut's only daily contact with the outside world had been his Cape Cod mailman. Now he shared the friendship of novelists Vance Bourjaily and Verlin Cassill, plus the advocacy of critic Robert Scholes, who was in the process of writing *The Fabulators*, the first critical study of the new innovative fiction. Above all, he was living in a world of literary experimentation, by both students and faculty. The first result for Vonnegut's own writing was a startling self-consciousness. For earlier novels, *Cat's Cradle* in particular, his publishers had warned him not to use his own name or personality in his fiction. In Iowa City Vonnegut learned there were no real reasons not to, and so for the hardcover reissue of *Mother Night* he added a personal preface about his own involvement with "the Nazi monkeybusiness." For the first time in print, he told about the Dresden massacre and his own act of witness to it. Two years later, as he left Iowa City, Vonnegut added a confessional preface to his story collection *Welcome to the Monkey House*, which explained much about how his own personality expressed itself in stories and novels. And by then he had figured out *Slaughterhouse-Five*.

The years at Iowa City coincided with other events, the sum of which was to bring Vonnegut his justly deserved fame. In 1966 and 1967 two publishers, Dell and Avon, reissued all his novels in paperback. For the first time readers could see that this misnamed "science-fiction writer" had been moving in and around practically every aspect of common American life. Some characters moved from novel to novel, and readers no doubt took delight in that. More important, readers could for the first time examine all his books—take them home for less than five dollars, read them in perhaps as many hours, and consider the full extent of Vonnegut's vision. The new preface to *Mother Night* made it clear that behind the catastrophes of all his novels stood the matter of Dresden. By 1969, when his Dresden novel finally appeared, Vonnegut had a following among the legions of paperback readers who had been carefully prepared —educated as performers of his works, Vonnegut might say— for the climactic work of his twenty-year career.

But paperbacks alone did not make Vonnegut's success. His name was becoming more familiar in the publishing world; one trick, as he revealed later, was to offer endorsements for every good novel around, so that cover blurbs would make "Vonnegut" a household term. About this time, the hardcover publishers took another look at this now-prolific writer. Harper & Row, who had reissued *Mother Night*, made plans to update *Canary in a Cat House* as a hardcover book,[27] and Holt, Rinehart & Winston followed the publication of his two previous novels with the reprinting of *Player Piano*, which had been unavailable since the mid-1950s. Yet if Vonnegut's life had been restricted to these prospects, however promising, it is doubtful that his reputation would have shot for the stars as it did in 1969. A certain amount of good luck, plus hard journeyman work, remained.

In 1965, when the markets for his short stories had collapsed, Vonnegut had turned to a completely new form of writing: first-person journalism. After a year or so of doing book reviews for the *New York Times Book Review* and *Life*, he began writing highly personalized essays for the *Times Sunday Magazine*, *Life*, and *Esquire*, most of which have been collected in *Wampeters, Foma & Granfalloons*. His subject matter was nothing new—just the same kind of middle-class American concerns he had been describing in stories for fifteen years. In the late 1960s Vonnegut wrote about the Maharishi Mahesh Yogi, the Apollo 11 moon launch, a mass murderer on Cape Cod whom the media had turned into a superstar, the peculiar nature of the Nixon Republicans governing America, and dozens of other topics close to the daily lives of most Americans. His attitude was much the same as in his short stories of the 1950s: extolling middle-class virtues and ridiculing the pretensions of the rich and powerful. Vonnegut admitted that he wanted to witness an Apollo launch because the very spectacle of it struck his little-boy fancy with firecracker explosions. His piece on the Maharishi carried the title "Yes, We Have No Nirvanas," and the Maharishi's appeal was shown to be just another product to feed middle-class consumerism. After attending a Transcendental Meditation session with the leader, Vonnegut came away irked by the movement's blithesome easiness and mundane practicality. "I went outside the hotel after that," he writes, "liking Jesus better than I had ever liked Him before. I wanted to see a crucifix, so I could say to it, 'You know why You're up there? It's Your own fault. You should have practiced Transcendental Meditation, which is easy as pie. You would also have been a better carpenter' " (pages 39–40).

These essays featured the same new development that was becoming evident in Vonnegut's fiction during these years: the ability to treat his subject by making himself the center of it and then reporting on himself. It was the method of the New Journalism, made popular about this time by Tom Wolfe, Hunter S. Thompson, Dan Wakefield, and a dozen others. As a device it popularized Vonnegut's personality, which remained as ruggedly simple as ever, especially when confronted with an alien subject. Asked to review the Random House Dictionary for the *New York Times Book Review*,

Vonnegut put the lexicographer's complicated terms into simple English, and into simple experience. "Prescriptive," he wrote, was like an honest cop, while "descriptive" seemed like "a boozed-up war buddy from Mobile, Alabama." Everything Vonnegut saw was reduced to simplicity, but in a homely, charming way. During his years on Cape Cod he had lived just across the peninsula from Hyannis; among his neighbors were the household employees of the fabulous Kennedy family, including Frank Wirtanen, the skipper of their yacht. For an essay sold to *Venture*, Vonnegut accompanied Wirtanen on a cruise to West Palm Beach, but instead of glamorizing the Kennedy vessel, he chose to point out its humble realities. During the summer most of its service was as a playground for the Kennedy children and their friends:

> The *Marlin*'s captain, Frank Wirtanen of West Barnstable, Cape Cod, says of his present duties, "I don't think a man without children of his own, without a real understanding of children, could hold this job very long without going bananas."
>
> Captain Wirtanen is a graduate of the Massachusetts Maritime Academy. He used to command tankers, both in peace and in war. He now has the Kennedy yacht fitted out with a system of rubber mats and scuppers that make it possible for him to hose away the remains of chocolate cake and peanut-butter-and-jelly sandwiches in a fairly short time. [page 8]

Throughout, Vonnegut measured the world by his own private standards: growing up in Indianapolis, going off to college and war, working for General Electric, and fashioning his own middle-class life in the village of West Barnstable, Massachusetts. His journalistic writing gave him the chance to organize his own personal mythology before dealing with the biggest event in it: the firebombing of Dresden.

The true achievement of *Slaughterhouse-Five* was that, after twenty years of trying, Vonnegut finally realized that the truth of his Dresden experience was not the firebombing itself but his own reaction to it. He described his adventures during the war to a student audience at Iowa City in 1969, then added:

> Anyway, I came home in 1945, started writing about it, and wrote about it, and wrote about it, and wrote about it. This thin book is about what it's like to write a book about a thing like that. I couldn't get much closer. I would head myself into my memory of it, the circuit breakers would kick out; I'd head in again, I'd back off. The book is a process of twenty years of this sort of living with Dresden and the aftermath. It's like Heinrich Böll's book, *Absent Without Leave*—stories about German soldiers with the war part missing. You see them leave and return, but there's this terrible hole in the middle. That is like my memory of Dresden, actually there's nothing there. It's a strange book. I'm pleased with it.[28]

To the students at the University of Michigan earlier that year Vonnegut had explained that "massacre on such a scale simply does not register with the mind."[29] He had learned the same lesson when writing about mass-murderer Tony Costa—that atrocities are simply too large for the human imagination to grasp. As a result, people shrink away from such happenings or excuse them with nervous giggles; since the reality of mass murders is never absorbed, they are never understood, and cannot be prevented from happening again. The matter of Dresden had proved just as much of a problem. But rather than losing it entirely, or—even worse—writing a detached account glorifying the adventure of war, Vonnegut kept the subject firmly in front of him by detailing his own attempt to face it. The result was *Slaughterhouse-Five*, the first truly innovative novel to reach the mass readership of contemporary America.

With the publication of his Dresden book, Vonnegut's words became a valuable public commodity. From the many interviews published everywhere from the *New York Times* to student newspapers (by 1977 these quoted commentaries numbered over five dozen) there emerged a viewpoint consistent with his novels, stories, and essays. Vonnegut was still projecting opinions based on his own familiar life. His study of anthropology earned him no job, and not even a degree until 1971, but it reinforced his attitude toward the relativism of culture. Childhood during the Depression was the basis for that feeling. For Vonnegut, reality was something impermanent and essentially unreal, since the basic facts of life could be changed by circumstances of birth, or by the whims of national economics even after one was half grown. But while other writers might find such conditions to be the roots of a pessimistic and even hopeless determinism, Vonnegut used his ingenuity to turn them around as the components of man's true freedom. If reality is indeed relative and arbitrary, then it is all the easier to change; man need not suffer an unhappy destiny, but can instead invent a new reality better suited to his needs. In *Slaughterhouse-Five* we are told that because of the horrors of war, Billy Pilgrim and Eliot Rosewater "both found life meaningless"; therefore, "they were trying to re-invent themselves and their universe. Science fiction was a big help" (page 87).

Writers should be the first change-makers, Vonnegut argued. As a philanthropist, Eliot Rosewater had shown a convention of science-fiction writers just how arbitrary one cornerstone of our reality, money, is, by writing a three-hundred-dollar check for each of them as an act of whimsy. "Think about the silly ways money gets passed around now," Rosewater told them, "and then think up better ways" (page 31). Such transformations of reality could then be translated from the esthetic to the ethical and social spheres—as Kilgore Trout suggests at the end of *God Bless You, Mr. Rosewater,* and as Bokonon and McCabe accomplish for a time in *Cat's Cradle.* The two of them "did not succeed in raising what is generally thought of as the standard of living" on San Lorenzo, we are told, "But people didn't have to pay as much attention to the awful truth. . . . They were all employed full time as actors in a play they understood, that any human beings anywhere could understand and applaud" (page 144).

The key solution to human problems, Vonnegut kept insisting, is to find human dignity for all human beings—even those who seem to least deserve it. That was the social ethic Kilgore Trout proposed in *Rosewater,* that people be valued not as producers of goods (a measure of worth appropriate to the nineteenth century) but simply for being people, since automation threatened to steal their jobs. In his public statements from 1970 through 1976, Vonnegut emphasized a solution so simple that it had become, in middle-class manners, a banality: the superstition of astrology. When asked if there could ever emerge a revolutionary leader such as his Reverend Lasher in *Player Piano,* Vonnegut responded, "Sooner or later someone's going to catch the imagination of these people with some new magic. At the bottom of it will be a promise of regaining the feeling of participation, the feeling of being needed on earth—hell, dignity." As for the seemingly petty superstitions which remain so popular, "The magic in astrology is not that the stars really influence our lives but that every person born suddenly has dignity."[30] Everyone has a birthday; everyone has a palm for palm-reading. Middle-class superstitions are ultimately democratic, and so Vonnegut finds them useful for his plan to salvage human life at a time when it threatens to become unlivable:

> People do not value each other very highly any more because there are very few ways we can use each other . . . there are fewer and fewer natural interdependencies. But everybody at a minimum has a birthday. So a perfectly colorless, friendless person can walk into a party. Some nice person welcomes this jerk to the party, but nobody can think of anything to say, or anything to think about him, until somebody says, "When is your birthday?" And it turns out he's a Leo, and so suddenly he becomes all these marvelous things—he has a stone and a precious metal and a very respectable set of characteristics. So some people in the room are naturally his friends, and others naturally his enemies, and life becomes marvelous. This is what a folk society does for any member in it . . . it makes a person feel important and gives a person roles to play.[31]

The need for primitive folk societies within our own culture, as a guarantee of personal worth, became for Vonnegut his major topic in the 1970s, culminating in his use of this theme in *Slapstick: Or, Lonesome No More!* The folk-community idea, having its basis in an arbitrary and ultimately meaningless distinction, combined the interests and talents of Vonnegut's full career. It was based on a simple and common idea; it demonstrated the self-created nature of reality; and, like Vonnegut's other inventions, its inspiration came directly from his own family life. In 1970, when Vonnegut was not only a famous writer but well on his way to being a millionaire, he wrote a Broadway play called *Happy Birthday, Wanda June.* In his preface to the printed version he explained the situation of his new life:

> This play is what I did when I was forty-seven years old—when my six children were children no more. It was a time of change, of good-bye and good-bye and good-bye. My big house was becoming a museum of vanished childhoods—of my vanished young manhood as well.

This was on Cape Cod. There were widows all around me—in houses like mine.

I was drinking more and arguing a lot, and I had to get out of that house. [page vii]

For the preceding twenty years, his family had been his folk community, supplying all his needs and demonstrating its need for him, just as his parents' family in Indiana had done a generation before. But with his children grown and departed, Vonnegut felt the need for an artificial family. Writing a Broadway play provided him with a new home and children to care for, right down to the roles he created and the repair work he did on them as rehearsals headed toward opening night. Working with a producer, director, and cast of actors was far less lonely than sitting alone with his fiction in West Barnstable, Massachusetts.

"I think most of the unhappiness—the indescribable malaise—that people are feeling these days is really a longing for a large family, a large *permanent* family," Vonnegut said in 1971. Looking at his own marriage and at the marriages and relationships of his children, he decided that young husbands and wives were seeking to create a folk society by themselves—a "Nation of Two," as in his novel *Mother Night*. But "a husband alone does not qualify—not enough people. That's a terrible strain on two people alone, really, pretending to be a society."[32]

The key to Kurt Vonnegut's genius, what indeed may have made him the foremost serious writer in America today, is his unique ability to fashion a work of art out of an ordinary middle-class life. The glamorous personalities of our day lead lives of fiction, seeming to us like storybook heroes. Vonnegut's achievement has been to make his own life into an esthetic success, when all he had to work with were the common experiences of his generation. The nature of his talent has been to realize just how strong the human imagination is; that no matter how pessimistic the conditions of the world may be, man still possesses the right to create his own reality. Such creation, like the writing of fiction itself, is based on whimsy and pretense. But here alone can there be hope for man. "I beg you to believe in the most ridiculous superstition of all," Vonnegut wrote in 1970, "that humanity is at the center of the universe, the fulfiller or the frustrator of the grandest dreams of God Almighty." Such a belief is, of course, a lie. But, told well, it is a lie which can sustain life in a humanely livable way. "The arts put man at the center of the universe, whether he belongs there or not."[33] Given the other possibilities, this seems the best hope for Vonnegut, and for the America in which he lives.

NOTES

1. Marion Adams, "You've Come a Long Way Since Shortridge High, Kurt Vonnegut, Jr.," *Indianapolis*, October 1976, p. 29.
2. Robert Scholes, "A Talk With Kurt Vonnegut, Jr.," in Jerome Klinkowitz and John Somer, eds., *The Vonnegut Statement* (New York: Delacorte Press/Seymour Lawrence, 1973), p. 109.
3. Kurt Vonnegut, Jr., "Foreword," in Bob Elliott and Ray Goulding, *Write If You Get Work: The Best of Bob & Ray* (New York: Random House, 1975), p. vii.
4. David Standish, "The *Playboy* Interview: Kurt Vonnegut, Jr.," *Playboy*, 20 (July 1973), 74.
5. Lawrence Mahoney, "Poison Their Minds With Humanity," *Tropic/The Miami Herald Sunday Magazine*, January 24, 1971, p. 13.
6. Wilfrid Sheed, "The Now Generation Knew Him When," *Life*, 67 (September 12, 1969), 66.

7. Patricia Bosworth, "To Vonnegut, the Hero is the Man Who Refuses to Kill," *New York Times*, October 25, 1970, Sec. 4, p. 5.
8. Standish, p. 74.
9. Kurt Vonnegut, Jr., "Science Fiction," *Wampeters, Foma & Granfalloons* (New York: Delacorte Press/Seymour Lawrence, 1974), p. 1.
10. Frank McLaughlin, "An Interview With Kurt Vonnegut, Jr.," *Media & Methods*, May 1973, p. 39.
11. Loretta McCabe, "An Exclusive Interview With Kurt Vonnegut, Jr.," *Writers Yearbook—1970*, p. 100.
12. McCabe, p. 100.
13. Standish, p. 214.
14. Joe David Bellamy and John Casey, "Kurt Vonnegut, Jr.," in Joe David Bellamy, ed., *The New Fiction/Interviews With Innovative American Writers* (Urbana: University of Illinois Press, 1974), p. 200.
15. Richard Todd, "The Masks of Kurt Vonnegut, Jr.," *New York Times Magazine*, January 24, 1971, p. 22.
16. "Ask Them Yourself," *Family Week*, June 28, 1973, p. 3.
17. Rollene W. Saal, "Pick of the Paperbacks," *Saturday Review*, March 28, 1970, p. 34.
18. Phil Thomas, syndicated story on Vonnegut, Associated Press, December 12, 1971.
19. "Can Merlin Save the Whales?," *Boston Sunday Herald Traveler/Book Guide*, March 29, 1970, p. 9.
20. William Wolf, syndicated interview with Vonnegut, Sunday Group, February 27, 1972.
21. CBS Television Network, "Man on the Moon: The Epic Journey of Apollo 11," transcript excerpt, p. 2.
22. McLaughlin, p. 45.
23. Standish, p. 58.
24. Israel Shenker, "Kurt Vonnegut, Jr., Lights Comic Paths of Despair," *New York Times*, March 21, 1969, p. 41.
25. Franklin Dunlap, "God and Kurt Vonnegut, Jr., at Iowa City," *Chicago Tribune Magazine*, May 7, 1967, p. 48.
26. Mahoney, p. 44.

27. This collection was eventually published as *Welcome to the Monkey House* by Delacorte Press/Seymour Lawrence in 1968.
28. Bellamy and Casey, pp. 202–203.
29. Marcia Abramson, "Vonnegut: Humor to Cope With Suffering," *University of Michigan Daily*, January 22, 1969, p. 2.
30. "Can Merlin Save the Whales?," p. 9.
31. Carol Troy, "Kurt Vonnegut, Jr.," *Rags*, March 1971, pp. 24–26.
32. Art Unger, "Kurt Vonnegut, Jr.: Class of '71," *Ingenue*, December 1971, p. 16.
33. Kurt Vonnegut, "Address to Graduating Class at Bennington College, 1970," *Wampeters, Foma & Granfalloons* (New York: Delacorte Press/Seymour Lawrence, 1974), pp. 163, 165.

A VONNEGUT ALBUM

Caption for photo on previous page:
Baby Kurt with brother Bernard and sister Alice, 1922 or 1923.

Young Kurt, 1926.

KV at age sixteen.

KV at age eighteen.

A month before KV went overseas. Taken at a photographic studio.

The house at 4365 North Illinois Street, Indianapolis, 1940.

The house at Williams Creek.

KV between his career at General Electric and the publication of his first novel, *Player Piano*, in 1952. Photo courtesy of Charles Scribner's Sons

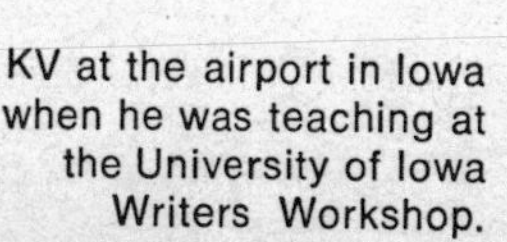

KV at the airport in Iowa when he was teaching at the University of Iowa Writers Workshop.

KV in his faculty office at the University of Iowa Writers Workshop, 1966. Photo courtesy of Loree Rackstraw

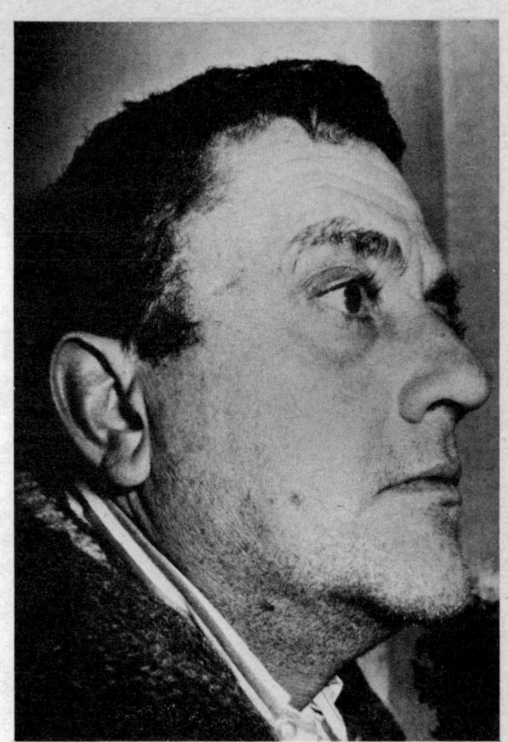

KV following his residency at the University of Iowa Writers Workshop, 1965–67.

KV on Cape Cod, 1969.
Photo credit: Bossi

KV in Cambridge, Mass., while serving as Briggs-Copeland Lecturer at Harvard, 1970–71. Photo © Jill Krementz

KV with his Russian translator Rita Rait at the Writers' Union in Moscow (under photograph of the Russian poet Mayakovsky), 1974. Photo © Jill Krementz

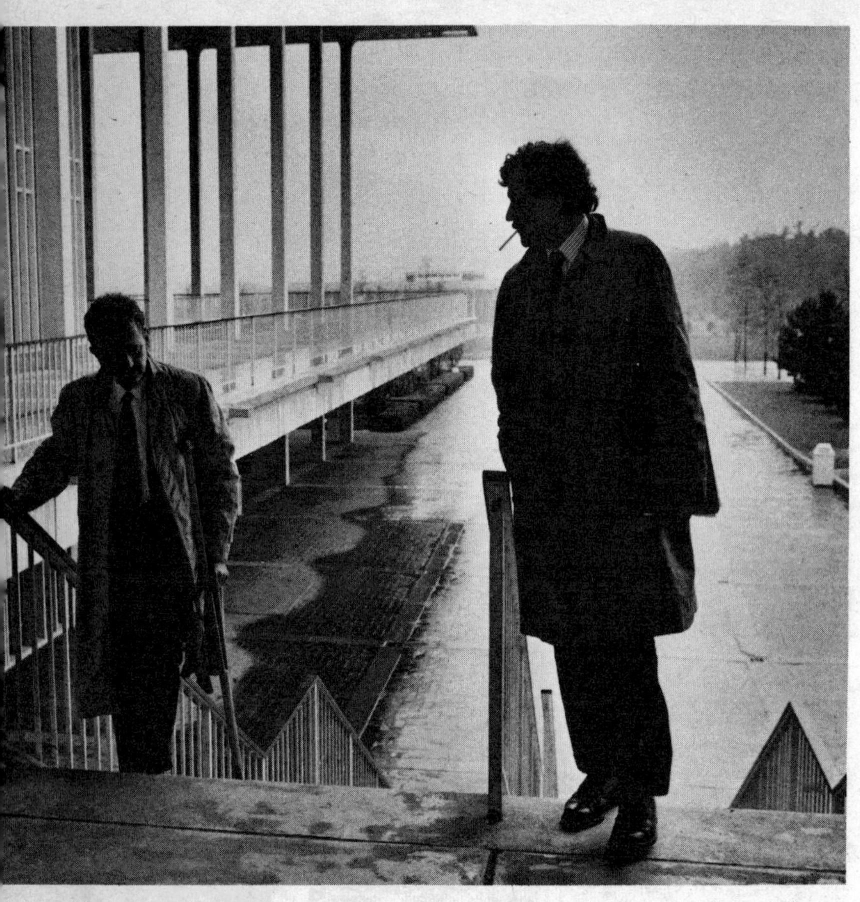

KV and his brother, Dr. Bernard Vonnegut, 1975.
Photo © Jill Krementz

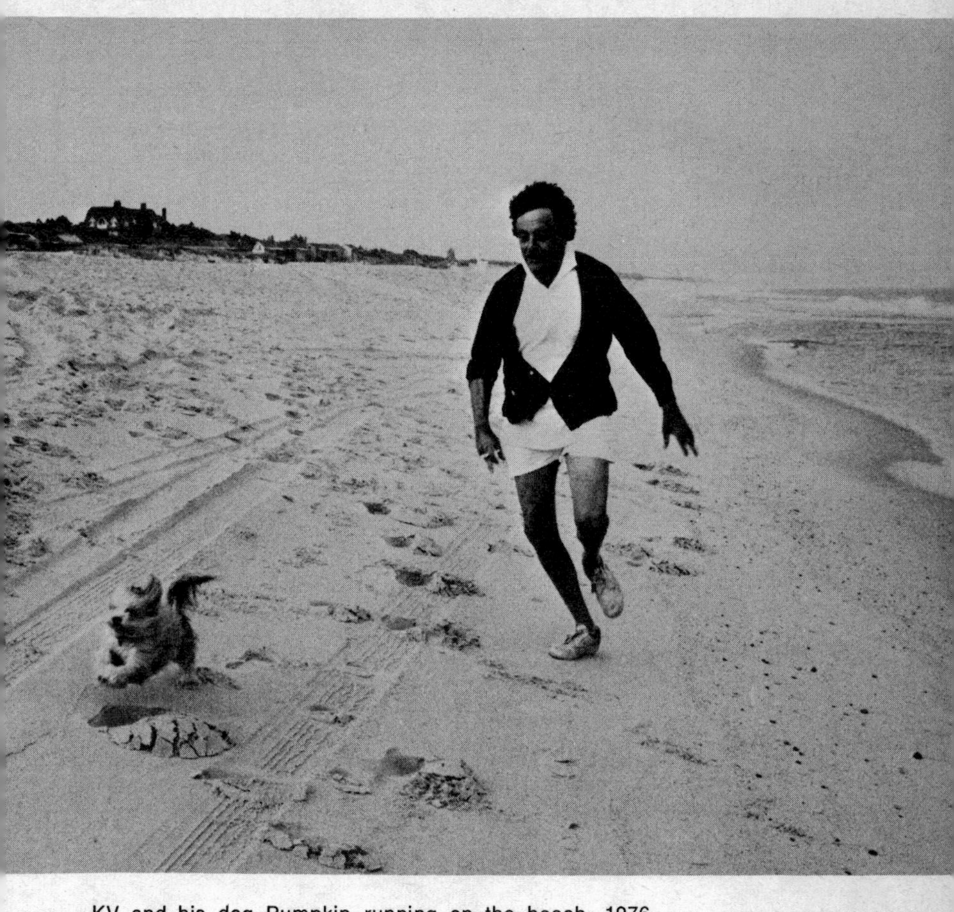

KV and his dog Pumpkin running on the beach, 1976.
Photo © Jill Krementz

KV with grandson Zachary Vonnegut, 1977. Photo © Jill Krementz

PART 2

ASPECTS OF VONNEGUT

Donald L. Lawler

Vonnegut in Academe (I)

On December 29, 1975, a seminar on the works of Kurt Vonnegut was held under the auspices of the Modern Language Association at its annual international convention in San Francisco. It was not the first MLA seminar on Vonnegut, nor will it be the last, but it was important for several reasons. In case there had been any doubts on the subject, the seminar revealed that the academic interest in Vonnegut's fiction was not merely faddish or an exercise in pop criticism. The seminar attracted participants from different areas of the country with established reputations in their academic disciplines. Their interests, focusing on different works of Vonnegut, complemented one another very well and covered nearly all the fiction, from the early short stories to the recent novels. The papers which formed the basis of the seminar brought to bear a remarkable diversity of critical approaches on Vonnegut from the perspectives of science fiction, structuralism, classical satire, bibliography, popular culture forms, literary surrealism, and biography. This kind of critical interest in a writer like Vonnegut was a sign at least that the author had something more to offer the culture of the time than the discarded mantle of a guru of the 1960s. Indeed, one of the main reasons for the seminar was to raise discussion and inquiry into Vonnegut's writing to the level of serious study and dialogue. This is not something that too many university professors feel comfortable doing with a current writer. It is much more respectable and a whole lot safer to speak of the achievements of Charles Dickens or Nathaniel Hawthorne than to attempt similar assessment of a writer on whom the judgment of history has not yet been made. But then, we should see that this very sort of critical risk-taking is an important part of the process through which history will reach whatever judgment generations of readers and critics finally settle on for Kurt Vonnegut.

The papers which follow were distributed in advance of our December meeting. All have since been updated or revised.

Jerome Klinkowitz

A Do-It-Yourself Story Collection by Kurt Vonnegut

First you must pretend it is, say, 1955. You're about to buy a fresh weekly issue of that venerable fifties institution, the *Saturday Evening Post*. And you're looking for a new story by the *Post*'s perennial writer, Kurt Vonnegut. Here, in the fifties tradition of do-it-yourself, are instructions for an entire book of undiscovered Kurt Vonnegut stories, never collected except in this homemade work you can assemble for yourself.

From 1949 to 1966 Vonnegut wrote over fifty stories for the *Post*, *Collier's*, *Ladies' Home Journal*, and the other slick magazines then in their heyday. He sold these stories, he says, "to finance the writing of the novels"— *Cat's Cradle*, *Slaughterhouse-Five*, and the others—which until 1969 were spectacularly unbought and not often read.

They are widely read now. Vonnegut's novels sell over a

million copies each year; and so with the need to sell them removed, his popular stories of the fifties have become a lost art. For his fans old enough to have been reading back then, Delacorte published a small selection of them, *Welcome to the Monkey House*, in 1968, which his younger readers also grabbed up. But if you really love the vintage Vonnegut, once is not enough, so here are directions for putting together your own new volume of Kurt Vonnegut stories.

Go to your nearest library. Even the smallest branch is likely to keep the popular magazines Vonnegut wrote for, and they all have Xerox machines for making copies. Copyright legislation makes it legal for you to request single copies of items, so take along a roll of dimes.

Begin with "Thanasphere" (*Collier's*, September 2, 1950), one of the first stories Vonnegut wrote after quitting his job as public-relations man for the General Electric Research Lab ("Progress Is Our Most Important Product"). You can tell what he'd been writing about for the last few years, since "Thanasphere" is set in the progressive future, measuring the effect of rocket travel on America's "first" astronaut. But the protagonist, Major Allen Rice, looks more like a Sabre-jet ace from the Korean War, and throughout the story Vonnegut's emphasis is on the here-and-now quite familiar to his middle-class readers. Rice has been sent up two thousand miles through the ionosphere. "With a telescope, he could pick out small towns and the wakes of ships without much trouble. It would be breathtaking to watch the enormous blue and green ball; to see night creeping around it, and clouds and storms growing and swirling over its face."

Heady stuff for 1950, and even today a more vivid account than some of our own astronauts have given us. But Vonnegut has a surprisingly sentimental story to tell: Major Rice is in a thanasphere, to which voices of the dead come like radio waves. He meets deceased husbands and wives, unavenged homicide victims, and even a cloying grandmother and a beckoning lover. Strange material to be mixed up with the exotic hardware of outer space. It's the first mark of Vonnegut's later method—combining middle-class themes with a science-fiction setting. But even in this embryonic setting, Vonnegut moves on to a more sophisticated technique. Rice's spirits tell him embarrassing truths about affairs on Earth, and of course his military superiors worry for the mission. But the chief scientist has a deeper worry. How would future space travelers survive, having to listen to such a gaggle of communication? "Every bum and genius, criminal and hero, average man and madman, now and forever a part of humanity—advising, squabbling, conniving, placating. . . ." In the unlikely context of a science-fiction thriller, Vonnegut has added his own touch of ironic humor.

After this, you might turn to "Any Reasonable Offer," from *Collier's* of January 29, 1952. Here Vonnegut presents broader comedy and shows how his fantasy schemes could be expressed directly through the most middle-class American realities—in this case, the story of a rich-looking couple who spend their vacations being wined and dined by real-estate agents who hope to sell them extravagant mansions. When the two weeks are up, the husband returns to his low-salaried job, the wife to her dirty diapers at home.

Whether of rocket ships in space or strike-it-rich dreams in your own backyard, Vonnegut's stories charted a profitable route through the formula of slick magazines everywhere: fantasy. In 1947, for the University of Chicago's Anthropology Department, Vonnegut had written a master's thesis entitled "Fluctuations Between Good and Evil in Simple Tales." The idea was, as he tells it, "that the shape of stories was ultimately an important clue to how societies act." For two years he took *New Yorker* stories, fiction from abroad, Kentucky ballads, folktales, American-Indian narratives—"I got a bunch of these stories and I graphed them," Vonnegut says. And, sure enough, each type of story had its own identifiable form. But the thesis was rejected. Did Vonnegut adopt any of these formulas when he had to write for the slicks himself? "Oh, no," he objects. "It turns out that I did, but I didn't know it." Looking back now, he sees the patterns, which are for us a ready-made structure for our do-it-yourself anthology.

Look up "Unpaid Consultant," in *Cosmopolitan*, March 1955. Here we meet a typical Vonnegut narrator, in this case a contact man for an investment-counseling firm. In other stories this figure sells aluminum siding and storm windows, and sometimes runs a Pontiac agency (as he will in the novel *Breakfast of Champions*), but here he is visiting clients of another class: the rich. His advice is less often financial than the counsel of homely, middle-class value. As an "unpaid consultant" he studies the portfolio of Celeste Divine, an old high-school girlfriend who is now a TV starlet. She is torridly unhappy because her career has dwarfed the achievement of her husband, an auto mechanic. Vonnegut's solution is to have the husband become an expert, knowing everything there is to know about one thing: catsup. "Harry's found himself," she raves. "Isn't it marvelous?"

Romance is one way to champion the common values of simple folk, and in "Custom-Made Bride" (*Post*, March 27, 1954) Vonnegut's spokesman, again an investments contact man, subverts the values of the richer classes. This time his client is a designer of flashy sports cars, "Di-Modular" beds, and atomic-age kitchens. He's also designed a new wife, dimodular and all-electric herself, but terribly unhappy in the flesh and blood beneath. The designer would have composed his life "like that Finnish carafe over there, clean, harmonious, alive with the cool, tart passion of reason in our time."

Vonnegut argues that human beings cannot fit such specifications—the thesis of *Player Piano,* and a familiar theme in his later novels as well.

The fifties, remember, are the years of the Great Corporation, bringing us Buick Roadmasters and all-electric homes, and an efficiency-conscious, technocratic society in which to enjoy them. As Vonnegut tested ideas of progress for General Electric in the forties, the fifties would give him ample time to project these ideas into common American life and consider their implications. "Poor Little Rich Town" (*Collier's,* October 25, 1952) is the site for a technological revolution such as the times considered possible. A new corporation is moving upstate, where a sleepy little town must be prepped by an efficiency expert rich in "know-how." With great heartlessness he crushes all the town's customs and its quietly happy way of life, until the people mount a counterrevolution to throw him and his corporation out. Two years before, Vonnegut had left Schenectady, thriving home of the General Electric Corporation, for just such an unspoiled village: West Barnstable on Cape Cod. He would certainly agree with his character's statement "What is a village profited, if it shall gain a real estate boom and lose its own soul?"

Time after time Vonnegut teases us with fantasy and then congratulates us for our good sense—and for what we really can't have anyway. A young kid, who can't afford it, burns up an expensive sports car in "The Powder Blue Dragon" (*Cosmopolitan,* November 1954), trying to impress a rich and unimpressible girl. "A Night for Love" (*Post,* November 23, 1957) finds a woman much happier with a poor boy than she would have been married to the richest man in town (their respective children are now dating). Two stories, "Bagombo Snuff Box" (*Cosmopolitan,* October 1954) and "The Package" (*Collier's,* July 26, 1952), treat the same situation: An old friend visits other old friends, the one humble and sincere, the others fabulously wealthy and successful. We know who's the happiest.

That such quaintly moral contrivances can become interesting and even funny in a short story is the mark of Vonnegut's genius. It shows up in his novels as an example of the talent which got him out of the magazine business. "Hal Irwin's Magic Lamp," featured in the June 1957 *Cosmopolitan*, is one of Vonnegut's best. In this story the hero, "a customer's man in a brokerage house" (the contrivance Vonnegut often used to bring the modest middle class in contact with the rich), has some luck in the market and strikes it rich himself. But he keeps it a secret from his wife. On the sly he fills the closets with every imaginable thing she's ever wanted, then hires a live-in cook and maid to surprise his wife with a genie's lamp, ready to grant her every wish. The climax is a dream mansion across town, where both husband and wife find themselves unhappy. "I wish," says the wife, "the lamp would take the house and everything else, if only it'll give me back the husband I thought I had." *Hey presto:* a stock-market crash, the Great Depression, and her every wish comes true.

Another brilliantly funny story, as inventive as anything in *Cat's Cradle* and the other novels, might take a bit of searching out. Not every library keeps old copies of *Argosy*, but if you can find one that does, look up the Christmas issue for 1954. "A Present for Big Nick" is the only seasonal story Vonnegut ever wrote. It begins with the strange case of a bunch of kids cowering in mortal fear of Santa Claus. To follow this out Vonnegut draws upon the same rich-poor, master-servant formula he's used so well before. The context is a Christmas party given by a boss for his employees and their children. But here Vonnegut reverses his usual structure of injecting middle-class familiarity into an exotic setting, since the employer is a mobster racketeer. An obnoxious bully, he makes it worse by dressing as Santa Claus to distribute presents and receive accolades of thanks. One kid's honesty breaks the Christmas party's chilling fear. Big Nick erupts; a henchman tries to restrain him and is slapped back: " 'Take your fil'ty hands off me!' roared Santa. 'You wanna commit suicide?' " This encourages a general rout of Santa, as his helpers turn on him and administer the thrashing he deserves. Coincidently, a present from a rival gangster turns out to be a bomb, which ends the story. "Santa Claus," announces the henchman, "is dead."

That's half the book, and a good index to what Vonnegut was doing in the fifties. To finish out an afternoon of reading, you might try three of Vonnegut's *Post* stories about a high-school bandmaster, George Helmholtz, who saves the day for teenage life, love, and music in "Ambitious Sophomore" (May 1, 1954), "The Boy Who Hated Girls" (March 31, 1956), and "The No-Talent Kid" (October 25, 1952). Fathers and sons, and more teenage love, get the *Post*-Vonnegut treatment in "This Son of Mine . . ." (August 18, 1956) and "Runaways" (April 15, 1961). When the most beautiful girl in town gets married, her disappointed beaux (every other man around) form a club, which Vonnegut calls "Lovers Anonymous" (*Redbook*, October 1963). And there's lovely sentimental mush in "Find Me a Dream" from the February 1961 *Cosmopolitan*, which carries the subhead: "No girl in her right mind would have fallen in love with Andy on purpose." Of course not, but this is a Kurt Vonnegut story.

In 1966, the year he started writing his first best-seller, *Slaughterhouse-Five*, Vonnegut published his last regular magazine story. It was for *Venture*, fanciest of the world travel magazines, and took his average-guy narrator into the most glamorous of circumstances, deckhanding on the Kennedy yacht as its skipper took it down the inland waterway to West Palm Beach. Although the story is the work of a fictionist, its narrative situation was real.

"I lived next door on Cape Cod to a guy named Frank Wirtanen," Vonnegut has revealed, "who was a skipper of Joe Kennedy's yacht, the *Marlin*. His son and one of my sons played on the same football team, and we were watching the first game of the season and he said, 'Hey you wanna go to West Palm?' and I said sure and so he said, 'O.K. You're hired.' " And so once again the humble guy-next-door was swept up into the world of money, fame, and glamor. It was quite a trip, and a fitting farewell by Vonnegut to the slick magazines.

Better take two rolls of dimes, because all this adds up to about one hundred pages of photocopying. But we don't have a cover yet, so try this: Imagine a young Kurt Vonnegut, tall and lanky, as he must have looked in 1950, lounging (white chinos, yellow sport shirt) at the fork of a country road, a field of soft greens and yellow flowers fading up into the title: *The Road Not Taken: The Early Fiction of Kurt Vonnegut*. If you are handy with a brush you just might paint it, but don't do an imitation Rockwell. For all the times both of them had work in the *Post*, the two never hit the same issue, and Norman Rockwell's covers had a soft sentimentality almost fully lacking in Vonnegut's stories.

Try instead for the effect of Amos Sewell, or of Harvey Kidder, both of whom illustrated many of these early Vonnegut works. Get the close detail of those wholesome Middle Americans, caught in the story's mundane action—but with that look of wild comedy just behind the eyes, ready to spill out into their lives.

Donald L. Lawler

The Sirens of Titan: *Vonnegut's Metaphysical Shaggy-Dog Story*

I

It seems to me that if one is going to study the construction of this novel at least three features must be understood. The first is the science-fiction narrative shell which I identify as a form of "space opera," used as an enabling form of satire. Unless I am mistaken, the pattern of the "space-opera" plot is the "shaggy-dog story." We can even identify the kinds of shaggy-dog story underlying the plot. The third feature is the surrealistic quality of so many of this novel's characters, actions, and episodes. The possible need for an expanded critical language or at least a reassessment of existing resources is underscored most effectively in the last two points.

Vonnegut's use of the extended joke structure analogous to the shaggy-dog story is a form of novelistic conceit, as I try to demonstrate further along in this essay. It functions as a structural metaphor and is a little like allegory in its extension. Unlike allegory, the hidden ground beneath the joke is not so much an idea as an attitude. Another difference is that whereas allegory extends metaphorical content in an elaborated development, the extended joke conceit expands metaphorical structure into a drawn-out and even bizarre negation of the reader's narrative expectations. At this point, the shaggy-dog and space-opera formulas complement and reinforce each other. They are used to evoke a set of conventional and clinchéd responses which are at the same time undercut and even made ridiculous by the author's ironic and satirical posture. The purpose of doing this is to create an event in which the proprieties of both fiction and society are experienced as mere cheap conjuror's deceptions. What remains after the shaggy-dog conceit deflates the reader's aroused expectations is the discovery of meaning in simpler and more elemental values not susceptible to perversion by either technology run amok or other agencies of mischief. This is one way Vonnegut has of bringing us to a confrontation with the moral axis of human life, and it has proven highly effective in this novel.

The second problem is not so much structural or formal as semantic. The only critical vocabulary that seems in any way descriptive of the devices Vonnegut uses and the effects he creates is to be found in literary surrealism and expressionism. Many of Vonnegut's techniques in this novel are surrealistic: the use of the fantastic, jokes, chance events as illuminations, repudiation of rational processes, insistence on the inwardness of truth, concern with fundamental problems of existence, use of humor as a dialectical statement of truth, and so on. But that does not make Vonnegut a surrealist any more than his appropriation of some favorite tricks of expressionism makes him an expressionist. He is neither, at least in the traditional sense in which both terms have been used by literary critics, and this is a special source of analytic difficulty. If we are going to hold to the traditional meanings of these terms as they apply to Breton and his surrealist disciples or to Strindberg, Kafka, and the expressionist drama, then we must beware of using them in those senses when we write of Barth, Brautigan, Kosinski, Pynchon, and Vonnegut. The difficulty lies not so much with the terms as with the critical community, which likes to have its references reasonably clear and consistent. This is surely not an unreasonable goal, but it sometimes leads to difficulties, such as the present embarrassment over the bankruptcy of our critical language.

Vonnegut, along with many of the other writers who have emerged over the past decade, took what expressive forms were available to them from their culture. Inevitably the idiom of the times would find an outlet in these forms. Contemporary writers, even those who see themselves as mainstream light-bearers, are much less elitist than those of preceding generations. Many contemporaries care little for the literary pedigrees of the forms they use. Vonnegut takes contemporary modalities like science fiction, expressionism, surrealism, and popular romance-story fiction and turns them to new and, in combination, unfamiliar purposes. For instance, the surrealism laid down by Breton in his various manifestos, as it was practiced in the thirties and forties and even as it evolved in the fifties, does not quite prepare us to deal with the uses to which its materials and methods have been put by writers like Barthelme and Vonnegut. Even in science fiction, where mainstream influence was thought to be rare until the "new wave," we find writers such as Cordwainer Smith, Philip K. Dick, and J. G. Ballard working on the periphery of the surrealist tradition.

There are many who deplore this very eclecticism in Vonnegut, just as they will insist that it is misleading to describe

Vonnegut's practice in terms of surreal or expressionistic devices. However, as we have seen, these devices are part of the cultural ambience supporting the literature of the times. It changes things to some extent when the ends to which the techniques have been used are satire and criticism of life rather than the doctrinaire solecism of Breton. The net result is to permit Vonnegut his special point of entry into the history of contemporary ideas and values. Vonnegut argues not for the absurdity of life, but for the absurd way modern men and women have come to live it. In order to recognize that truth, Vonnegut must show the folly of our patched-up ethical values in conflict with our equally patched-up notions of social stability and religious truth. He does this in *The Sirens of Titan* through the use of devices I try to place in a critical perspective in the following pages. If associations in the novel with the surreal, science fiction, and the extended-joke conceit are somewhat discontinuous, it is because Vonnegut is putting these elements to fresh uses in an unorthodox way, to produce a new kind of fictional product that is both expressive of and at the same time critical of the character of the times.

II

Let us begin with the curious debate that has arisen in recent years over the proper classification of the novels of Kurt Vonnegut and indeed of the author himself. The controversy over whether Vonnegut writes science fiction is not one for which the author has much respect, and it would not be raised here except that sometimes questions of classification can take us into unexplored areas of even greater interest.

Vonnegut's attitude is well-known. He wishes to avoid identification with the parochialism of the science-fiction writer, and he wants to be taken seriously.[1] Both are reasonable aspirations. Mainstream critics and reviewers are still troubled by the image of the popular cult hero compounded by an apparent weakness for the fleshpots of science-fiction adventure. On the other hand, science-fiction critics and writers, some of them anyway, treat Vonnegut's pretensions as an apostasy and condemn his infidelity to a genre which is also a kind of cause.[2] The social implications of the quarrel are possibly of greater interest than its literary merit, and yet it will offer a convenient opportunity to look into the work of a major writer from a potentially revealing perspective. Since we are concerned with the question of Kurt Vonnegut's practice as a writer rather than with his loyalties, it seems reasonable to limit this inquiry to the one novel everyone seems to believe is a science-fiction novel if the author ever wrote one. We may hope to learn from our study whether Vonnegut does indeed write science fiction, and if he does, to what purpose.

The first question is answered easily enough, at least on the surface. Anyone can tell that *The Sirens of Titan* is science fiction. The cover illustrations make that identification unmistakable. The story is a space opera with all the trimmings: space travel, interplanetary warfare, aliens manipulating human history, brainwashing, thought control, future societies, new religions, adjustment to life on other planets and their moons. The purposes behind such fictions and the uses to which they are put, however, are another matter. Before taking this line of thought any further we must remember that whether the author is writing science fiction for science fiction's sake or not, all the various levels of meaning in this novel rest on his invention of a cosmic order in which there are Tralfamadorians, chrono-synclastic infundibula, Mercurian Harmoniums, Titanic bluebirds, and Churches of God the Utterly Indifferent. Without them none of the experiences of the novel is accessible or even possible, because the meanings are generated by the novel's own imagined universe.

In the *Playboy* interview, Vonnegut reveals that his writings serve a social purpose, which he broadly defines as being biological agencies of change. "Writers are specialized cells in the social organism. They are evolutionary cells. Mankind is trying to become something else; it's experimenting with new ideas all the time. And writers are a means of introducing new ideas into the society, and also a means of responding symbolically to life" (*Wampeters*, page 237). Man is controlled by his "wish to improve [himself]" (page 238), an idea which appears in *The Sirens of Titan* as "the universal will to become." The purpose of art as Vonnegut sees it then is very much like a criticism of life, and the ideas introduced by Vonnegut in *The Sirens of Titan* are taken primarily from metaphysics, moral philosophy, and theology.

The novel begins at a point in the future, less than a century from now, when everyone knew "how to find the meaning of life within himself."[3] Vonnegut's critique of contemporary life philosophies is spelled out very clearly. People were ignorant of the fact that truth was within. "Gimcrack religions were big business" (page 7) and were partly responsible for having misdirected humans to seek meaning outside themselves. Looking outward, mankind eventually sought answers in space exploration. For Vonnegut, space is a "colorless, tasteless, weightless sea of outwardness without end" (page 7). It is nugatory not only for the senses but also for the spirit, being totally alien to all that is human. It is against such outwardness of belief and aspiration that the author sets himself and the reader.

Vonnegut's utopian introduction serves a number of purposes, one of which is to offer the reader a vision of a future time when mankind has turned inward for its answers rather than outward. What follows in the novel is a demonstration, a commentary, and a burlesque of the futility of seeking outward answers to the great abstract questions about the meaning of human life or the designs of providence. Vonnegut's answer to the questions of the great purpose of human history or the purpose of creation is essentially "Don't ask!"

After fifty thousand years of human endeavor, the existential mysteries remain unsolved. Vonnegut implies that, in an objective sense at least, they cannot be solved, because the traditional terms in which mankind has tried to answer them (free will, God, Heaven, salvation, etc.) cannot be understood. Such questions, therefore, are not relevant to man because they are unanswerable. The thesis of this novel seems to be that human history is absurd if we assume the existence of an objective, divine consciousness. The novel supposes an imaginary and utterly fantastic explanation for the pageant of history, in which the meaning of these cosmic questions is reduced to the absurdity of a science-fiction natural-theology spectacular. The story suggests that the meaning of human history is to send a message to a robot stranded on Titan that a spare part is on its way. Indeed, mankind's childhood ends with the delivery of that spare part and the consequent disengagement of Tralfamadore from the affairs of Earth. We have all been manipulated, everyone used.

Without doubt, Vonnegut's intention in offering us this burlesque of metaphysics and theodicy is to ridicule mankind's obsession wth finding an answer to the mystery of existence in superhuman agencies. The novel is telling us, in effect, that since these questions are unanswerable by their nature, it is best to dismiss them by proposing a resolution which is a patently absurd parody of the kind of answer the race has conjured up in the past. The force of the Tralfamadorian connection as explained by Rumfoord lies in its bizarre plausibility. It explains everything, and its absurdity dramatizes the irrationality of all such accounts to Vonnegut's way of thinking.

Vonnegut's critique of the school of thought that sees human history as allegorical is uncompromising, but we must be careful here not to oversimplify. Vonnegut does not suggest that human life or destiny is necessarily absurd. It is only man's attempt to find an objective meaning to life that is. From this point of view, the novel makes a seriocomic demonstration that the universe in its workings is unintelligible and arbitrary. It intends neither good nor bad. The allegorical sense of life which leads to the "big eye in the sky" philosophy can just as easily be explained by the machinations of Tralfamadore as by orthodox theology. Like the sirens of Titan, which appear to offer Constant the prospect of satisfied appetites, traditional ways of thinking about the supernatural have lured the race with the idea that happiness and purpose in life are to be discovered outside the self. It is obvious that Vonnegut the moralist does not believe in such solutions and the novel offers an alternate resolution of its own.

If Vonnegut is critical of metaphysics and theology, he is prepared to affirm that there are certain ethical absolutes, and these are demonstrated as thoroughly in the novel as other values are parodied. The chief ethical virtue is the duty of loving whatever is around to be loved. All the sympathetic characters in the novel seem to exemplify this quality in varying degrees. Boaz adopts the Harmoniums, while Beatrice and Constant achieve at last a mature love relationship. Together and separately, they also learn their proper parental roles as they live out their lives on Titan. Even Salo, the Tralfamadorian robot, becomes the benefactor, first of Rumfoord and later of Constant. Most specifically, this ethical imperative applies to Chrono, who leaves his delinquent past behind and becomes the leader of the bluebirds of Titan—an apotheosis indeed.

Those who find Vonnegut a prophet of the absurd should note well that the author does not confront his readers with a universe that makes no sense but rather one that makes no sense as it has been conceived. While on Titan, Beatrice began writing a refutation of Rumfoord's dogma that the purpose of human life in the solar system had been manipulated by Tralfamadore to get a needed spare part to their grounded messenger. The Rumfoord view epitomizes the best that human reason can determine of the meaning of life, looked at externally or objectively. We know it is the best because Rumfoord has the unique advantage of being infundibulated, which permits him to see all the ways of being absolutely right up to the time of his exit from the solar system. Unfortunately, he never learns the validity of the subjective truth arrived at by Beatrice and Constant after years of suffering and exploitation. From their point of view, the machinations of Tralfamadore may be understood to serve another purpose. Once Tralfamadorians turn their attention away from the solar system, humans are free for the first time in five hundred centuries to go their way without external control and intergalactic meddling. The freedom, Vonnegut seems to imply, is not a free gift. It has been dearly bought.

Perhaps the central paradox of this novel is that both Beatrice and Constant feel themselves controlled by chance, the victims of random forces. If they really had been, they would have learned sooner that the bars are on the inside, as the surrealists remind us, not on the outside. Being conventionally modern, however, they must reach the point of resigning all their expectations of making sense of things or of receiving a compensatory justice in life before such a realization is possible. "Reason is the enemy which must be driven out before man can hope fully to possess the surreal. And of course, the Surrealist identifies the full possession of the sur-real with the full possession of the self—the true nature of human identity."[4] However, Beatrice and Constant are, of course, the victims not of mere chance but of purposive ma-nipulation by both Tralfamadore and Winston Niles Rum-foord. The redundancy is important, because it shows that outward rational direction and planning leads inevitably to absurdity. The result is the same whether humanity is con-trolled by Tralfamadore for Tralfamadorian ends or manipu-lated by Rumfoord for humanitarian ends. Theirs is the sort of logic that eventually renders human history intelligible only as a bad joke and reduces religious impulses and even humanitarian values to the absurdity of "The Church of God the Utterly Indifferent," with its handicapping and circus-tent revivalism. Both Tralfamadore and Rumfoord endow the race with bogus virtues, and it is only by reason of having de-veloped a new perspective that Beatrice, Constant, and the others are able to set aside phony ideas and embrace truth.

Vonnegut's criticism of ideas is shaped by two correlative literary forms, science fiction and comedy. The forms are re-ciprocal in the novel and together create the context in which the ideas are dramatized. Since Vonnegut's use of the two forms is both complex and revealing, we will examine each briefly and then attempt to see how they complement each other. Vonnegut certainly does not use science fiction for purposes of teaching science, as Hugo Gernsback advocated. Indeed, Vonnegut's advocacy may be almost the reverse. Speaking of *Slaughterhouse-Five,* Vonnegut compared the science-fiction elements to the clowns in Shakespeare: "When Shakespeare figured the audience had had enough of the heavy stuff, he'd let up a little, bring on a clown or a foolish innkeeper or something like that, before he'd become serious again. And trips to other planets, science fiction of an obviously kidding sort, is equivalent to bringing on the clowns every so often to lighten things up."[5] An extreme view, perhaps, which may fit the strategies of the later novels, but a view which needs modifying if it is to be applied to *The Sirens of Titan*, because the plotting of the novel, its organization of parts and internal development, is predicated on science-fiction conventions and probabilities. The type of science fiction Vonnegut chose was the space opera, which he considered an obviously kidding sort. There is a variety of reasons why space opera is an appropriate narrative form for this novel.

Space opera is a form of fantasy science fiction which is noted for sensational action and extraordinary incident. It is the sibling of the soap and horse operas, and it is usually referred to with about the same degree of contempt. It seems fair to say that Vonnegut shares the generally patronizing attitude that mainstream critics have for space opera. He has found it, however, ideal for his own brand of comic parody and satire; but, considered as a strategy, it is also something more, providing for Vonnegut the "enabling form" for his serious ideas as well as his burlesque.

Let us look at the potentials of the space-opera conventions for Vonnegut in *The Sirens of Titan*. In a sense, space opera epitomizes attitudes to which Vonnegut is clearly opposed. To begin with, it is a literature of outwardness. In the space-opera story, human existence gains a dimension and a significance in space exploration that it seems to lack when it is brought back down to Earth. Another thing about space opera is the way in which it treats heroic and even superhuman adventure with all the trappings of engineering marvels and advanced ideas. The heroes and even the villains are nearly always idealized types whose exploits are both exaggerated and implausible as judged by ordinary standards of human achievement. However, in the hyperbolic settings of space opera, humans regularly achieve the unattainable and perform the impossible as heroic affirmation of the idea that humans are capable of transcending their natural limitations by sheer inventiveness, ingenuity, courage, and willpower. Vonnegut's objection is not to portraying people as better than they are but as better than they can be.[6] His critique of bankrupt idealism is one of the consistent themes of his fiction generally, and of *The Sirens of Titan* especially.

Space opera is, therefore, doubly suited to Vonnegut's purposes. Because the type itself is hyperbolic in its treatment of subject, it is an ideal vehicle for burlesque, especially when the values to be parodied are the very ones that space opera has promoted consistently. All Vonnegut had to do was generate an appropriately detached attitude toward the narrative properties and he had a ready-made vehicle for burlesque. This technique extends as well to the manner in which he parodies metaphysics and theology, already discussed. The strategy is to take their symbolic forms literally, replacing teleological visions with punning fantasies. But we must not get too far ahead of ourselves, since our inquiry into Vonnegut's use of space-opera narrative forms has another facet.

I spoke of the space opera as the enabling form of Vonnegut's ideas, and this needs some explanation and perhaps demonstration. By "enabling form" I mean simply a contrivance which extends a writer's capacity for treating a subject or for expression beyond the limits of either traditional discourse or his own private views. To some extent, all fiction is an enabling form. I merely wish to emphasize at this point a construction which facilitates potential frames of reference beyond the ordinary conventions of his crafts. It need not be a form in which the writer himself believes, as it is clear that Vonnegut does not accept the assumptions or probabilities of space opera except in a comic manner. That is why space opera is for Vonnegut an enabling form. It permits him to develop textures of thought otherwise denied him.

The technique is a well-established device of satire. Swift and Twain may be cited as satirists who made use of similar enabling forms of fantasy and science fiction. That which common sense may deny Vonnegut, space opera will happily grant. The form supplies the cosmic perspective needed to dramatize the tragic-comic implications of modern thought and attitudes. For example, the conventions of space opera enable Vonnegut to show humans being controlled by extraterrestrials for a trivial purpose, and this then puts the author at liberty to develop all the implied potentials of such a hypothesis. In addition and by the same narrative stroke, Vonnegut is in a position to propose for imagined belief the great Tralfamadorian contribution to broadening the human world view by seeing the historical process as a sequence of events continuously present. The sense of resolution for private and social history is almost religious in its impact, and we may nearly forget the fact that it is predicated on an utterly fantastic premise. No matter, though, because it is the force and quality of the imagined elucidation that accounts in part for the novel's power. This aspect of the science fiction receives an even greater and perhaps more coherent emphasis in *Slaughterhouse-Five.*

The science-fiction manner is enabling in at least three other areas deserving attention. They are so closely related that if it were possible for argument to treat three ideas simultaneously, we should do so in order to stress the special degree of apposition they enjoy in the novel. For our purposes, however, they must be noted separately, and perhaps in less detail than they deserve.

The novel opens with a brief plunge into the mid-twenty-first century, when everyone enjoys peace of mind. We are then quickly recalled to the imagined near future of the story, but that glimpse is enough to achieve the desired effect. We may remind ourselves that space opera is not only science fiction but also fantasy and that fantasy is a literature of relocated perceptions. Relocation of perception is one of Vonnegut's characteristic techniques of narrative and is associated on a thematic level with a characteristically human response to the absurdity of existence. In *The Sirens of Titan* it is related to the failure of outward-looking metaphysics and theology to answer the fundamental questions about the purpose of life.

Relocated and dislocated perceptions are a creative action, a kind of fictional frenzy in which an artist may discover an appropriate if fantastic metaphor for his observations of human frustration. He is also free to adopt a necessary scale of values. In this case, Vonnegut employs the hyperrealism of space-opera narrative necessary to offer an appropriate assessment of human history and human folly. Such perceptions also make it possible, as we have seen, to raise grand questions within an appropriate reference frame.

Another related value of the space opera is that it seems to fulfill surreal archetypes by focusing on a narrative formula suggestive of a dreamlike process. The abrupt and apparently discursive transitions are expressive of the conventional space-opera narrative and of surreal values. Many times in the story, apparently accidental, random, or trivial incidents have a significance that is literally cosmic. Chrono's selection of a discarded piece of metal as a good-luck charm and Constant's decision to reassemble Salo are both critical in world history. It is not my purpose here to prove that Vonnegut is a surrealist in sheep's clothing, but it is impossible to ignore the richness and complexity of this novel's surrealistic techniques. They really deserve the kind of full-length study which is impossible here, but we may add a little to what has already been asserted about surrealism in the novel.

Some of the chief weapons of literary surrealism are satire and burlesque, and they are clearly important intentions in

The Sirens of Titan, a novel in which many of the pillars of Western social structure are undermined. Satirized in an obvious way is the assumption that good luck and bad luck are awards of Providence, a kind of inexplicable bestowal. Good luck is lavished on the ascendant types of our culture (almost always successful businessmen), and bad luck falls on the descendant and unfortunate.One form of luck bolsters a false confidence in one's superiority, while the other breeds confusion and despair. We all know where Vonnegut's primary sympathies lie. Also satirized, albeit more subtly, is the idea that chance events are entirely without significance. Chance comes as a kind of surreal revelation that the world has no purpose which can be defined as being exterior to man. Unwillingness to acknowledge chance events is always, in this novel at least, a sign of immaturity and misdirected values. Those who learn truth develop a serene passivity, a receptivity to the revelations chance produces among those who understand its nature. For the surrealist, chance is associated always with a revelation that brings an increased awareness of one's inner potentials. The validity of objects of chance is that they have the capacity to dislocate and liberate the imagination. Whether Vonnegut has the same kind of faith in the imagination as the surrealist is another matter. I doubt that he does. What cannot be doubted is how congenial he finds surrealist techniques of perception and revelation of meaning.

Our final view of space opera as an enabling form carries us out of science fiction and into comedy. Even for a space opera, Vonnegut's story is patently absurd, exaggerated, and disjointed in the development of its action. However, this very quality makes it possible for Vonnegut to dramatize most effectively the absurdity of contemporary values, philosophies, and aspirations. Like all comic exaggeration, it must be understood as exaggeration if a norm is to emerge in relief against ideas, beliefs, and mores we know at a given point in the novel to be foolish, misleading, or wrong. The tag line "somebody up there likes me" illustrates this technique very well.

Once again we find ourselves falling back on the terminology of surrealism for reference. If the aim is to alienate, the form chosen by the writer must be one that produces alienation. If the aim is to parody an idea or a point of view, his form must be expressive in a way which is itself absurd or foolish or which easily demonstrates folly. Vonnegut expresses both alienation and parody in *The Sirens of Titan* partly through his selection of space opera as a narrative form.

I have suggested already several advantages associated with the utopian introduction. It may be, however, that Vonnegut's principal motive in proposing the benefits of discovering the truths of inner space is to accomplish at the outset a necessary estrangement of the reader from his own present. Trapped into accepting the narrator's utopian perspective, the reader is compelled to adopt the aloof, disinterested pose of the narrator. The alienation of the reader is a necessary technique of satire, lest the author attack ideas and values with which the reader is engaged in active sympathy as he reads. The technique makes it possible for us to see the characters becoming puppets, and comic ones at that, driven by forces of which they are ignorant. Vonnegut's alienation of the reader is accomplished both by his selection of form and by his own narrative performance. The implied narrator-reader relationship is clearly established on the basis of the estranging distance of satire from its subject. The further on we read, the more we are drawn into adopting the perspective of the ironical but sympathetic observer. Even the narrator's handling of language contributes to the alienation. As the style descends to the level of the Voice of America's "Special English" broadcast, it is almost always a signal of satirical intent. This technique is more fully developed in later novels, especially in *God Bless You, Mr. Rosewater, Slaughterhouse-Five, Breakfast of Champions*, and *Slapstick*.[7]

Although Vonnegut makes use of many devices of satire and parody, there is one formula so closely related to the novel's narrative structure that it forms an underlying pattern of the plot. As we have already observed, the burlesque depends on taking the grand existential questions and refracting them through the medium of the space opera. Here is driven home the classic disproportion between style and sentiment of which Samuel Johnson spoke. The burlesque is achieved by treating the serious with levity, in this novel a self-conscious levity, the tone of which is identified elsewhere by Vonnegut with "gallows humor."[8] *The Sirens of Titan* is an extravaganza with a serious intent in which the comparatively trivial conventions of space opera are used to achieve disproportionately serious ends. Vonnegut uses space opera as his vehicle for both satire and apologue as a storyteller uses the formula of the shaggy-dog story—the playful hoaxing of the audience is a correlative intention of the storytelling process.[9] The reader is baited for being gulled by an author who cheerfully leads him off on one snipe hunt after another, treating him to a multiform shaggy-dog revelation of his own naive enjoyment of space opera, his own immature or perverted religious values, and his own bankrupt metaphysics as assessed and evaluated from the satirist's viewpoint.[10]

I have chosen the shaggy-dog story as a referent for two reasons. First, it seems to be the best model available to describe Vonnegut's gross plotting devices. Second, it illustrates the relationship between the comic superstructure of the novel and the surrealistic substructure. The shaggy-dog story has been defined as "A nonsensical joke that employs in the punch line a psychological *non sequitur*, a punning variation on a familiar saying, or a hoax, to trick the listener who expects conventional wit or humor. Such jokes usually describe ridiculous characters and actions and often are told (to heighten the effect of the final letdown) in a long drawn-out style with minute details, repetitions and elaborations."[11]

One of the keys of the shaggy-dog story is that it ends in a "psychological *non sequitur*."[12] Another way of putting it is that the story creates expectations which it does not intend to fulfill or does not gratify in the anticipated way. The story of Rumfoord is a minor example of this. From the time he was chrono-synclastic infundibulated, he became involved in directing the fortunes of the human race for as far as he could foresee. Well intentioned though they were, Rumfoord's efforts became a grotesque mockery of philanthropy. Like great metaphysical Rube Goldberg machines, his designs for the Martian mobilization and invasion are masterpieces of folly. They are almost unreasonable enough to work, except that the automated Martians used as cannon fodder were once human.

Even more grotesque is his plan for a new religion. "The Church of God the Utterly Indifferent" is another Goldberg device for doing something simple by an extravagantly indirect method. Vonnegut uses a like handicapping scheme for similar parody in his short story "Harrison Bergeron." In case we may need reminding, Vonnegut wants us to know that not all answers are solutions. Rumfoord in the infundibulum behaves as the god of the medieval theologians, foreknowing without forewilling; only Rumfoord does his share of the latter, in manipulating the Martians as well as Constant and his family. Ironically, in so doing he is himself being used by Tralfamadore, and he ends up not nearly the omniscient architect of the golden age he had hoped. Instead, he is unceremoniously kicked out of the universe on a mission to nowhere, still wondering about the purpose of it all.

Beatrice, who begins as Rumfoord's virginal wife, comes to discover that not to be used by anyone for anything is the worst fate that can happen to a human being. She spends the last year of her life on Titan, writing a book refuting Rumfoord's view of human history. Her book, unfinished, is left on Titan, forgotten. The anticipated vindication of Beatrice's hard-won philosophy of life is not realized, deliberately perhaps, because it then remains the illumination of a single person which foreshadows the great awakening to come in the next generation. That, the author seems to be saying, is enough.

The sirens are another one of Vonnegut's calculated letdowns. They are first seen in a photograph given to Malachi Constant by Rumfoord. Quickly they become symbols of Constant's desire at the beginning of his odyssey for ultimate sexual wish-fulfillment. They turn out to be idealized figures of women carved of Titanic peat by a bored robot. They end the way the original sirens did, at the bottom of the water, in this case a swimming pool. Their real power was to serve as a focal point for the rather limited aspirations of Constant's youth. Ultimately, they become castaway objects symbolic of those burnt-out passions that Constant survived. Unable to satisfy the desires they aroused, the sirens also symbolize the deceptive power of all idols man creates for himself and serve as a reminder that real satisfaction comes only from within the self through perfection of the moral sense. By the time Constant has reached Titan, he has changed so much that he does not even feel the irony of discovering the true nature of the sirens.

Malachi Constant's refrain that "somebody up there likes me" is an example of the shaggy-dog story's psychological non sequitur. The idea of being heaven-blessed is the delusion of several other characters, but in Constant's case it turns out to be literally true, although in a quite unexpected way.

There are two chief shaggy-dog plot lines in the novel. One is the revelation that human history has been manipulated for fifty thousand years by Tralfamadorians, who have been using the race to send semaphore signals to Salo. The second is the disclosure of the purpose behind Salo's mission across the universe. Both jokes are interrelated. The tale of Tralfamadorian control of human history is a hoax story. As Rumfoord tells Chrono: "In your pocket is the mysterious something that every Earthling was trying so desperately, so earnestly, so gropingly, so exhaustingly to produce and deliver" (p. 297). It was the spare part for Salo's ship, and so much for your marches of mind, *élan vital*, Oversouls, and the like.

The purpose of Salo's mission is learned too late to satisfy the curiosity of Rumfoord, who had asked him for friendship's sake to disclose it. By the time Salo overcomes his programmed prohibition to reveal the meaning of the message he is to deliver, Rumfoord has been bounced out of the universe. Perhaps the most expressive symbolic action of the book is Salo's humanization, the effect of observing the human comedy from his vantage point on Titan. Salo does reveal the message to those humans remaining on Titan—to Beatrice, Constant, and Chrono.

> "Would you like to know what the message is that I have been carrying for almost half a million Earthling years—the message I am supposed to carry for eighteen million more years?"
>
> He held out the square of aluminum in a cupped foot.
>
> "A dot," he said.
>
> "A single dot," he said.
>
> "The meaning of a dot in Tralfamadorian," said Old Salo, "is—*Greetings*." [pages 300–301]

A shaggy-dog story, to be sure, but one in which the humor is a refined exercise of the absurd. In form, at least, this is a species of the shaggy-dog story known as the "catch tale," ending with another of those letdowns which Eric Partridge calls a psychological non sequitur.

The shaggy-dog story is rarely if ever employed for the more serious purpose Vonnegut intends, and this is yet another example of the author's originality in blending together the structural features of literary types in the service of satire with a bedrock serious intention. The quality that most distinguishes this author's use of the shaggy-dog formula from its traditional function is the type of intended humor. Speaking on the subject, Vonnegut has said that laughter is one possible adjustment to grief, tragedy, and disaster—"the biggest laughs are based on the biggest disappointments and the biggest fears." [13]

The surrealist overtones of Vonnegut's use of jokes and joke formulas are possibly even greater than those inherent in the author's use of science-fiction elements and in his criticism of ideas. We must content ourselves here with but a few superficial observations. First of all, the shaggy-dog story, if not positively surrealist, is a close relation.[14] Not only is there an underlying similarity of form but also there is at least in this novel a purpose analogous to that of the surrealist joke: "The joke in Surrealism has that quality of disruptive humor in which the Surrealists place confidence. It calls into question our sense of what *is* and what *is not*, by prompting an awareness of what *might be*."[15] Surrealist humor like Vonnegut's attacks conventional ideas and challenges the accepted rational formulas from which social structures are born and nourished. At the comic level, this is precisely the way in which a shaggy-dog story amuses. When it is not willfully tedious, it is slyly irrelevant. It will delight in reducing the heroic to a punning variation of a well-worn cliché, as in the conclusion of that shaggiest of dog stories: "I wouldn't let a knight out on a dog like this." Vonnegut does likewise in reducing the purpose of human evolution to the absurdity of Tralfamadorian "Greetings."

Humor for surrealism and for Vonnegut is not supine. It is a dialectic beyond the reach of sophistry, because it tells the kinds of truth that attain an immediate recognition. In humor, there is an element of liberation, even of assertion, which cannot be overcome even at the point of a gun, for humor offers the pleasure of taking a kind of indirect action against oppressive realities.

> By laughing at the world, man destroys its power over his own subjectivity; if he can go one step further and laugh at his own despair, he can destroy the power of his own emotions—he succeeds then in completely alienating himself from the world and from his ordinary self. If he can laugh at himself, it is because he treats himself as if he were someone else. By this process, he abandons to the world that part of himself that is irretrievably engaged and retreats into his alter ego where he enjoys absolute detachment and freedom. Or, to put it in Freudian terms, black humor is the extreme means by which the ego surmounts the traumas of the external world and demonstrates that for the great distress of the ego, the remedy can come only from the id.[16]

Vonnegut's own remarks on humor, particularly gallows humor, develop some of the same points.[17] The purposes of humor in this novel are therefore both public and private, purposes which he was to demonstrate even more compellingly in the later novels. Jokes express the tragic content of human experience, which paradoxically is its meaninglessness, in a form that makes it acceptable.[18]

We may now return to our point of departure and propose an answer to the queston, does Vonnegut write science fiction? The answer must be that he does, or at least did in *The Sirens of Titan*. However, in view of our analysis, a simple *yes* or *no* to that question is not adequately responsive and may even be misleading. The science-fiction narrative is certainly not an add-on feature. As we have seen, space opera establishes the aggregate pattern of action and order of probabilities, but it also serves the larger purpose of satire and criticism of ideas. It is for the author the enabling form of both visions and something more, because space opera communicates its form as part of its content, both dramatizing and illustrating the absurdity of trying to discover or impose a pattern of outward meaning or purpose on historical events. Underlying these structures is the formula of the shaggy-dog story in at least several of its variations, including the hoaxing and catch tales, each producing its characteristic psychological effect as a dislocation of response in the reader. In all this, we should certainly see a remarkable orchestration of narrative techniques and forms which gain a consistent resonance from the surrealist elements to be found at all levels of the novel.

If we answer *yes* to the question of classifying *The Sirens of Titan* as science fiction, it must necessarily be a heavily qualified *yes*. While the science fiction of the novel must be affirmed, we have seen that it is employed for unusual ends, including the author's criticism of ideas, satire, burlesque, shaggy-dog jokes, and surrealist effects. If a term had to be found for such a blending of types and genres, I should be least unhappy to call it comic-satire. Whatever it may be called, we should come away from our analysis with a renewed appreciation of the author's powers of invention, plotting, and narrative architecture. What may appear on the surface to be a rather simplistic fable turns out to be a far more original and satisfying work of art. In the future, critics will want to take into account the author's remarkable success in putting together such a complex and expressive form in this early work when they approach the less intricate structures of his later fiction.[19] If Vonnegut is a writer of science fiction, we must conclude that it is of the same type found in Swift's *Gulliver's Travels,* Voltaire's *Candide,* and Twain's *A Connecticut Yankee in King Arthur's Court,* in which fantasy or science fiction was the enabling form for satire and serious comedy.

NOTES

1. See, for instance, Vonnegut's essay on "Science Fiction" in *Wampeters, Foma & Granfalloons,* pp. 1–2. Future references to material in this collection, including "*Playboy* Interview," will be identified parenthetically by short-title convention in the text where appropriate.
2. See Brian Aldiss, *Billion Year Spree* (New York, 1974), p. 316.
3. Kurt Vonnegut, Jr., *The Sirens of Titan* (New York: Delacorte Press/Seymour Lawrence, 1971), p. 7. All future references are taken from this edition.
4. J. H. Matthews, *An Introduction to Surrealism* (University Park, Pa., 1965), p. 118.
5. "*Playboy* Interview," in *Wampeters,* p. 262.
6. Vonnegut spoke of this during the interview: "There are people, particularly dumb people, who are in terrible trouble and never get out of it, because they're not intelligent enough. And it strikes me as gruesome and comical that in our culture we have an expectation that a man can always solve his problems. There is that implication that if you just have a little more energy, a little more fight, the problem can always be solved. This is so untrue that it makes me want to cry—or laugh" (*Wampeters,* p. 258).
7. This is not really the place to make anything like an analysis of Vonnegut's stylistic mannerisms, however valuable such a

study might be. The curious reader may note, though, how both the tone and language give the effect of slowed-down thought process. It is the kind of exaggerated declarative style used in Voice of America broadcasts designed for listeners trying to learn the language. Vonnegut uses it, I believe, with a doubly ironic intent. First this sort of primer-English has the effect of a stylistic parody of the thought, and it acts as a signal to the reader that the ideas are grotesque even if they happen to be otherwise convincing or attractive, as they often are. We hear echoes of these accents of Vonnegut's common-man comic figure in the refrains which clutter these same later novels with such profusion that it becomes a direct assault on the reader in the latest two novels (*Breakfast of Champions* and *Slapstick*). The strategy I take to be a literary analogue of the conditioned-reflex experiment, with Vonnegut as experimenter and the reader as subject.

8. *Wampeters*, p. 256.
9. The author has spoken of his use of jokes in the *Playboy* interview as follows: "I'm in the business of making jokes; it's a minor art form. I've had some natural talent for it. It's like building a mousetrap. You build the trap, you cock it, you trip it, and then bang! My books are essentially mosaics made up of a whole bunch of tiny little chips; and each chip is a joke" (*Wampeters*, p. 258).
10. When Marshall McLuhan preached that "the medium is the message," he might have been writing a review of *The Sirens of Titan*. Considered as satire, the most important feature of this novel is not its idea content but rather the way in which the author makes the ideas accessible to the reader. The overriding message, so to speak, is the author's (or his narrator's) perception of the world as imitated. In that angle of vision we feel the exercise of the satirist's moral authority. It is there, as well, that the character of the satire is also discovered, there in the author's implied models of human behavior that we feel the bitterness of a Swift, the energetic wit of a Voltaire, the shrewd common sense of a Twain, and the compassion of Vonnegut.
11. Jan Harold Brunvand, "A Classification for Shaggy Dog

Stories," *JAF*, 76 (1963), p. 44. Brunvand's definition relies heavily on Eric Partridge's *The "Shaggy Dog" Story. Its Origin, Development and Nature*, Freeport, New York, 1970 (a reprint of the 1953 edition).

12. See Partridge, p. 87.
13. *Wampeters*, p. 257.
14. John Waller in his *Shaggy Dog and Other Surrealist Fables* (London, 1953) offers tantalizing suggestions of the relationship between the two forms but never develops them beyond the initial attribution.
15. Matthews, p. 146. A little further on in the text, Matthews comments, "In Surrealism, laughter is anarchic, calling for a revision of standards in every sphere it touches, and appealing directly to a sense of the marvelous. Surrealist laughter is militant, working towards the destruction of the present and the fuller revelation of the future which is surreal" (p. 148).
16. Paul C. Ray, *The Surrealist Movement in England* (Ithaca, 1971), p. 60.
17. See especially "*Playboy* Interview," in *Wampeters*, pp. 256–258.
18. The joke is also an archetypal form to be used when a writer wishes to convey the ironic potential of the contrast between human expectation and human performance, between hopes for the future and the testimony of the past, and between the human inclination to make an allegory of human life and the utterly unconscious forces of nature.
19. This formula is to some extent recovered by Vonnegut in his most recent novel, *Slapstick* (1976).

Willis E. McNelly

Kurt Vonnegut as Science-Fiction Writer

I love you sons of bitches. . . . You're all I read any more. You're the only ones who'll talk about the *really* terrific changes going on, the only ones crazy enough to know that life is a space voyage, and not a short one, either, but one that'll last for billions of years. You're the only ones with guts enough to *really* care about the future, who *really* notice what machines do to us, what wars do to us, what cities do to us . . . You're the only ones zany enough to agonize over time and distances without limit, over mysteries that will never die, over the fact that we are right now determining whether the space voyage for the next billion years or so is going to be Heaven or Hell. [*God Bless You, Mr. Rosewater*, page 27]

Thus Eliot Rosewater invaded a convention of science-fiction writers at Milford, Pennsylvania—an actual conference first organized by Damon Knight, founder of the Science Fiction Writers of America.

"Once mistakenly typed as a science fiction writer, Vonnegut is now recognized as a mainstream storyteller often fascinated by the tragic and comic possibilities of machines." Thus the dust jacket for *Slaughterhouse-Five*.

And what's the truth? Is he or isn't he? Does he or doesn't he? The answer is probably somewhere between the two, for despite what his publisher seems to think, Vonnegut has never been limited to the comic or tragic possibilities of machines. Perhaps he didn't wish to be limited to mere space opera—thud and blunder among the stars—for, as Brian Aldiss has remarked in *Billion Year Spree*, "Vonnegut sped right out of the field as soon as he had cash for the gasoline" (page 316).

It might be said, in fact, that since *Rosewater* Vonnegut has done everything possible to disassociate himself from science fiction as a genre. His books are almost never found in the SF paperback shelves—and I wonder if his clout with the publishers is such that they insist on the physical separation, almost as if Vonnegut's books might be soiled if they were placed next to those of Clarke, Bradbury, or Asimov.

Why has he distanced himself from SF? There are a number of answers, of course, not the least of which is the still-shabby unrespectability of the genre. The interviewer in the famous *Playboy* interview of Vonnegut a number of years ago remarks that the standard critical appraisal of SF is that "it's low rent," and Vonnegut's response gives us a clear statement of his position: "Well, the rate of payment has always been very low compared with that for other forms of writing."

So then, contrary to being what more than one SF writer has termed "An uncle tom-morrow," Vonnegut is simply a writer who wishes to make money and found that the half a cent a word of the pulps didn't begin to equal a fifty-thousand-dollar advance for a mainstream novel and a quarter-of-a-million-dollar sale for movie rights. Of course, you really can't blame a writer for wanting to make money, and if making money means you're going to turn your back on what made you a cult hero, so be it, Vonnegut seems to say. Wasn't it Samuel Johnson who said that anyone who wrote for anything except money is a fool? Whatever else Vonnegut is, he's no fool, although he often plays the clown, sort of a latter-day Touchstone.

Yet in that same *Playboy* interview Vonnegut avers that science fiction seemed to be the best way to write about his thoughts on various subjects: General Electric and the loss of human dignity; loss of faith in government; loss of faith in God; loss of faith in the innocence of science; loss of faith in . . . well, you supply your own favorite Vonnegut metaphor.

At this point, let me tread foolishly into the problem of definition. Science fiction probably has as many definitions as literature itself, and whether it's simply a pulp genre striving for respectability, or future-scene fiction, or speculative fiction (as Robert Heinlein and Harlan Ellison would have it), or a branch of imaginative literature which deals with the interface between man and the machine, concerned with ideas and their impact rather than character—or any of a hundred other definitions—makes little difference. But perhaps we can all agree with Robert Scholes, whose recent *Structural Fabulation* is a superlative analysis of the form, that SF is "fiction that offers us a world clearly and radically discontinuous from the one we know, yet returns to confront that world in some cognitive way" (page 29).

Anything else written under the guise of SF is trash and should be consigned to the nearest rubbish heap of a remainder shelf. But Vonnegut? Do his works, regardless of what label he or his publishers prefer, offer us worlds radically discontinuous from our own, and are those worlds confronted cognitively? With a few exceptions, I think so, but whether his vision has changed perceptibly since, say, 1955, is open to doubt. In fact, Aldiss maintains in *Billion Year Spree* that "Kurt Vonnegut has not improved since he has been voted one of America's heap big gurus" (page 314). And I might add that I find *Breakfast of Champions* a spectacular failure, a condition I ascribe to the fact that it *isn't* science fiction. But let that pass.

Vonnegut's vision seems to be a thoroughgoing pessimistic one, resembling either a mordant existentialism, revisited, or black humor which may or may not indicate a belief in a small-"g" god whose name may be, at best, random chance. After all, whether the world ends with the whimper of Ice-Nine or the bang of a Tralfamadorian chain reaction makes little difference. Remember the last sentence of The Books of Bokonon: "I would take from the ground some of the blue-white poison that makes statues of men; and I would make a statue of myself, lying on my back, grinning horribly, and thumbing my nose at You Know Who" (*Cat's Cradle*, page 231).

Is Vonnegut, then, only in the business of making jokes—bad jokes, sad jokes, irreverent jokes? He seems to think so, and once called it a minor art form. "My books," he said in the *Playboy* interview, "are essentially mosaics made up of a whole bunch of little chips; and each chip is a joke . . . I've gotten into the joke business." Later on in the same interview he responds to the question of why he used the science-fiction mode in *Slaughterhouse-Five*: "These things are intuitive. There's never any strategy meeting about what you're going to do; you just come to work every day. And the science-fiction passages in *Slaughterhouse-Five* are just like the clown in Shakespeare. When Shakespeare figured the audience had had enough of the heavy stuff, he'd let up a little, bring on a clown or a foolish innkeeper or something like that, before he'd become serious again. And trips to other planets, science fiction of an obviously kidding sort, is equivalent to bringing on the clowns every so often to lighten things up" (page 68).

Well, if Vonnegut is in the business of making jokes, we may, of course, discount his remarks as merely another joke. To be sure, I'm not another De Quincey, trying to write something analogous to his essay about the Porter's scene in *Macbeth*, tentatively entitled "On the Chrono-Synclastic Infundibula Scene in *The Sirens of Titan*." However, comedy has traditionally provided great writers—and Vonnegut may be one of them although his veiled comparison of himself with Shakespeare leaves me a bit limp—with the means of commenting on the world without fear of getting caught up by it. Most classic clowns, whether they be Lear's Fool, Touchstone, Chaplin, Ringo Starr, or Woody Allen, have views that are radically discontinuous from our own, but views that do confront our world very cognitively indeed. In this sense, perhaps the greatest science-fiction motion picture ever made is Chaplin's *Modern Times*, followed closely by Woody Allen's *Sleeper*, and the sagest comment Touchstone's remark, "The fool doth think he is wise, but the wise man doth know himself to be a fool." Vonnegut, then, is the wise man who knows himself to be a fool, a wise fool, a witty fool, a deeply contemplative fool who moralizes on the time with lungs that crow like Chanticleer.

A detailed examination of just how Vonnegut utilizes science-fiction devices as foolish-wise commentary in *Slaughterhouse-Five* might indicate just where Vonnegut stands as a science-fiction writer. Of course, Vonnegut had been prodigious in creating science-fiction devices showing, as Aldiss has indicated, "an exuberance of invention which he shares with most of the better SF writers" (page 316). This very exuberance has led him to produce an entire pantheon of characters who stalk his pages in novel after novel: Rosewater, Howard W. Campbell, Jr., Malachi Constant, and, of course, the enigmatic figure of Kilgore Trout, author of eighty-seven paperbacks, all of them unknown outside the science-fiction field. Parenthetically, I once felt that if I were Theodore Sturgeon I would sue Vonnegut for libel, because Sturgeon is still perhaps the finest stylist that SF has yet produced, but when Vonnegut gave Trout the Nobel Prize for medicine I changed my mind, even though the award may be nothing but another of Vonnegut's complicated "in" jokes.

Before being set free in *Breakfast of Champions,* many of these characters have one final say about science fiction in *Slaughterhouse-Five.* "So they were trying to re-invent themselves and their universe. Science fiction was a big help. Rosewater said an interesting thing to Billy one time about a book that wasn't science fiction. He said that everything there was to know about life was in *The Brothers Karamazov,* by Feodor Dostoevsky. 'But that isn't *enough* any more,' said Rosewater" (page 87).

How is science fiction a help? As I indicated in an earlier study of Vonnegut ("Science Fiction: The Modern Mythology," *America,* September 5, 1970), I feel that Vonnegut is using science fiction and science-fiction devices as a kind of objective correlative, enabling him to achieve an empathetic symbiosis whereby the disparate esthetic emotions in the mind of the artist are recreated by the reader.

Thus Vonnegut, faced with the horror of Dresden, its omnipresence of cruel disaster and casual slaughter, wills that the reader share both his incomprehension and his horror. I also suspect that the distance of years made Vonnegut gradually become aware of a horror greater even than that of Dresden itself: an American public that has managed to ignore the moral responsibility for Dresden as well as the ethical implications of such an attack. What must have been the culmination of a chain of horrors to Vonnegut was the fact that few Americans even knew of the attack in which over 135,000 people died. How to communicate the hurt, the guilt, the sense of loss of belief, must have been an enormous problem to Vonnegut, and if he was a comedian, he was, as the old saying goes, too old to cry and too hurt to laugh.

So science fiction in Vonnegut's hands enables us to distance ourselves from ourselves, to face problems we cannot otherwise face directly. T. S. Eliot once pointed out in "East Coker" that "Human beings cannot stand very much reality." Perhaps they can stand the unreality of science fiction, Vonnegut seems to reason, and face a little bit more reality after reading a novel like *Slaughterhouse-Five* than they could before they read it. To enable himself and his readers to cope with the slaughter of innocents, Vonnegut reinvents Tralfamadore as a sort of looking-glass extension of Earth. If we cannot be moved by Dresden, perhaps the awareness of what happened to the universe with the coldly logical madness of Tralfamadore may cause us at least to stop and think.

One problem still remains, however, in this consideration of Vonnegut as a SF writer. Just how good a SF writer is he? How does he rank in comparison with such "pure" SF writers as Isaac Asimov, Robert A. Heinlein, Arthur C. Clarke, Ray Bradbury, Philip K. Dick, and Brian Aldiss? A detailed comparison is impossible, of course, but certain general observations might be made about the half-dozen writers mentioned here. All of them differ radically from one another, just as Vonnegut differs radically from each of them. No one who has read any science fiction at all could possibly mistake a work by Ray Bradbury for one by, say, Philip K. Dick. While Bradbury's stories are redolent with a nostalgia for a past recreated in the future, Dick's are studied, powerful Pirandelloesque pieces of hallucination, illusion, paranoia, and altered states of reality.

The problem, then, obviously, is one of definition. Is it possible to construct a definition of science fiction (of speculative literature, if you prefer) which can include both Bradbury, Dick, Heinlein, and Vonnegut? Scholes may help us here, but standard popular definitions of science fiction fail utterly. Nothing, in other words, resists categorization or definition more than science fiction, and if Vonnegut wishes to define himself out of the SF field, that's his privilege or his hang-up, not ours. Vonnegut almost seems to say, "Kilgore Trout writes science fiction. What he writes is trash, junk. I don't write trash or junk. Therefore I don't write science fiction."

So he approaches the mainstream in SF clothing and tries to shed the SF clothing all the way to the bank.

To return to the problems of definition: Just as it is virtually impossible to construct a definition of science fiction which can include Dick, Bradbury, Asimov, and anybody else you might happen to mention, including Theodore Sturgeon, Kilgore Trout, E. E. "Doc" Smith, and Arthur C. Clarke, so it is equally impossible to construct a definition of science fiction which might encompass *God Bless You, Mr. Rosewater*, *The Sirens of Titan*, *Cat's Cradle*, *Mother Night*, and *Slaughterhouse-Five*. Again Vonnegut seems to say, impishly perhaps: "You can't define SF to include me. Therefore I don't write SF."

And the problem is somewhat more than difficult. *Cat's Cradle* abounds in the tensions of a pessimistic-optimistic religiosity which approaches self-parody. It admits of no definition except that of description: It spoofs; it spoofs Vonnegut, objectivity, religion, illusion, and fictive reality, to name only a few items. Its truth and shameless lies are lies and shameless truth. In the end, all perish in the science-fiction device of Ice-Nine. And Vonnegut says he doesn't write science fiction! Nonsense.

So also with *The Sirens of Titan.* Rich in absurd invention, the novel becomes a romp, and, as Aldiss puts it, "its hither-thither technique is a pinch from the Wide Screen Baroque School" (page 314). To be sure, the chrono-synclastic infundibulum may be merely a very precious way of saying that if you can see the future, you either won't like it or you'll be bored by it, but it's still a science-fiction device utilized or invented to permit Vonnegut to moralize on the time, as Touchstone once said.

A similar brief analysis of all of the novels up to *Breakfast of Champions,* which may (or may not) be a different story, would indicate that, if Vonnegut hasn't written science fiction, he's been obsessed by it, and I for one fail to see any real difference. *Player Piano* is pure extrapolative science fiction, as Vonnegut seems to say, in company with writers like Bradbury or Clarke, "If this goes on . . ." *The Sirens of Titan* is moralizing science fiction; *Cat's Cradle* is mordantly predictive science fiction; *Mother Night* is obsessed by science fiction in the person of the ambiguous antihero, Howard W. Campbell, Jr.; *God Bless You, Mr. Rosewater* sends a message in the form of science fiction; and *Slaughterhouse-Five* is science fiction as allegory or even parable. I might even maintain here, somewhat tentatively to be sure, that *Breakfast of Champions* shows us science fiction as nostalgia, at least in those sections where Vonnegut sets his science-fiction creations free.

In the end, what are we to think of Vonnegut's disclaimers about science fiction? They seem largely to be protests against being categorized too easily. And easy definitions of science fiction resist the kind of oversimplification that any writer would resent. Scholes's more metaphysical definition may help us here once again and finally put to rest Vonnegut's allegations about the genre which made him both rich and famous. Tralfamadore, Kilgore Trout, and the rest of the science-fiction impedimenta that Vonnegut is so obsessed by are certainly radically discontinuous from the world we know, yet Vonnegut forces us, through his use of these very devices, to face our world both emotionally and cognitively.

In our world mission and futility brother each other, but the cyclic vision of a spring bird chirping "Poo-tee-weet" augers a rebirth. If Vonnegut uses science fiction, then, as a counterthrust to his mordant humor with his comedic vision providing a final affirmation or hope, so it goes.

William Veeder

Technique as Recovery: Lolita *and* Mother Night

Goethe said once that he had never heard of a crime he couldn't imagine himself committing. A comparable recognition of common fallibility is often fostered by art. Despite our horror at Macbeth's murderous conduct, despite our recognition that he must die, we find ourselves—amazingly, perversely—drawn to him as Macduff attacks. That "even villains have real passions" is true not only in *Pelham* but throughout the tradition of fiction. Charlotte Brontë cautioned herself in her diary—"about villains—Moderation to be observed here"—because she knew that only in melodrama do the motives of villains lack the moderating complexity of our own. Especially since World War II, the morally ambiguous protagonist has become a paramount feature of fiction. We can neither bless wholeheartedly nor righteously banish such powerful contemporaries as the demonic prophets of Flannery O'Connor, the fouled voyagers of Samuel Beckett, or the homicidal and fantastic perceivers of Robbe-Grillet. These and many other figures of modern fiction foster in us an awareness like Goethe's—that we are all capable of almost anything. This awareness gained through literature is particularly important because it counters our workaday tendency of mind. In our daily rush and self-absorption we inevitably simplify, separating sheep from goats with a convenient ease which usually gives the benefit of the doubt to ourselves. Art challenges such simplification. "Technique as recovery" is obviously indebted to Mark Schorer's famous concept of "technique as discovery," but the critical focus is altered. Schorer demonstrates that the artist discovers his true meaning and true self through formal innovation; I focus on how these formal innovations help the reader recover his best self by recovering his bond with all mankind. Through technique we recover our essential humanity, though the experience often requires us to recognize, as Goethe said, how inhuman we can be.

Recovery is central to both *Lolita* and *Mother Night*. Nabokov and Vonnegut each present protagonists "guilty" of particularly antisocial crimes: rape and anti-Semitism. Besides complicating enormously what these crimes mean (in ways which I will discuss soon), both novelists reveal repeatedly that none of us is entirely restricted to or entirely free from the most savage instincts. Vonnegut insists that Hitler's minions were not unqualifiedly loathsome, even as he displays the murderous instincts of "good citizens" throughout America. Good citizens fare no better in *Lolita*—their children copulating behind bushes, their educational theories advanced by the obscene Miss Pratt, their laws on lovers' ages neglecting utterly the real moral issues involved. Nabokov will not agree with repressive "Mr. 'Windmuller' . . . that 'the long shadow of this sorry and sordid business' should not reach the community to which he is proud to belong" (page 6), because this sorry, sordid business began in Windmuller's community and aspects of the business will abide there until Nabokov's perceptions about the communal heart are taken to heart.

Studying the techniques of recovery in *Lolita* and *Mother Night* is especially useful because these novels share more than an emphasis on our common guilt. There is an amazing number of other similarities. (My point is not that Nabokov influenced Vonnegut directly—although Vonnegut surely read the notorious *Lolita* at least half a decade before publishing *Mother Night*—but that the two novels are so similar that their differences reveal much about the novels and about the function of technique in fiction.) In particular, *Lolita* and *Mother Night* share similar situations, themes, and techniques. The situations of Humbert Humbert and Howard Campbell are identical: Both men, accused of nasty crimes, write their Confessions in prison. Both prisoners self-consciously give evidence against themselves, pass judgment on themselves, and cheat the executioner by dying after their last Confessions. Both men are "innocent" of the crimes charged against them. Humbert was the one seduced, Campbell was an American spy. Yet, in a more basic sense, both prisoners are guilty—Humbert because he violated, not Lolita's maidenhead, but her maidenhood; Campbell because a man who fosters worldwide anti-Semitism is, in fact, an anti-Semite. Each prisoner has had two love affairs, the second of which (with Lolita and Resi) is pursued in light of the first (Annabelle and Helga). Both aging lovers know they cannot relive their past, each finds his past inescapable; both lovers employ detectives to find their lost loves, and inevitably fail.

Thematically, love is a major concern in both *Lolita* and *Mother Night*. Since I discuss "romantic" love later, let me briefly note now an epistemological aspect of this theme. Both novels reveal the perils of human intercourse. Problems of perception, of identity, of self-knowledge, and of the unreliability of appearances all compound the lovers' plights with their fair ladies and with ill-informed and untrustworthy societies. Social and personal problems of epistemology fuse when the voices of little children convey problematic lessons about love. Formally, each novel is composed of two basic parts—an editor's preface and a lengthy Confession. Each preface, though in different ways, prepares us to read the Confessions which follow. This two-part structure is also reflected in the double titles to the novels: *Lolita* is subtitled "Confession of a White Widowed Male"; *Mother Night*, "The Confessions of Howard W. Campbell, Jr.," who is a white widowed male. Although both novels share specific techniques, these techniques are less important for now than the fact that *Lolita* and *Mother Night* have major formal differences. Since the novels share basic situations and themes, we can seek in their formal differences for that difference of final effect which ultimately distinguishes the achievements of Nabokov and Vonnegut. Let us begin with techniques used in the prefaces to each novel; we can then focus upon two formal aspects of the Confessions themselves.

I

In the "Foreword" to *Lolita* and the "Editor's Note" to *Mother Night*, John Ray, Jr., and Kurt Vonnegut, Jr., establish their credentials as editors in most conventional fashion.

> As for my own tinkerings with the text, they are few. I have corrected some spelling, removed some exclamation points, and all the italics are mine.

> I have in several instances changed names, in order to spare embarrassment or worse to innocent persons still living. [page x]
>
> My task proved simpler than either of us had anticipated. Save for the correction of obvious solecisms and a careful suppression of a few tenacious details that despite "H.H." 's own efforts still subsisted in his text as signposts and tombstones (indicative of places or persons that taste would conceal and compassion spare), this remarkable memoir is presented intact. [pages 5–6]

Beyond these conventionalities, the editors introduce us to the ambiguous protagonists. The techniques used here affect our response to the editors and indicate the formal issues which lie ahead in the Confessions. In Ray's Foreword we encounter

> I have no intention to glorify "H.H." No doubt, he is horrible, he is abject, he is a shining example of moral leprosy, a mixture of ferocity and jocularity that betrays supreme misery perhaps, but is not conducive to attractiveness. . . . A desperate honesty that throbs through his confession does not absolve him from sins of diabolical cunning. He is abnormal. He is not a gentleman. But how magically his singing violin can conjure up a tendresse, a compassion for Lolita that makes us entranced with the book while abhorring its author! [page 7]

Early critics who attacked the Foreword as "inconsistent" were at least recognizing how problematic the writing is. Could any one consciousness produce all the judgments in the passage above? Could a mind primitive enough to accuse Humbert of being "not a gentleman" also achieve the astute insight that Humbert is "a mixture of ferocity and jocularity that betrays supreme misery perhaps, but is not conducive to attractiveness"? The simple-minded moralizing of "he is a shining example of moral leprosy" seems fundamentally incompatible with the sophistication of "a desperate honesty that throbs through his confession does not absolve him from sins of diabolical cunning." To explain the presence of judgments so diverse, we cannot minimize the diversity. That no single mind—short of incapacitating schizophrenia—could have produced such disparate judgments does not mean that Nabokov is guilty of inconsistent characterization. Inconsistency is his point. Nabokov is not creating a "character" in J.R., Jr. He is creating an experience for us readers. In trying to make sense of the Foreword, we learn how to read the Confession. When we cannot fit Ray's diverse judgments into a single, coherent "character," we recognize how inappropriate our effort is. There is no J.R., Jr. There is no one authoritative consciousness ordering the world of words and judging the actions of men reliably. We are thrown back on ourselves. Our only guide is our response to the words. "He is not a gentleman" and "he is a shining example of moral leprosy" are judgments so trite and banal, so rigid and righteous, that we dismiss the judge and withold our evaluation of the prisoner. On the other hand, "how magically his singing violin can conjure up a tendresse, a compassion for Lolita that makes us entranced with the book while abhorring its author" is a judgment complex enough to be potentially appropriate; when we come upon that violin playing two hundred pages later, our evaluation of the judgment is confirmed.

The Foreword to *Lolita* throws us especially on our own resources because incompatibilities are not always separated off clearly into different sentences.

> If . . . an editor attempted to dilute or omit scenes that a certain type of mind might call "aphrodisiac" . . . one would have to forego the publication of *Lolita* altogether, since those

> very scenes that one might ineptly accuse of a sensuous existence of their own, are the most strictly functional onces in the development of a tragic tale tending unswervingly to nothing less than a moral apotheosis. [pages 6–7]

Up to "tragic tale," the judgment here is sane and sophisticated. The sexual encounters in *Lolita* are as indispensable as comparable moments are in *Ulysses*. But "tending unswervingly to nothing less than a moral apotheosis" comes from a radically different mentality. Here is that righteous moralism which Nabokov parodies so often and which reappears in "a shining example of moral leprosy." Only by developing sufficient sensitivity to the language to recognize multiple mentalities within the supposedly homogeneous confines of a single sentence can we hope to recognize and interpret the ambivalence which glimmers throughout Humbert's Confession. Nabokov does not abandon us to moral incoherence. But he does force us into active engagement with the words themselves. Nabokov is practicing here what Henry James preached a century before—that "[when the art is great] *then* the reader does quite half the labor." By making us actively engage the language of the Foreword, Nabokov makes us part of the process of producing meaning. Ambivalence can exist as a fully realized theme in *Lolita* only if it exists as a fully experienced fact for us readers. Techniques which make us do half the work of realizing (in several senses) the ambivalence allow us, in turn, to recover our contact with the mystery which inheres in real-life situations and which the situations of daily life often dissipate. In preparing us to experience the ambiguity of Humbert Humbert, Nabokov puts us back in touch with the ambiguity which is us all.

Vonnegut takes up the same issue of ambiguity in his Editor's Note:

> To say that he [Campbell] was a writer is to say that the demands of art alone were enough to make him lie, and to lie without seeing any harm in it. To say that he was a playwright is to offer an even harsher warning to the reader, for no one is a better liar than a man who has warped lives and passions onto something as grotesquely artificial as a stage. [page ix]

While Nabokov makes us experience ambivalence through his formal techniques, Vonnegut relies here upon assertion. He wants no ambiguity about ambiguity. Artists are liars. Although we may acknowledge and even embrace this fashionable truism, we are troubled by its form. Assertions have exactly that formal rigidity and epistemological certitude which a world rife with lies should undermine. Uncertain about the status of assertions in such a world, we are also uncertain about our own status as the passive recipients of assertions. Since we are told about an ambiguity which we do not experience, the ambiguity does not seem very real. On the other hand, if Campbell's world is really as ambiguous as Vonnegut says, why are we made passive when the active engagement of all our powers seems essential?

> And, now that I've said that about lying, I will risk the opinion that lies told for the sake of dramatic effect—in the theater, for instance, and in Campbell's confessions, perhaps—can be, in a higher sense, the most beguiling forms of truth. [page ix]

How much is Vonnegut actually risking here? Despite the tentativeness of "will risk . . . perhaps . . . can be," Vonnegut seems in fact to be asserting fairly unequivocally the old truism that the lies of art are deep truths. Our response is uncertainty. On the one hand we wonder how our continuing passivity before Vonnegut's assertions can prepare us for the supposedly unreliable Confession ahead. On the other hand we wonder how much ambivalence remains once the lies of art are revealed as deep truths. True lies may well mean that Campbell's world is less radical and subversive epistemologically than Vonnegut's preceding sentences suggested. And, finally, what indication is there that Vonnegut recognizes our questions, that he intends to foster this much uncertainty? I see no indication of such awareness here at the beginning of the Note. How about at the end?

> I would prefer to dedicate it [*Mother Night*] to one familiar person, male or female, widely known to have done evil while saying to himself, "A very good me, the real me, a me made in heaven, is hidden deep inside."
>
> I can think of many examples. . . . But there is no single name to which I might aptly dedicate this book—unless it would be my own.
>
> Let me honor myelf in that fashion, then:
>
> This book is rededicated to Howard W. Campbell, Jr., a man who served evil too openly and good too secretly, the crime of his times.
>
> Kurt Vonnegut, Jr. [page xii]

This rededication raises one of the central issues of *Mother Night*—that of the moral worth of the prisoner. To what extent is Campbell, for all his failings, a figure worthy of permanent commemoration? Vonnegut signs his name right after Campbell's rededication, but Vonnegut makes no comment. What are we to think about Campbell? Authorial silence does not necessarily endow the protagonist with a separate—and therefore potentially mysterious—existence. Silence in the Note contributes less to mystery than to confusion. While we do not want to be told "the answer" about Campbell (any more than we wanted to be told the answer about lies and truth), we do expect the writer to establish the nature of our dilemma. We are challenged by the Foreword to

Lolita because we are taught there the reading skills which we need to deal with Nabokov's world. The skills define the world. We feel that we know where we are, even though where we are is a chimeric, inscrutable place. The Note to *Mother Night* leaves us largely in the dark. Vonnegut talks too much and too little, makes us too passive and too restive. We passive recipients of asserted truths search anxiously for the tools, the reading skills, by which we can know and deal with Campbell's world. Assertions and silence: Neither separately nor together do these techniques make us active in a way whereby we can do half the work.

I do not want to overstate our difficulties with the Note to *Mother Night*. What is crucial here is less the difficulties themselves than the problem which they are symptomatic of. Not only are we ill prepared to function in the complex epistemological situation which apparently awaits us in the Confession, but the absence of any education comparable to our experience in the Foreword to *Lolita* means that we are drawn less intensely to Howard Campbell than we are to Humbert Humbert. Technique in Vonnegut's Note has not made us recover a sense of shared humanity with the prisoner and with all our brother criminals. Campbell tells us that many men are guilty of his crime. But we do not *feel* that. Campbell is not very real for us. Not yet. Although a powerful interest in the protagonist would obviously be an asset here, the crucial question is whether our lack of interest is symptomatic of a more serious failure throughout the rest of *Mother Night*. The extent to which Campbell, and Humbert Humbert, exist for us in the confessional sections of their novels depends largely on the formal techniques used there by Vonnegut and Nabokov. Let us focus on two technical considerations: how love is presented in the Confessions, and how the ambiguous narrators are used.

II

In many respects, Nabokov and Vonnegut agree about "love." Both novelists present "romantic lovers" of the most chivalric sort. Lionel Trilling's notion of Humbert as courtly lover helps us also understand Howard Campbell, whose plays feature " 'pure hearts and heroes . . . you believe in romance' " (page 30). Both novelists show their courtly lovers haunted by fair ladies living and dead. Most important, both novelists are concerned with the limitations of romantic love. Humbert and Howard fail to go beyond one-woman love to an intercourse with humanity. Solipsism threatens both lovers. Take, as a key here, the initials "H.H." Throughout *Lolita*, mirrors reflect Humbert Humbert's infatuation with himself. In loving Lolita, Humbert is in fact making love to himself. Annabelle Leigh was himself projected outward, and Lolita perpetuates Annabelle as alter ego. Thus, when Humbert takes Lolita into the motel room, "there was a double bed, a mirror, a double bed in the mirror, a closet door with mirror, a bathroom door ditto, a blue-dark window, a reflected bed there, the same in the closet mirror" (page 110). So completely is the lover locked within himself that not only the alias Humbert Humbert but even the aliases which he rejects—Otto Otto and Mesmer Mesmer—echo solipsistically. The "H.H." initials also appear in *Mother Night*, but with a variation. Howard Campbell's last name does not echo his first. Howard loves, not Howard, but Helga. He can reach beyond himself to genuinely revere one other human being. The Howard-Helga union is not ideal, however. Once consummated, it seals Howard away from the rest of humanity as disastrously as Humbert's more complete solipsism does. Even when the beloved is more than a mirror of the protagonist, romantic love can allow too complete an indulgence of the self. "Uncritical love is what I needed—and my Helga was the angel who gave it to me. . . . No young person on earth is so excellent in all respects as to need no uncritical love" (page 33). Campbell, like Humbert, can commit himself to love and yet can commit atrocities. Howard-Helga and Humbert Humbert help us recognize both the common theme of self-absorbing love and the different stages of that love in each novel.

What primarily distinguishes love in *Lolita* and *Mother Night* is the form of its presentation. Nabokov and Vonnegut use quite different narrative strategies. Although both men tell their tales retrospectively, Nabokov begins at the beginning. Virtually all of *Lolita* is devoted to dramatizing Humbert's love. Sustained exposure makes that love intensely real for us. Nabokov's strategy of cumulative effect requires, in turn, that the accumulated moments throughout the novel be effective in themselves. As a paradigm of his technique throughout, here is a sentence which follows two pages of description of Annabelle:

> I was on my knees, and on the point of possessing my darling, when two bearded bathers, the old man of the sea and his brother, came out of the sea with exclamations of ribald encouragement, and four months later she died of typhus in Corfu. [page 15]

Nabokov succeeds here in making us experience the lover's stunned sense of loss. The words down to "ribald encouragement" function differently from the words after. The sentence dehumanizes Humbert and Annabelle by encouraging us to see the couple in terms of stereotypes: Here are Young Lovers Caught in the Act. The stereotyping is done in ribald good fun, of course, but the effect is still dehumanizing. We cease thinking of Humbert or Annabelle as one of us. Then death enters. We are hit so hard because the ultimate of human realities appears just when we have lost touch quite completely with the humanity of the characters. As the Foreword to *Lolita* required us to recognize and switch between two mentalities in a single sentence, we move here in one sentence from stereotyping to empathy. Technique makes us recover our sense of mortality.

This recovery is especially important—and the sentence particularly paradigmatic—because our dilemma here is Humbert's dilemma throughout the novel. He relentlessly dehumanizes Lolita by seeing her in light of Annabelle and himself. Stereotyping is rape, because making an individual into The Beloved violates her basic identity. Does Humbert, in turn, manage eventually (like the reader of the sentence above) to recognize Lolita's independent existence? He claims that he does, during their last hour together. Postponing for now the question of Humbert's reliability, we can say with some certainty that our overall experience of the novel coincides with our experience of the sentence on page 15. We recover our sense of human identity and worth. Because Nabokov devises formal techniques which provide us with experiences analogous to the protagonist's, Humbert's "love" becomes real—both the complex emotion and the fair lady.

Neither is adequately realized in *Mother Night*. Vonnegut focuses on the time period after Helga's death. What is treated directly and extensively in *Lolita*—the love affair itself—is treated retrospectively and selectively in *Mother Night*. The technique which Vonnegut relies on primarily is the flashback. Despite its obvious potential, the flashback technique fails to realize Campbell's "love" in *Mother Night*. We never really experience his complex emotion or his lady fair. Once Vonnegut forgoes Nabokov's strategy of cumulative effect—less than ten pages of *Mother Night* are devoted to the actual love of Campbell and Helga—he places an impossible burden on the flashback technique. Brief moments, and such graphic details as the hairs around Helga's navel, cannot make us experience anything like a passion intense enough to sustain anti-Semitic activities. Flannery O'Connor can make non-Christians experience momentarily the wonderful workings of grace; Gerard Manley Hopkins can convert us to Catholicism for the duration of a lyric; and Shakespeare's Cleopatra surely puts us in touch with "love." But Vonnegut's flashback technique cannot provide enough intensity to compensate for the cumulative power which his narrative strategy denies to *Mother Night*.

Since this failure has particularly important ramifications for *Mother Night*, I want to make clear that I am not simply criticizing Vonnegut for writing a novel different from *Lolita*. Vonnegut has not simply reversed Nabokov's priorities—making primary that interaction with the outside world which Nabokov keeps subsidiary. In exploring the moral issue of how good people serve bad ends, Vonnegut is in fact exploring the consciousness of his protagonist. Romantic love is what allows Campbell to persevere as a Nazi propagandist. Only if Campbell's emotional life in the kingdom of love is real for us will his activities in Hitler's Germany be real. Should Campbell's anti-Semitic activities lack reality for us, the novel is obviously weakened. Vonnegut's flashback technique cannot forestall such weakness. Rather than create an experience, the flashbacks assert the existence of the experience. They point back to establish the "givens" of Campbell's situation, when in fact the givens *are* the situation. A mimetic device thus comes to function as a propositional assertion. Flashbacks corroborate Campbell's claim that love sustained him. Our problem is not that we doubt the potential power of love. With Goethe, we will acknowledge the power of any human drive. But experience is all. Campbell's is one crime which we can imagine ourselves not committing, because the nation of two is one country which we never actually inhabit. Campbell refers repeatedly to "my several selves." But Campbell the Propagandist is never as real for us as he should be, because Campbell the Lover never is. Neither Lover nor Propagandist is much more real than the truism about artistic lies being the highest truth—because, in each case, an assertion is substituted for an experience. Technique has not meant recovery. Unfortunately for *Mother Night*, this same failure recurs when we turn from Campbell's past to his present and focus on the paramount technical issue: Vonnegut's use of the unreliable narrator.

The question put to Howard Campbell—" 'how could I ever trust a man who's been as good a spy as you have?' " (page 158)—can, with minor alterations, be asked of Humbert Humbert too. Both Howard and Humbert are potentially unreliable, Howard because all artists are liars, Humbert because he remains inveterately rhetorical. Both protagonists exist, in turn, in worlds as ambiguous as themselves. In *Mother Night*, for example, the conduct of Kraft and Resi remains inscrutable.

> He was indignant, and, for all I know, he was sincere in his indignation. . . . Maybe he was sincere. [page 42]
>
> He never did quite cry, but he was close to doing it—genuinely close to doing it, I think. [page 60]
>
> She wept for joy. For real joy? Who knows. [page 129]

Very often in *Mother Night*, however, we encounter quite different situations:

> He [Kraft] told me what was supposed to be the story of his life, none of it true. . . .
>
> "No children?" I said.

"None," he said sadly. He actually had three children. [page 39]

Kraft claimed to be mystified, too. He wasn't really mystified. [page 54]

Not only is Campbell the artist-liar obviously giving us the straight facts about Kraft here, but the scenes themselves demonstrate anything but the epistemological uncertainty which occasioned the dilemma they present. The dilemma is potentially moving—a human being is betrayed by his only friend. But to actually move us, Kraft's lies must be as real for us as they are for Campbell. Vonnegut makes Kraft's lies unmistakable by exposing each lie immediately. There is no doubt that Kraft is guilty. And Campbell's pain and indignation are evident. But the cost of speedy judgment is high. That the lies are manifest facts does not—paradoxically—make the lies experientially real for us. Immediate judgment precludes the epistemological uncertainty which made Campbell's dilemma possible and which seemed inevitable after Vonnegut's Note. Immediate judgment denies us an experience analogous to Campbell's. We are not made to believe in Kraft, to care for Kraft—and then experience his perfidy. Vonnegut diminishes the intensity of our contact with human suffering and fallibility, so that he can pass irremediable judgment on Kraft. Compare Vonnegut's technique here with comparable moments in *Lolita.* When Humbert, for example, brings Lolita back from the phone booth to patch up their quarrel and to set up their second trip, he assumes she has been talking to a girlfriend; when she asks whether the hotel was named The Enchanted Hunters, Humbert assumes that she is recalling with pleasure their first lovemaking. Whether we are quite so sanguine as he, we certainly share his ignorance for many pages. When we do learn with Humbert that Lolita was in fact telephoning

Clare Quilty to set up their elopement, and that she was recalling, not lovemaking at The Enchanted Hunters, but the coincidence of Quilty's presence there, the shock of recognition strikes us with a force comparable to Humbert's pain. Moreover, Lolita's perfidies are complicated in a way that the perfidies of Kraft (and Resi) are not. Kraft and Resi *are* complicated, in the sense that they betray a man whom they genuinely like, but the scales are clearly weighted against the Soviet spies because they deceive Campbell for the grossest of cold-war motives. Kraft and Resi are patently betraying a trusting and generous man. Lolita, on the other hand, is betraying a man who has entrapped her in a starkly predatory relation. Her perfidy is, in fact, a bid for freedom. And so, although we experience Humbert's pain, we also experience Lolita's pain and her right to freedom. The shock of recognition thus provides dual, contradictory experiences which put us effectively in touch with the contradictory nature of the human condition.

Having not experienced a comparable sense of recovery in the scenes with Kraft, we should examine Vonnegut's narration in the rest of *Mother Night.* Compare the following passages:

> A uniformed colored man was sweeping the walk in front of an apartment. His blue and gold uniform bore a striking resemblance to the uniform of the Free America Corps. [page 99]

> My father-in-law was stood on a footstool four inches high. The rope was put around his neck and drawn tight over the limb of a budding apple tree. . . . He was revived eight times, and hanged nine. Only after the eighth hanging were his last bits of courage and dignity gone. Only after the eighth hanging did he act like a child being tortured. . . . The barber

> called out to me. He shook another man's hair out of the cloth he was going to put around my neck.
>
> "Next," he said. [pages 83–84]

On page 99, the reader does none of the work. We are told about the uniform and confronted with the ironic connection of American racists and American victims of discrimination—ironic, but not very "striking." Had Vonnegut been satisfied with describing the black man's uniform, we would have had half the work to do. Our act of connecting the uniform with the Free America Corps would have made us *experience* the irony inherent in the connection. We do experience irony on pages 83–84. Rather than rendering us passive by asserting the connection for us, Vonnegut juxtaposes the hanging of the father-in-law with the barbering of the son-in-law. We make and thus experience the ironic connection of two situations which we would assume very different because we in our daily simplifications assume that we are not all killers. Through Vonnegut's technique we eschew such righteous simplicity and recognize, like Goethe, that any one of us—the barber—can victimize any one of us. Moved by Vonnegut's technique here, we are legitimately disappointed with scenes like those on pages 39, 54, 99. Why does Vonnegut lapse from experiential to assertive presentation? Is he less conscious of the different effects of the techniques than we are? Does he feel that assertions convey irony adequately? Is he sufficiently threatened by epistemological uncertainties that he wants to establish certitude at any cost? Probably all of these factors operate to some extent. We must withhold any final judgment until we have defined another—quite opposite—problem with Vonnegut's narrative technique.

Where is Vonnegut in this passage?

> "This once-proud country of ours is falling into the hands of the wrong people," said Jones. He nodded, and so did Father Kelly and the Black Fuehrer. "And, before it gets back on the right track . . . some heads are going to roll."
>
> I had never seen a more sublime demonstration of the totalitarian mind . . . [page 168]

Where Campbell is is all too clear. The mysteries of the human heart, the brotherhood of fallibility, vanish as individuals become types. "The" totalitarian mind. Instead of making us experience how we all share totalitarian impulses and how even "Ahab has his humanities," Campbell derides the cardboard Fascists. Where is Vonnegut here? Can we attribute to Campbell the cardboard quality of the Fascists? Can we assume that Vonnegut demurs from the comparable simplification of Campbell's "the totalitarian mind"? When "the boss G-man" then oversimplifies even this situation and says to Jones " 'you're completely crazy' " (page 169), how does Vonnegut relate to Campbell's reply?

> Jones wasn't completely crazy. The dismaying thing about the classic totalitarian mind is that any given gear, though mutilated, will have at its circumference unbroken sequences of teeth that are immaculately maintained . . . The missing teeth, of course, are simple, obvious truths, truths available and comprehensible even to ten-year-olds, in most cases. [page 169]

The boss G-man misses the point so that Campbell can make it. The whole scene seems staged to put down "the classic totalitarian mind." But the dehumanization involved in such stereotyping is ultimately more offensive than Jones or the G-man—especially in a novel which insists periodically that Nazis have their human aspects and that all men have their homicidal moments. Jones and the G-man cannot match in their cardboard crudeness the crudeness of representing the human consciousness by the image of a machine. If Vonnegut demurs from Campbell's image, where does he make his separation clear? That Campbell goes on to explicate the image:

> The missing teeth, of course, are simple, obvious truths . . . The willful filing off of gear teeth, the willful doing without certain obvious pieces of information . . .

indicates that Campbell condescends not only to the characters, but to the reader. Having dehumanized the characters with "the classic totalitarian mind," he presumes that we need the machine image explained to us. Campbell later apologizes for the image (page 170), but the chapter ends, like the Editor's Note, with self-congratulation. Where is Vonnegut here?

> Since there is no one else to praise me, I will praise myself—will say that I have never tampered with a single tooth in my thought machine, such as it is. There are teeth missing, God knows . . . But never have I willfully destroyed a tooth . . . Never have I said to myself, "This fact I can do without." [page 170]

Are we to doubt Campbell's probity here, any more than we are to doubt the perversity of the classic totalitarian mind? Compare this scene from *Mother Night* with moments in *Lolita* where Nabokov presents characters whom he cannot approve of completely—Jean Farlowe, for example:

> She was very tall, wore either slacks with sandals or billowing skirts with ballet slippers, drank any strong liquor in any amount, had had two miscarriages, wrote stories about ani-

> mals, painted, as the reader knows, lakescapes, was already nursing the cancer that was to kill her at thirty-three, and was hopelessly unattractive to me. [page 97]

Nabokov traps us here as he did with "and four months later she died of typhus in Corfu." The opening clauses create a stereotype, like Young Lovers Caught in the Act or Vonnegut's American Nazis. Our very recognition of condescension toward and even distaste for the Arty Housewife implicates us in the stereotyping of Jean. Then, tucked in with the cancer, is the revelation of Jean's mortality. We are again forced to recover our sense of the humanity of our fellow mortals.

Another fellow, and one as odd as anyone in *Mother Night*, inhabits Nabokov's Wild West:

> In Kasbeam a very old barber gave me a very mediocre haircut: he babbled of a baseball-playing son of his, and, at every explodent, spat into my neck, and every now and then wiped his glasses on my sheet-wrap, or interrupted his tremulous scissor work to produce faded newspaper clippings, and so inattentive was I that it came as a shock to realize as he pointed to an easeled photograph among the ancient gray lotions, that the mustached young ball player had been dead for the last thirty years. [page 194]

Again death appears, putting foibles into perspective. By prompting us to do to the character what we do so often in daily life—become sufficiently distracted by superficial quirks that we fail to appreciate the hidden sorrow and humanity of an individual—Nabokov provides us with an experience analogous to the protagonist's. Active engagement fosters experiential meaning. This shock-of-recognition technique is probably most effective in *Lolita* when 243 pages of familiarity with and affection for Lolita brings us to her letter to

Humbert, and to her signature "Mrs. Richard F. Schiller." Death enters again. No assertion renders us passive. Only our connecting the name here with a fact back on page 6 makes meaning happen. We were told in the Foreword that a Mrs. Richard F. Schiller died in childbirth on Christmas Day, 1952. Thus, on page 243 we see with shock that Lolita is dead, and that Humbert never knew. The pathos of them both, our kinship with them both, make this letter one of the great moments of modern fiction. How indispensable technique is to the effect here can be demonstrated by reading the Foreword in the *Annotated Lolita.* Alfred Appel, Jr., like the best disciple of Howard W. Campbell, Jr., and the less knowledgeable student of Nabokov's art, glosses "Mrs. 'Richard F. Schiller' " on page 6 as "Lolita's married name." Lolita's letter is thus denied all of its sudden shock of meaning, and the whole novel is read in light of that death, which Nabokov scrupulously hides from us for 237 pages.

Vonnegut, in turn, is consistently problematic because his combined techniques of assertion and silence make us uncertain about what our response to Campbell should be and what the meaning of *Mother Night* is.

> Dr. Goebbels had a dream of producing the pageant annually in Warsaw after the war . . . Can the writing of this ghastly pageant be added to the list of my war crimes? No, thank God. . . . I am willing to admit, however, that I probably would have written it if there had been enough time, if my superiors had put enough pressure on me.
>
> Actually, I am willing to admit almost anything. [page 14]

Here Campbell takes the crucial theme of our common guilt and flaunts human weakness with a liberal self-abasement which makes the theme seem glib and jejune. Where is

Vonnegut here? Campbell has, remember, been proclaimed a moral hero only three pages earlier:

> "You are the only man I ever heard of . . . who has a bad conscience about what he did in the war. Everybody else, no matter what side he was on, no matter what he did, is sure a good man could not have acted in any other way." [page 11]

What indication is there that Vonnegut dissents from this laudatory judgment? That Campbell can be morally exemplary for knowing guilt and yet can plead guilty to "almost anything" is unattractive enough. But Campbell, in turn, is willing to pass judgment on almost everything.

> The only advantage to me of knowing the difference between right and wrong, as nearly as I can tell, is that I can sometimes laugh when the Eichmanns can see nothing funny. [pages 126–127]

This "as nearly as I can tell" seems disingenuous. Howard Campbell obviously feels superior to "the Eichmanns." The definite article once again stereotypes individuals into a class, separating such goats from us sheep *qui rient*. Campbell is thus doubly problematic. Having proclaimed the common guilt of all men, he both sullies that truth by his willingness to plead guilty to anything and starkly denies that truth by rigorously setting himself off from "the Eichmanns" and "the" totalitarians.

> [concerning patriotism] . . . real estate doesn't interest me. It's no doubt a great flaw in my personality, but I can't think in terms of boundaries. [page 100]

> . . . dramatizing exquisitely my own sense of the world's being a junk shop. [pages 166–167]

> His mother understood my illness immediately, that it was my world rather than myself that was diseased. [page 194]

Especially since Vonnegut in the Note was ready to assert truths as insubstantial as these, we find ourselves again questioning his relation to the narrator. Campbell's willingness to judge mankind is probably most objectionable during his encounter with the young policeman:

> "It's all right for me to go upstairs?" I said.
>
> "It's your home," he said. "Nobody can keep you out of it."
>
> "Thank you," I said.
>
> "Don't thank me," he said. "It's a free country, and everybody gets protected exactly alike." He said this pleasantly. He was giving me a lesson in civics. [page 177]

Is the scene so complex that we need Campbell's last sentence here? The assertive overexplaining is only slightly irritating in itself, but it is symptomatic of Campbell's very irritating attitude toward the reader and the rest of mankind. Rather than letting us do half the work by actively interpreting the scene, Campbell keeps us passive by asserting the meaning unambiguously. His condescension to the policeman and to the reader increases as the scene progresses. And so does our irritation.

> "That's certainly the way to run a country," I said.
>
> "I don't know if you're kidding me or not," he said, "but that's right."
>
> "I'm not kidding you," I said. "I swear I'm not." This simple oath of allegiance satisfied him.
>
> "My father was killed on Iwo Jima," he said.
>
> "I'm sorry," I said.
>
> "I guess there were good people killed on both sides," he said.

"I think that's true," I said.

"You think there'll be another one?" he said.

"Another what?" I said.

"Another war," he said.

"Yes," I said.

"Me too," he said. "Isn't that hell?"

"You chose the right word," I said.

"What can any one person do?" he said.

"Each person does a little something," I said, "and there you are."

He sighed heavily. "It all adds up," he said. "People don't realize." He shook his head. "What should people do?"

"Obey the laws," I said.

"They don't even want to do that, half of 'em," he said. "The things I see—the things people say to me. Sometimes I get very discouraged."

"Everybody does that from time to time," I said.

"I guess it's partly chemistry," he said.

"What is?" I said.

"Getting down in the dumps," he said. "Isn't that what they're finding out—that a lot of that's chemicals?"

"I don't know," I said.

"That's what I read," he said. "That's one of the things they're finding out."

"Very interesting," I said.

"They can give a man certain chemicals, and he goes crazy," he said. "That's one of the things they're working with. Maybe it's all chemicals."

"Very possible," I said.

"Maybe it's different chemicals that different countries eat that makes people act in different ways at different times," he said.

"I'd never thought of that before," I said.

"Why else would people change so much?" he said. "My brother was over in Japan, and he said the Japanese were the nicest people he ever met, and it was the Japanese who'd killed our father! Think about that for a minute."

"All right," I said.

"It *has* to be chemicals, doesn't it?" he said.

"I see what you mean," I said.

"Sure," he said. "You think about it some more."

"All right," I said.

"I think about chemicals all the time," he said. "Sometimes I think I should go back to school and find out all the things they've found out so far about chemicals."

"I think you should," I said.

"Maybe, when they find out more about chemicals," he said, "there won't have to be policemen or wars or crazy houses or divorces or drunks or juvenile delinquents or women gone bad or anything any more."

"That would sure be nice," I said.

"It's possible," he said.

"I believe you," I said.

"The way they're going, everything's possible now, if they just work at it—get the money and get the smartest people and get to work. Have a crash program," he said.

"I'm for it," I said.

"Look how some women go half off their nut once a month," he said. "Certain chemicals get loose, and the woman can't help but act that way. Sometimes a certain chemical will get loose after a woman's had a baby, and she'll kill the baby. That happened four doors down from here just last week."

"How awful," I said. "I hadn't heard—"

"Most unnatural thing a woman can do is kill her own baby, but she did it," he said. "Certain chemicals in the blood made her do it, even though she knew better, didn't want to do it at all."

"Um," I said.

"You wonder what's wrong with the world—" he said, "well, there's an important clue right there." [pages 177–180]

However overbearing and simpleminded the young policeman is, his limitations seem less serious than Campbell's. Campbell condescends to the policeman and to the reader by patronizing each in different ways. To the policeman's well-intended gropings, Campbell responds with a tongue-in-cheek glibness which seems to acknowledge neither the fact that the cop is honestly, if remedially, seeking answers to life's basic questions, nor the fact that the cop's perception about the Japanese is as sophisticated as Campbell's comparable revelation about the Germans. Campbell patronizes us in a different way. Rather than draw smugly back, he smugly assumes that we share his amusement at these simple types. We liberals know about "the" totalitarian mind and the G-man and "the" Eichmanns and all those "the's" who explain life with a single fixed idea. Again we wonder where Vonnegut is. If he has enough distance from his narrator to recognize Campbell's limitations, can Vonnegut possibly have intended us to feel the degree of distance, of disaffiliation, that we do? Moreover, since we can find no clear sign that Vonnegut does indeed have ironic distance on Campbell here, we may well feel confirmed in the fear which has surfaced every time we have asked where Vonnegut was. He seems fairly clearly "with" his protagonist. Where the author remains—and the consequences of his presence or absence—is the chief critical issue as we proceed on to the end of *Mother Night* and *Lolita*.

III

Let us begin by comparing these two passages:

> One day, soon after her disappearance, an attack of abominable nausea forced me to pull upon the ghost of an old

mountain road . . . After coughing myself inside out, I rested a while on a boulder, and then, thinking the sweet air might do me good, walked a little way toward a low stone parapet on the precipice side of the highway. . . . A very light cloud was opening its arms and moving toward a slightly more substantial one belonging to another, more sluggish, heaven-logged system. As I approached the friendly abyss, I grew aware of melodious unity of sounds rising like vapor from a small mining town that lay at my feet, in a fold of the valley. One could make out the geometry of the streets between blocks of red and gray roofs, and green puffs of trees, and a serpentine stream, and the rich, ore-like glitter of the city dump, and beyond the town, roads crisscrossing the crazy quilt of dark and pale fields, and behind it all, great timbered mountains. But even brighter than those quietly rejoicing colors—for there are colors and shades that seem to enjoy themselves in good company—both brighter and dreamier to the ear than they were to the eye, was that vapory vibration of accumulated sounds that never ceased for a moment, as it rose to the lip of granite where I stood wiping my foul mouth. And soon I realized that all these sounds were of one nature, that no other sounds but these came from the streets of the transparent town, with the women at home and the men away. Reader! What I heard was but the melody of children at play, nothing but that, and so limpid was the air that within this vapor of blended voices, majestic and minute, remote and magically near, frank and divinely enigmatic—one could hear now and then, as if released, an almost articulate spurt of vivid laughter, or the crack of a bat, or the clatter of a toy wagon, but it was all really too far for the eye to distinguish any movement in the lightly etched streets. I stood listening to that musical vibration from my lofty slope, to those flashes of separate cries with a kind of demure murmur for background, and then I knew that the hopelessly poignant thing was not Lolita's absence from my side, but the absence of her voice from that concord. [pages 279–280]

> There was one pleasant thing about my ratty attic: the back window of it overlooked a little private park, a little Eden . . . That park, that Eden, was walled off from the streets by houses on all sides.
>
> It was big enough for children to play hide-and-seek in.
>
> I often heard a cry from that little Eden, a child's cry that never failed to make me stop and listen. It was the sweetly mournful cry that meant a game of hide-and-seek was over, that those still hiding were to come out of hiding, that it was time to go home.
>
> The cry was this: "Olly-olly-ox-in-free."
>
> And I, hiding from many people who might want to hurt or kill me, often longed for someone to give that cry for me, to end my endless game of hide-and-seek with a sweet and mournful—
>
> "Olly-olly-ox-in-free." [pages 17–18]

With their common word "sweet," both passages present sentimental, nostalgic moments. We react differently to the passages because the techniques used by Nabokov and Vonnegut differ characteristically. The very fact that the passage from *Lolita* is out of chronological order means we must be careful, be active. Humbert could have placed the passage anywhere, so his saving it for the last pages of the novel suggests special importance. But Nabokov does not *end Lolita* with the passage, so we cannot assume that the "point" of the passage is the "point" of the novel. We must be particularly careful because the point of the passage is as problematic as its placement. Humbert's sentiments here near the end of Part Two run contrary to his sentiments at the end of Part One.

> 33.
>
> In the gay town of Lepingville I bought her four books of comics, a box of candy, a box of sanitary pads, two cokes, a mani-

> cure set, a travel clock with a luminous dial, a ring with a real topaz, a tennis racket, roller skates with white high shoes, field glasses, a portable radio set, chewing gum, a transparent raincoat, sunglasses, some more garments—swooners, shorts, all kinds of summer frocks. At the hotel we had separate rooms, but in the middle of the night she came sobbing into mine, and we made it up very gently. You see, she had absolutely nowhere else to go. [page 130]

Seeing Lolita's plight here in light of the number 33, we are not surprised when events confirm her crucifixion.

> "Come in," she said with a vehement cheerful note. Against the splintery deadwood of the door, Dolly Schiller flattened herself as best she could (even rising on tiptoe a little) to let me pass, and was crucified for a moment, looking down, smiling down at the threshold, hollow-cheeked with round *pommettes*, her watered-milk-white arms outspread on the wood. I passed without touching her bulging babe. Dolly-smell, with a faint fried addition. My teeth chattered like an idiot's. "No, you stay out" (to the dog). [page 246]

The posture of crucifixion and the position of sexual lovers: superimposing these two attitudes, Nabokov provides an image which is basic to the meaning of the novel but which requires our active interpretation. When we see Humbert juxtaposed to Lolita and the baby in the crucifixion tableau, we recognize how his passion has in effect sired the child who will kill her on Christmas Day. His decision in Chapter 33—and not the actual "rape"—initiated a course of events which led eventually to Lolita's marriage to Schiller, her pregnancy by him, and her death in childbirth. When Humbert, in turn, relates Lolita to the children's voices near the end of the novel, we are tempted to see a significant moral advance. The value which he places upon children's lives and upon childhood fellowship contrasts with the girlhood which he denied to Lolita and which the stillborn girl-child emblemizes. Humbert seems to join us in understanding the true nature of his crime, and in affirming the values which he has offended against. What keeps us wary here is Humbert's relentlessly rhetorical stance. He is still making his case. (We do not know yet that he will refuse to defend himself with this document at the trial.) There are obvious rhetorical advantages to coming up with the right sentiments. We—"frigid gentlewomen of the jury"—will be most sympathetic if we feel that Humbert has learned the right lesson—our lesson. Such moralism is, of course, what has prompted Nabokov's many disclaimers of any moral intention in the novel. But the moralistic is not the moral. *Lolita* is a passionately moral book in the sense that it passionately demonstrates the right of the individual to free development. What is wrong, evil, sinful, criminal is not what arbitrary laws or conventional codes or outdated mores indict moralistically. What is wrong is rape: the crucifixion of a human being on the gibbet of another's power drives. How can Nabokov convey this moral sense without lapsing into the moralism of propositional assertion? He must assure that the narrator on page 280 cannot be simply equated with the novelist. Such an equation would violate Humbert in the act of proclaiming Lolita. We cannot forget Humbert's humanity even as we insist on hers. What saves Nabokov is again technique. Because Humbert remains the rhetorician, we can never know for certain what he believes. Repeatedly throughout the novel we have been unable to distinguish between his actual feelings and the feelings which he would portray if he believed them persuasive with us frigid gentlewomen.

> Adieu, Marlene! Fat fate's formal handshake (as reproduced by Beale before leaving the room) brought me out of my tor-

por; and I wept. Ladies and gentlemen of the jury—I wept. [page 96]
To rout the monster of insomnia should he try himself one of those amethyst capsules? There were forty of them, all told—forty nights with a frail little sleeper at my throbbing side; could I rob myself of one such night in order to sleep? Certainly not: much too precious was each tiny plum, each microscopic planetarium with its live stardust. Oh, let me be mawkish for the nonce! I am so tired of being cynical.

This daily headache in the opaque air of this tombal jail is disturbing, but I must persevere. Have written more than a hundred pages and not got anywhere yet. My calendar is getting confused. That must have been around August 15, 1947. Don't think I can go on. Heart, head—everything. Lolita, Lolita, Lolita, Lolita, Lolita, Lolita, Lolita, Lolita. Repeat till the page is full, printer. [page 101]

Here, as in the nostalgic "sweet" passage on page 280, we encounter heavy sentiment. By what criteria can we determine with some clarity what "the real" Humbert is feeling? The language here is even tricker than the Foreword. No words clue us authoritatively to the switches between unreliable and reliable mental sets. We cannot even determine that such switches are occurring. Nabokov thus permits Humbert to sustain to the end that mystery which characterizes every human heart and which prevents any sheep-goats division of villains and heroes. Humbert remains as inscrutable as we all. On the other hand, we do not end up where ambiguous narrators, as Wayne Booth demonstrates, can lead us: into the chaos of complete relativism. Whether or not Humbert Humbert really perceives the moral reality which Nabokov is presenting, we know that we do. And with this knowledge comes a second perception—that it does not finally matter whether Humbert sees. Although our inability to achieve complete epistemological certainty assures Humbert's ambivalence, we escape complete moral confusion. Some recognition of human community, some sense of moral contiguity, abides amid the epistemological uncertainties. Nabokov has it both ways. He insists both on the inevitable fact of perceptual uncertainty and on the equally inevitable necessity of freedom and love. We share, as Goethe does, a bond with our fellow mortals, even as we recognize, with Goethe, that crime is criminal.

Vonnegut also tries to have things both ways. Throughout *Mother Night* he both proclaims the fact of epistemological uncertainty and divides sheep from goats with rigorous certainty. He thus seems two-faced. Or at least Howard Campbell does. The narrative confusion throughout *Mother Night* recurs in the scene with the children, and at the end of the novel. The scene with the children is potentially moving. That man, the human child, seeks ever to return "home" has been a theme of great literature from the pilgrimages of Ulysses, Chaucer, and Bunyan to the quests for home in "Judgment Day" and *The Lime Twig.* But the nostalgia and sentimentality of this theme are inherently dangerous. To prevent our sinking into bathos, the artist must find ways to complicate, to toughen the situation. Nabokov on page 280 prevents us from sinking into bathos by making us actively recognize the rhetorical—and hence potentially false—nature of Humbert's view of the children. Howard Campbell seems to succumb to bathos. Luxuriating in the sweet sadness, he does nothing to relieve the passivity which leaves us in the warm bath of sentimentality too. No formal devices in the scene evoke the skepticism which a mature consciousness must inevitably feel when an adult situation is equated too completely with childhood. And again, our question: Where is Vonnegut? I can find no complication in the scene which would demonstrate the author's distance from his narrator. Both seem to offer us the simple sweet truth that life is sad.

However moved we may be by this truth in life or in other works of art, the truth in *Mother Night* and *Lolita* cannot exist "simply because" epistemological issues have inevitably activated our mature skepticism; we cannot be satisfied by truths presented simply.

Our dissatisfaction continues on to the end of *Mother Night*, because the quest for home continues until the last page of the novel. Campbell finally reaches home. Since suicide is among the most difficult of life's actions to render effectively in literature, Vonnegut needs complications here which will enable us to know where we are. We appreciate Campbell's loneliness in a basically mendacious world and share his distaste for the awful trial on the morrow. But is suicide a moving alternative? Since Humbert Humbert, the nymphet-lover, has had something the matter with his heart during his whole life, coronary thrombosis is an intelligible physical end to his spiritual pilgrimage. The end of Campbell's pilgrimage is more problematic, because it seems as sentimental as his response to the children in their Eden. Olly-olly-ox-in-free. Campbell has been called home at last. Life is sad and cruel. And *Mother Night* fails once again to deeply move a consciousness mature enough to see complications in an act presented without apparent formal complication. Amid epistemological uncertainty, we again remain passive and uncertain of Vonnegut's complicity. By now, however, our questions about the author have stopped. Vonnegut's novel is as problematic as his narrator. In the world of jurisprudence, silence means assent; in the world of modern fiction, authors who wish to remain silent must use formal techniques to signal the nature and extent of their assent to the words and deeds of their narrators. Especially since Vonnegut and Campbell are all too ready with assertions, this bond of author and narrator only seems cemented by Vonnegut's silence. This bond is, in turn, confirmed by other works by Vonnegut. The sentimentality in *The Sirens of Titan* ("He groaned. It was a tiny groan—and so sad. . . . It was all so sad. But it was all so beautiful, too" [pages 296, 305]) is echoed in Vonnegut's nonfiction. "This is a lonesome society that's been fragmented by the factory system . . . I wanted Sarge Shriver to say . . . 'Here's a war cry for the American people: "Lonesome no more!" ' " (*Wampeters*, pages 241, 274). The general tendency to assert propositional truths is also evident in both the other novels and the nonfiction. *The Sirens of Titan* readily assures us that " 'The worst thing that could possibly happen to anybody . . . would be to not be used for anything by anybody' " (page 310). In the essays and interviews Vonnegut's confidence in his grasp of "the truth" is often frightening.

> I worry about stupid people, dumb people. Somebody has to take care of them, because they can't hack it. One thing I tried to get going at one time was a nonprofit organization called Life Engineering. If you didn't know what to do next and you came to us, we'd *tell* you. Our only requirement would be that you had to do what we told you. [*Wampeters*, page 255]

This spiritual totalitarianism failed, and Vonnegut thinks he knows why: "We had no way of enforcing it" (*Wampeters*, page 256). Enforcing his beliefs is what prompts Vonnegut to forgo techniques which produce experiential (and therefore potentially ambivalent) "truth" and to rely on techniques, such as propositional assertion, which assure that we sad lonely readers know who "the" totalitarians are. Ideology wins out over mimesis. Nabokov, on the other hand, utilizes techniques which make us active, because he knows that he lives with us in an ambivalent world which will yield meaning only when we engage it actively, with humility and daring. One with Nabokov, we became one with Humbert and with all our fellow criminals of the heart. Technique has meant recovery.

Conrad Festa

Vonnegut's Satire

For many years now we have been trying to categorize Kurt Vonnegut. Though he has stubbornly resisted all our best efforts, the fact that he is free from the pigeonhole is not due so much to his clever denials and denunciations as it is to the fact that we have not found the right-shaped box yet—he is a very awkward person. My objective is to demonstrate that Vonnegut is a satirist, and, further, that the satire in his work is dominant, central, and sustained. To my knowledge, no one has failed to recognize that Vonnegut's fiction contains satire. However, reviewers and critics alike continue to treat the satire as if it were incidental to the work. Consequently, the satire is largely forgotten and certainly not allowed its full play. I believe that the distinction is critical for both the evaluation and interpretation of his fiction.

From the beginning of his professional writing career, Vonnegut evinced a strong inclination to write satire. Stories such as "Harrison Bergeron," "Report on the Barnhouse Effect," "The Euphio Question," "Welcome to the Monkey House," and his first novel, *Player Piano*, fit easily and recognizably into the satiric genre. That is, they (1) sustain a reductive attack on their objects, (2) convey to their intended readers significances at odds with the literal or surface meanings, and (3) are pervaded and dominated by various satiric techniques. Furthermore, the satiric objects in those works are easily identifiable and familiar, and their satiric significances are obvious. Judged solely on his early fiction, Vonnegut emerges as a somewhat traditional satirist. Were he to have continued writing in that way, we all would have joined hands long ago to slam down the lid on his box.

The early satire is primarily concerned with the evils of technology and the follies of the American way of life, but, beginning with the second novel, Vonnegut broadens his field of attention to issues of a more cosmic dimension, such as the question of the meaning of life. Also, the satire in his work becomes less apparent: as a consequence, the reader's attention is focused more steadily on the fiction. Yet, while his style and form and fiction are more imaginative creations, while his work manifests so much growth and development in technique and thought, it fails to satisfy certain expectations of consistency of idea, and it fails to yield a comprehensive unambiguous interpretation. Peter Reed draws our attention to the problem of interpretation in *The Sirens of Titan*, in which the pervasive determinism of its universe conflicts with the meaningfulness of certain life activities affirmed at the end of the book. However, Reed rejects any interpretation of the work which would undercut or negate its affirmations. "Perhaps, we should conclude that 'T' were to consider too curiously, to consider so—at least in a comically conceived work of science fiction," he tells us.[1] Citing similar problems, Raymond Olderman says of Vonnegut's fiction: "Its basic weakness is a confusion of attitude, a failure to make clear the author's position."[2] Nevertheless, both critics sense the irrelevancy of the need for consistency in his works. Olderman, in fact, goes on to say: "We should read Vonnegut with some different criteria."[3]

Olderman is, I believe, correct. Our attention to the fiction leads us wrongly to apply criteria appropriate to the novel proper, to the romance, and the confession. But, as Northrop Frye has shown, the criteria applied to these forms of prose fiction differs significantly from the criteria applied to a fourth form: satire.[4]

Frye uses the term "Menippean satire" generally; it should be, however, reserved for a particular kind of satire. Some satire is very tightly structured and follows the conventions of the form it is using rather closely, whereas other satire approaches chaos structurally and mixes forms in a seemingly random way. Menippean satire is the latter kind: a loosely plotted narrative in a mixture of forms, including poetry as well as prose, which does not strive for coherence and consistency in a conventional sense. I believe it is also helpful for us when we think of Vonnegut's satire to keep in mind that Menippus was a Cynic: an advocate of the doctrine that virtue is the only good, that the essence of virtue is self-control, and that surrender to any external influence is beneath the dignity of man. The Cynic postulates this morality on no absolutes such as the gods and their laws or on ideal or utopian worlds. I do not mean to imply that Vonegut knows all about Menippus, Menippean satire, and Cynics; I simply wish to suggest that he sure knows how to write Menippean satire.

Because satire is such a protean, unruly, and willful form, the understanding of it as a form is greatly confused. This accounts for at least some of the reasons why Vonnegut's work is not recognized as satire. Robert Scholes's response to Vonnegut's satire is useful here in that it illustrates the attitude taken by critics thus far, and it points to some of the problems we have in identifying the essential characteristics of satire. Scholes says that Vonnegut's fiction is black humor and not satire because "it has none of the scorn, resignation, or hope of reform that accompanies satire. It is amoral and resists moral abstractions although it exercises our consciences."[5]

Others note the lack of ridicule and invective, which to them indicates that the work is not satire.[6] Some of these charges are irrelevant. That Vonnegut's work does not contain the acid invective, the bitter ridicule, and the Olympian scorn of Swift's is obvious, but that does not mean that Vonnegut is only passively concerned about the follies and vices of men. Further, the qualities of scorn, resignation, ridicule, and invective are not in themselves necessary to satire, though frequently present. The satirist has many other weapons in his arsenal as effective as those used so brilliantly by Swift and Juvenal.

Nevertheless, satire is not possible without implicit moral norms and without the hope of reforming aberrant behavior. Jonathan Swift once wrote: "There are two ends that men propose in writing satire; one of them less noble than the other, as regarding nothing farther than the private satisfaction and pleasure of the writer. . . . the other is a public spirit, prompting men of genius and virtue to mend the world as far as they are able." That Vonnegut finds delight in his own work is evident from that marvelous piece of self-indulgence *Breakfast of Champions*, his birthday present to himself. But there has been some question concerning Vonnegut's belief in the possibility that the world can be mended. I share the grave doubts of those who say that Vonnegut's work does not offer a great deal of hope. Even when reform does happen in his novels, it is soon corrupted; notice, for example, the reformed Church of God the Utterly Indifferent, which is established upon marvelously humane principles but falls quickly into the most horrible granfalloon imaginable. The Church of God the Utterly Indifferent is founded on the principle "Take care of the people, and God Almighty will take care of Himself." The import of that is staggering, and the positive effects for humanity are limitless. But, just as Christ's admonition to "Love thy neighbor as thyself" (which as the keystone of Chistianity has limitless positive implications for humanity) has been betrayed, this principle too becomes totally perverted, and "taking care of the people" becomes warped to the brutal and cruel handicaps system developed by the Church.

Nevertheless, most critics are agreed that some hope is offered in Vonnegut's work. Of course, that hope may be interpreted as insincere or as a slight failure of courage, but opinions of this kind do not stand up well in the face of statements which support that hope in his speeches, articles, and interviews, as well as in his fiction. Obviously he is not a cockeyed optimist. But the real question is not how firmly convinced he is about the possibility of reform, but whether he believes in it at all; any amount of conviction is enough.

We must remember that all of the major satirists evince a strong ambivalence about the possibility of man's reform. Over and over in Swift's work we see demonstrations and hear direct statements which deny the possibility of reform. Yet no one denies Swift's belief in reform. The tendency in satirists toward self-satire is born out of those ambivalent feelings. Every one of Vonnegut's novels contains numerous references to the craft of writing and to writers both fictional and real, and almost every reference is touched with irony and reflects satirically on Vonnegut himself. This seems to suggest that Vonnegut's ambivalence is especially keen, but the tension between the conflicting views is not at equipoise: He *does* believe.

That very belief implies necessary corollaries: that man is rational; that he can exercise choices; and, further, that he can make decisions deemed likely to result in his own happiness and in good for society.

Quite naturally, Vonnegut is aware of the many limitations of man's free will, and he does not deny that the limitations sometimes become so severe as to close off the possibility of free will completely. Yet critics such as Charles Harris read Vonnegut's fiction as a statement debunking the whole idea of free will. An interpretation of this kind is postulated on the idea that Vonnegut shares a certain point of view with artists who have been called absurdists and black humorists. These artists see our universe as chaotic, unknowable, and indifferent to man, who is the helpless victim of unknowable forces. The tone of their work is gloomy: pessimism and despair on one hand, pessimism and a joke on the other. All that gloom is the direct result of certain adjustments the twentieth-century mind has had to make in response to relativity theories, deterministic theories, and uncertainty principles. We have lost our absolutes and our certainties. The total explanations of classical physics, which destroyed and replaced the total explanations of divine revelation, have in their turn been destroyed. However, they have been replaced this time by uncertainties, not other certainties.

For those dependent on total explanations, life becomes either a monstrous mistake or a cruel joke. However, some minds react differently: They feel freed from the shackles of Urizen. For clarity let me shift from William Blake's symbol to an observation by Jerry Bryant, who sees that freedom from total explanations "offers an exciting and affirmative conception of the human being and of his relationship to his world. It suggests an unprecedented freedom and openness in both physical reality and, by analogy, human reality."[7] Bryant goes on to say, "The relativistic viewpoint attempts to correct for our not being God and urges us to open ourselves to as wide a range of views as our limitations will permit us, to avoid imprisoning ourselves any more than we are already imprisoned. In doing so, our abstractions will correspond ever more closely to the thing itself, and the observer will free himself more and more from the prejudice and distortion of unexamined traditional viewpoints."[8] If we assume that Vonnegut shares this view (and there is ample evidence to support this assumption), then a conviction that human beings possess a will at least relatively free becomes axiomatic for him.

To assume, then, that Vonnegut is philosophically equipped to write satire and that he has a strong inclination in that direction is well within the bounds of credibility, and we may now move closer for a look at the fiction itself. Vonnegut's first problem is getting our attention, a problem he shares with all other writers. Satirists have frequently solved this problem by offering the reading public what its current tastes demand. Swift, for instance, set *Gulliver's Travels* in the form of a travel adventure book, a form which at the time enjoyed an almost unrivaled popularity. Vonnegut follows this same technique by appropriating the popular fiction of our day: science fiction and the confessional. From these popular forms he launches his satire. His technique is much like the one used by Winston Niles Rumfoord on Malachi Constant: Vonnegut ofers us the sirens, who ultimately become irrelevant, and gives us Titan, where survival and satisfaction are derived from one's own efforts. He offers us escape, and gives us confrontation.

Critics have said that Vonnegut has designs on us. I like

that. It suggests strategies, plans, carefully thought-out courses of action. A criticism I react badly to is that which suggests that Vonnegut is an inferior writer because he gives the appearance of unconcern through the carelessness of his writing. After such studies as those of Glenn Meeter and John Somer,[9] criticism of that sort should have been silenced. If nothing else, those studies should alert us to the craftsmanship, the skill, and the art that hides the art with which he seduces us to his message. Vonnegut, who once worked in public relations, is keenly aware of the need for good packaging.

Although when evaluating art we may be disdainful of the marketing principle of providing what we sell, we must remember that it is a matter of some importance to satire. It is, after all, a literary form that is basically argument. Vonnegut *does* want us to share his convictions. Therefore, he is not going to try to beat us into submission or shout us down. He knows that these methods have, at best, little effect. Instead, he becomes the engaging, charming, funny storyteller, because he knows that that is the most effective way to "poison minds with the truth."

Vonnegut recognizes the ineffectiveness of the satirist who is not also a skillful artist; in fact, Kilgore Trout is precisely the ineffective satirist. Trout is a voice crying in the wilderness, not so much because his intended audience is ignorant and philistine, but because, as Eliot Rosewater has said so well, "He has great ideas, but he's a lousy writer." And who among us would deny this judgment after *Venus on the Half-Shell*? People like Rosewater, who possesses intelligence and a sensitivity to the wrongs in our society and the will to resist those wrongs, are already in Trout's camp. They can delight in his work. But people like Billy Pilgrim, whose convictions are latent and unformed and whose will is so weak that his first reaction to difficulties is to surrender, fasten on the sleazy narrative, which provides them with nothing more than fodder for fantasy; Billy's fantasy of Tralfamadore, we recall, is suggested by a Trout story.

Vonnegut's strategy is to package his satire in an entertaining, well-told story which will persuade readers who are not already committed to his convictions. Perhaps the packaging is so intriguing that the product goes begging for attention. I do not believe that, since almost every critic mentions his strong moral sense and his humanistic values. Evidently the message gets through, if only subliminally. Nonetheless, Robert Scholes and Sharon Weinstein point out that Vonnegut's fiction does not possess the tone of moral certitude felt in traditional satire.[10] Because he often undercuts his judgments with irony, these critics feel that he fails to project a commitment to a specific moral system. No doubt this observation is correct, but the reason is not necessarily that Vonnegut lacks moral convictions. It seems to me that his purpose in employing an almost noncommittal tone is actually twofold: First, he feels that the hard sell is strategically ineffective; second, he is aware that the age's loss of certainties has allowed our society to accept a broader range of human activity.

Major psychological studies have concluded, and these conclusions are common knowledge, that persuasion is enhanced by indirection and humor. It is not difficult to suppose, then, that Vonnegut would use the method proven effective regardless of how passionately he felt about his convictions. Furthermore, as I have said earlier, science has corroborated the suspicion, long held, that there are no final answers. The force of this conviction is felt by us all, and it affects the way we look at morality. In fact, we have been challenged to revalue our morals in the light of our new concepts of existence. The new respectability of situational ethics and the tolerance of sexual practices heretofore seen as immoral are results of that revaluation. As a result, a whole long list of human follies which to Swift were an abomination, an offense, are to Vonnegut, at their worst, merely amusing. When it comes to matters that are really important, Vonnegut is uncompromising, and his satire is clear and devastating.

Yet it may be Vonnegut's indirection that prompts Weinstein (who argues effectively against Alfred Kazin's dismissal of Vonnegut as simply a superfatalist and against C. D. B. Bryan's charge that Vonnegut fails to become the satirist he could be) to conclude that Vonnegut is "not a satirist, really—nor is he a fatalist, a nihilist, a pessimist, or an optimist."[11] What he really is, she says, is a master of the "ironic vision"—a vision which "allows contradictions to coexist, and functions as a dialectic that endeavors to hold incongruous attitudes in balance."[12] Though it may be possible for a person to remain in balance, in stasis, between the demands of conflicting statements or evidence (a state perhaps something like that of Keats's "negative capability"), it is doubtful that we can see Vonnegut as projecting that kind of attitude in his irony.

The irony of Thomas Hardy may approach a kind of nonjudgmental position, since he seldom uses the device to issue a critical judgment. The purpose of most of Hardy's irony is to challenge the optimistic nineteenth-century notion of a caring and benevolent God and universe. Vonnegut simply assumes Hardy's God-abandoned, impersonal, disinterested, vast, and ultimately unknowable universe. His irony, therefore, is not aimed so much at the human condition as it is at human interaction, human relationships: the differences between how we say we should act toward each other and the way we do act, the difference between our ideals and our performance. It is not we who give the universe meaning, nor is it the universe which gives us meaning. It is, rather, we who give each other meaning, and that is done quite simply through the acknowledgment of self and the acceptance of others. Let me illustrate the distinction briefly by recalling for you two deaths, one in *The Return of the Native* and the other in *Cat's Cradle*. After Mrs. Yeobright has discovered the infidelity of her daughter-in-law and experienced the apparent rejection by her son, she succumbs to a stroke on a brilliant summer afternoon amid the wild beauty of the heath. The scene is described in such a way as to show that the death is so insignificant a matter that nature goes on as if nothing had happened at all. Hardy takes us out of our little world in which every event is of importance into the larger universe where those events really mean nothing at all. The death of Bokonon, too, is in the presence of a totally disinterested universe. But what is significant in Bokonon's death is that he renounces his life spent philosophizing and creating stories to help make life bearable for people living under unbearable conditions. If he had it all to do over again, he says, he would write a history of human stupidity and thumb his nose at the gods. The effect of this death is to turn us away from the indifferent universe and back to ourselves, our immediate problems of survival and our concerns for human behavior.

The tone of the irony in most novels (and those of Thomas Hardy are representative) is cool and detached, but underlying Vonnegut's irony is the active, keen, and barely suppresed sense of moral outrage characteristic of satire. A good example of Vonnegut's irony is found in the scene in *Slaughterhouse-Five* in which old Edgar Derby finally becomes a character by asserting himself and denouncing Howard W. Campbell, Jr. Derby's speech is in itself the epitome of the Fourth of July chauvinism found in high-school essays competing for D.A.R. or American Legion prizes. The speech, coming after all we have seen about the "American fighting man," is sardonic. But the real ironic power is generated by the air-raid siren that punctuates the end of Derby's speech and heralds the coming of American bombers which will attack and destroy a defenseless city and massacre over 135,000 people, an act of cowardice and viciousness equal, at least in moral terms, to Pearl Harbor and Auschwitz.

Space does not permit a close examination of the satire in all of Vonnegut's books, but a brief demonstration of the satire in *Slaughterhouse-Five* will suggest what can be found in the others. It is possible now to see that even *Slaughterhouse-Five*, once considered the least satirical of Vonnegut's fiction, fits very comfortably within the category of Menippean satire. In fact, none of his other books manifests the Menippean characteristics of mixed forms and complex structure better. Vonnegut tells us that the structure of his book is on the Tralfamadorian telegraphic-schizophrenic model, a structure designed to focus the reader's attention on the meaning of the work and not the story being told. And the list of forms he uses, in a seemingly random and indiscriminate way, is surprisingly long: songs, stories within stories, science fiction, fantasy, jokes, recitations of historical documents, the juxtaposition of real and fictional events, passages of pure undisguised autobiography set along side pure fiction, and the poetic refrain running throughout the entire work.

Vonnegut's use of the refrain "So it goes" is an example of how he can take conventions of other forms and use them for ironic and satiric purposes. In its resignation, Vonnegut's refrain recalls that from *Deor's Lament*, "And this, too, shall pass." At first it strikes us as resignation born out of experience, and it is sometimes even humorous. But the frequency of its repetition and its use to explain every death from that of a bottle of champagne to that of Martin Luther King finally creates in us a rising fury at its utter banality and meaninglessness. We feel increasingly that it explains nothing, and in fact obscures the difference between the death of a bottle of champagne and the death of Martin Luther King. By the end of the book we feel the urge to rise in impatience and cry, "That isn't the way it is!" And we want to move beyond the feeble shrug and make those moral distinctions a clear reality. The effect is what Scholes describes as "exercising our consciences."

In itself, our reponse to the refrain points us away from what some feel to be the central message of *Slaughterhouse-Five*—that the proper response to a meaningless, cruel, and apparently doomed world is total resignation. That is Billy Pilgrim's response, but it is decidedly not Vonnegut's. However, Vonnegut does not minimize the difficulty of taking a more positive position, considering the facts of our past experiences and the apparent condition our existence is in. Vonnegut acknowledges that and much more; in the first chapter of *Slaughterhouse-Five* he shows how the whole matter is complicated by the overwhelming difficulty of telling the truth in fiction, especially when the work is subjected to irrational and mindless responses from even the so-called intelligent readers (the professor of literature who dismisses all science fiction as a buggering of the truth). And the difficulties do not stop there, for the prevailing cynicism of the times (Harrison Starr, movie producer, would just as soon do an antiglacier film as an antiwar film) and its "eye for an eye" morality (the liberal social scientist who justifies Dresden by citing Auschwitz) makes for an incredibly unreceptive audience. But Vonnegut's response—instructive, I think—is "I know, I know," and he goes on to tell his story despite the difficulties.

The story that he tells is an antiwar story, but the antiwar theme is something understood even before the story of Billy Pilgrim begins. Certainly the satire in *Slaughterhouse-Five* attacks the notion of war as glorious, noble, or just. However, an even greater object of satire, the central object of the satire, is man's inclination to avoid painful reality. In *Mother Night* Vonnegut speaks ironically of schizophrenia as the great boon to modern life. It is in the same novel that he talks of the human ability to willfully neglect simple, available knowledge in order to maintain insane ideas and attitudes. The enormity of this folly of self-delusion and the painful, often fatal results is a theme dealt with directly in *Mother Night*, and it is one which plays an important part in all his satirical work.

Vonnegut departs from traditional satire, in which the sin of pride is singled out for special attention and considered man's transcendent problem. For this reason, a satirist such as Swift will attempt to puncture our inflated self-image by giving us a picture of ourselves as weak, ugly, forked creatures daubed with excrement—in other words, Yahoos. There are no Yahoos in *Slaughterhouse-Five*, because Vonnegut seems to feel that pride in the mid-twentieth century is not as great a problem as self-deception. Therefore, he gives us fragile creatures who have learned how to survive by adopting the protective coloring of the group (including the display of bumper stickers distributed by power sources), who have learned how to succeed by following the ten easy steps of the how-to books (including the classic step of marrying the boss's daughter), and who have learned how to escape the demands of conscience through rationalization and fantasy.

Vonnegut's work proclaims loudly that choices must be made. If he is anything, he is an activist interested in the specific good that can be done and impatient with all abstractions, including "humanity," "race," "nationality," and dogma of any kind. *Slaughterhouse-Five* is an attack on the very understandable but nonetheless unacceptable response of being so overwhelmed by life's pain, dangers, and problems as to retreat into private escapes. The Tralfamadorians are apostles of the most attractive rationalization for private escape: fatalism. That they are meant to be satirical objects is evident simply from the moments they select to live: the kidnapping of a humanoid, a day at the zoo cheering wildly when the captured urinate and mate. Though they are technologically advanced, their smug condescension and bastardized existentialism cum popularized Eastern mysticism work to reduce even further our opinion of these plumber's-helper-shaped people from outer space.

What has been observed concerning the satire in *Slaughterhouse-Five* may be discovered in all of Vonnegut's major fiction. His books, including *Player Piano* and *Breakfast of Champions*, share the Menippean characteristics of an extensive use of irony for satiric effects, of a mixture of forms, of a complexity of structure, and of a sense of moral outrage. These qualities are so pervasive in the books that they can be characterized as satires without straining the definition of "satire" and without doing violence to the works themselves. Furthermore, when they are read primarily as satires, they yield an interpretation which is consistent from book to book. Vonnegut focuses our attention on evils in our society which make life unnecessarily painful, dangerous, and destructive—evils which, for the most part, can be corrected if only we would avoid our greatest folly: our tendency to escape unpleasant, threatening reality which demands corrective action, either by slipping into private dream worlds or by pretending that nothing can be done about it anyway.

Vonnegut's satires offer us hope, not despair—but not hope without action. They tell us simply that we are not necessarily bound to a determined future and that we are capable of making a better world if we have the will and the courage. To a very large degree Vonnegut has accepted life as it is. But, just as strongly as he has accepted life, he rejects the idea that we have no control over the evil in it that makes life unnecessarily painful. The tension between the two positions held simultaneously by Vonnegut creates not only the impulse toward satire but also the special tone of his satire—a Horatian spirit infused with a sense of urgency, anger touched with pity, and moral indignation bathed in a deep sense of personal inadequacy.

NOTES

1. Peter J. Reed, *Kurt Vonnegut, Jr., Writers for the Seventies* (New York: Warner Paperback Library, 1972), pp. 74–75.
2. Raymond M. Olderman, *Beyond the Wasteland: A Study of the American Novel in the Nineteen-Sixties* (New Haven: Yale University Press, 1972), p. 190.
3. Olderman, p. 192.
4. Northrop Frye, *Anatomy of Criticism: Four Essays* (Princeton: Princeton University Press, 1957), p. 310.
5. Robert Scholes, *The Fabulators* (New York: Oxford University Press, 1967), p. 40.
6. Charles B. Harris, *Contemporary American Novelists of the Absurd* (New Haven: College and University Press, 1971), p. 51.
7. Jerry H. Bryant, *The Open Decision: The Contemporary American Novel and Its Intellectual Background* (New York: The Free Press, 1970), p. 30.
8. Bryant, p. 31.
9. John Somer, "Geodesic Vonnegut; or, If Buckminster Fuller Wrote Novels," in Jerome Klinkowitz and John Somer, eds., *The Vonnegut Statement* (New York: Dell, 1973), pp. 221–254. Glenn Meeter, "Vonnegut's Formal and Moral Otherworldliness," in *The Vonnegut Statement*, pp. 204–220.
10. Scholes, p. 54. Sharon Weinstein, "Comedy and Night-

mare: The Fiction of John Hawkes, Kurt Vonnegut, Jr., Jerzy Kosinski, and Ralph Ellison," diss. Univ. of Utah (1971), p. 112.

11. Weinstein, p. 151.
12. Weinstein, p. 151.

Peter J. Reed

The Later Vonnegut

By "the later Vonnegut" I mean the books published since *Slaughterhouse-Five*, an arbitrary and personal division, perhaps, but one which I think is shared by those who see an organic development through the first six novels and detect a break between them and the mixed works which have appeared subsequently. This means, in effect, five titles: *Happy Birthday, Wanda June*, *Between Time and Timbuktu*, *Breakfast of Champions*, *Wampeters, Foma & Granfalloons*, and *Slapstick*. Some of these "later" works are actually not new. *Happy Birthday, Wanda June* derives, Vonnegut says, from an earlier play, *Penelope*, written fifteen years before (*Birthday*, page viii). It appears quite derivative, incorporating episodes, characters, and ideas seen in earlier Vonnegut fiction. *Between Time and Timbuktu* was at least partially assembled by others, though Vonnegut had a controlling hand, and is even more derivative than *Happy Birthday*, being a TV screenplay which was in large part a pastiche of earlier Vonnegut scenes. *Breakfast of Champions* may also in a sense lack newness, since Vonnegut says, first, that *Slaughterhouse-Five* and *Breakfast of Champions* used to be one book, then were separated,[1] and second, that it is his good-bye to all the "junk" and characters of his previous work (*Breakfast*, page 5). Certainly many familiar characters, ideas, phrases, and situations reappear. *Wampeters, Foma & Granfalloons* is a collection of interviews, speeches, and articles, and therefore not a new work in itself.

Yet each of these books does have something new about it. *Happy Birthday* is Vonnegut's first published play, so it is a new direction in form, and it also introduces some new content, particularly a feminist theme. *Between Time and Timbuktu* is also a new form, discounting the film adaptation of *Slaughterhouse-Five*, and an interesting difference in tone emerges from it. *Wampeters, Foma & Granfalloons* is "new" in the sense that it brings together for the first time a fascinating collection of Vonneguteana which, through its variety and sensitive selection, gives a fine portrait of the author. Predictably, the two novels, *Breakfast of Champions* and *Slapstick*, provide the most significant indications of the directions which Vonnegut's later work has taken.

First, however, it might be well to try to provide some kind of context for these later works. Professor Iwamoto argues that in *Slaughterhouse-Five* the two dominant influences in Vonnegut's life, technology, or his experience with General Electric in Schenectady, and war, or being under the bombing of Dresden, come together.[2] In my book on Vonnegut's novels I tried to argue for a similar pattern of inevitable confluence of themes.[3] *Slaughterhouse-Five* from the start suggested the possibility that Vonnegut had written the crucial personal experiences out of his system, and I think that this is one reason we have all tended to wait with particular interest, and perhaps a little uncertainty, for what would subsequently come from him. In prefacing *Happy Birthday*, Vonnegut declared that he was through with novels and with characters who were "spooks" (*Birthday*, page vii). The end appeared at hand, if one dared take the author seriously. In *Breakfast of Champions* he announced the discarding of old characters and themes, while also bringing certain other lines of development in his fiction to their seeming logical ends. With Vonnegut's observation that *Breakfast of Champions* spun off from *Slaughterhouse-Five*, one could imagine that it represented a final housecleaning. But then came *Slapstick*, a continuation which seems to promise more of the same.

Leslie Fiedler is fond of saying that Vonnegut began as a science-fiction writer but then began to take himself seriously, pay too much heed to his critical acclaim, and became concerned with trying to become a "mainstream writer."[4] Fiedler had acclaimed Vonnegut as illustrative of what he called the return to popular art, bringing the novel back from the Joycean preserves of the esoteric and allusive to the traditions of folk culture.[5] I am not certain that Vonnegut ever fit quite so comfortably into the box—or drawer—that Fiedler put him in. As Vonnegut himself says, "I have been a soreheaded occupant of a file drawer labeled 'science fiction' ever since, and I would like out, particularly since so many serious critics regularly mistake the drawer for a urinal" (*Wampeters*, page 1). Vonnegut has always shown concern—defensiveness, even—over the form of his novels, as revealed in the numerous comments on characterization and dialogue, and the many writers and artists, which appear in his fiction. That seems not to have changed. Further, Vonnegut does not see himself—and ultimately, I think, should not be seen—as a science-fiction writer. Some of the short stories clearly *are* science fiction; the novels, however, rather make use of that technique and of a recognition of technology's impact on contemporary life.

Yet there may be some truth in Fiedler's allusions to Vonnegut's self-consciousness. It appears to have grown. That is suggested by his talk of abandoning the novel in his preface to *Happy Birthday, Wanda June,* and by his decrying the qualities of his books, which read as if "written by Philboyd Studge," in the introduction to *Breakfast of Champions.* The preface to *Between Time and Timbuktu* reveals more of the same: Vonnegut talking about the inadequacy of film since the author cannot place himself in the work (page xv). And in prefacing *Wampeters, Foma & Granfalloons* he speaks of the problems of being a "guru" addressing college audiences, about critics writing of him as if he were already dead, and about "British critics" who find him sometimes too sentimental. More important than these prefatory musings, however, are the signs of such preoccupations in the content and style of the works.

In this respect, the projection of self into the novel changes markedly in nature between *Slaughterhouse-Five* and *Breakfast of Champions.* Vonnegut has been "present" in many of the earlier novels, in the sense that they have directly or obliquely autobiographical content. The change at this point is in the manner of the intrusion of the autobiographical "I." In *Slaughterhouse-Five,* the appearance of Vonnegut himself in an intermittent minor role in the action—"that was me"—is framed by the first and last chapters, in which Vonnegut speaks from the present of the writing of the novel. The technique seems entirely appropriate in a novel with a subject matter which is at one level intensely personal and which is viewed reflectively. It enables Vonnegut to combine his retrospective perspective as author rationalizing and ordering past experience and his contemporaneous reactions as participant in the events shown. It is also appropriate (and an effective structural device) in a novel which emphasizes time, the interrelationships of time periods, and the effects of time on perception or "truth." In the later novel, the introduction of self as character seems a little less comfortable or natural. The difference in context *almost* provides a satisfactory answer: *Slaughterhouse-Five* is probably Vonnegut's most serious novel, while *Breakfast of Champions* may be his most whimsical. *Breakfast of Champions* is also intensely personal, as its preface explains. But even when an author writes a book as a birthday present to himself, if he publishes it, it will be read by others, who, even if disposed to wish him Many Happy Returns, are still likely to approach it much as they would any other work of fiction. The test then becomes one of how well the introduction of author as character is supported not by exterior, prefatory assertion but by thematic, structural, and generic context. This does not mean an expectation of a traditional concept of the fictional world as "real," not to be violated by authorial admissions of artifice to shatter our willing suspension of disbelief. Modern readers are generally prepared for this if they have encountered the multiple endings of John Fowles or the disarming unpretentiousness of the French New Novel. But what Vonnegut does here is rather different. An author's admission that a fictional world *is* a fiction, *is* artifice, frequently works in the direction of emphasizing the involvement of the reader in the creative process. In *Breakfast of Champions* the direction is almost opposite. The author is present in the fictional world as character and creator simultaneously, telling us how he chooses to have other characters perform.[6] This tends to put the reader in the position of observer, even if an observer who is "let in" on why actions occur or what will happen next. Vonnegut's projection of self into this novel is such that the reader finds it hard to escape the sense that *Breakfast of*

Champions at least in the later chapters, is personal in a rather exclusive way. This particular kind of personal quality has a certain awkwardness, one which may be resolved in either first-person fiction (by a consistent character-narrator relationship) or autobiography, but which in *Breakfast of Champions* remains unsettled. The effect results in the reader's feeling partially estranged in the ficional world into which he has apparently been invited.

Vonnegut's increased self-consciousness also reveals itself stylistically. Here *Wampeters, Foma & Granfalloons* makes interesting reading. Some of the earlier pieces (for example, "Brief Encounters on the Inland Waterway") seem strikingly fluent and almost languid in comparison with the later prose. In *Breakfast of Champions* the statements are terse, the rhythms brusque, the sentences short and staccato in the manner of the later abrupt style. The novel also abounds with the repetitions which distinguish the later work. Where *Slaughterhouse-Five* uses the "So it goes" refrain effectively, this novel has the repeated injunction "Listen," the reiterated fade-out "And so on," and the inconclusive "Etc." There are other forms of repetition, such as the echoing of the last word of a paragraph as a solitary declaration preceding the next paragraph and the restatement of the thematic motto, "Good-bye Blue Monday." While this device has its purpose in the context of the novel, repetition succeeds rather less well here than in *Slaughterhouse-Five.* As with the curt phrasing, the resurrection of familiar characters and scenes, and even the characteristic, bitingly understated asides on current social events, it gives the impression of being self-consciously employed—as indeed Vonnegut's prefatory statement that he is saying "good-bye to all that" implies it is.

This impression becomes disturbing for several reasons. The most obvious one is that it might suggest a decline of powers, or efforts, on Vonnegut's part, since the phenomenon of the American novelist's succumbing to self-parody in later years is not an unfamiliar one. The personal, prefatory remarks in *Breakfast of Champions,* revealing ambivalence and weariness, might contribute to this impression. So might the relative lack of originality, of scope, power, of sheer size, in the content of the novel itself. The tendency to self-imitation might naturally invite the judgment that Vonnegut is playing to the known responses of an established following. Doubtless the perennial Vonnegut detractors would say that. Some have always accused him of playing "guru" to one generation, although his publishing history and the content of his fiction make the charge ludicrous. What seems apparent is that in the wake of the success of *Slaughterhouse-Five,* as book and film, Vonnegut has felt the pressures of fame and of those who would cast him in the guru role, as he discloses in the preface to *Wampeters, Foma & Granfalloons.* This, and other personal circumstances, doubtless contributed to making the years following the publication of *Slaughterhouse-Five* distracting ones for Vonnegut. The precise relationship between personal trauma and the form of *Breakfast of Champions* would be difficult, if not impossible, to define. But Vonnegut's preface alone suggests that there is a relationship, and the plot almost certainly confirms it. The conclusion that these personal circumstances, or the state of mind in which they leave him, contribute to the form which his personal intrusion into the novel takes seems unavoidable. In the preface to *Between Time and Timbuktu* he says: "I want to be a character in all of my works. . . . I don't mean that I am a glorious character. I simply mean that, for better or for worse, I have always rigged my stories so as to include myself, and I can't stop now. And I do this so slyly, as do most novelists, that the author *can't* be put on film" (page xv). In *Breakfast of Champions* the inclusion of Vonnegut as character is not so sly. It is direct and self-conscious, at least *seeming* to permit the author to publicly talk to himself about his personal woes. The potential for sentimental self-pity in such a stance is mitigated by the upbeat resolution and the comic undercutting of self. More important, the character Vonnegut is not the *whole* projection of the author into the novel, as I shall explain later. Yet this new kind of intrusion of the autobiographical self into the fiction has a certain awkwardness not always associated with first-person narrative or a more veiled incorporation of the author into his own fictional world. Somehow it detracts from the enjoyment of the felt presence, or the slyly interjected presence, of Vonnegut which we have experienced before.

The foregoing remarks imply a relatively negative view of *Breakfast of Champions*, yet overall the novel has more strengths than it has generally been credited with. Perhaps the "surface" of the novel, with its whimsical sketches, apparent randomness of structure, personal musings, and "echolalia," distracts too easily from the richness which lies beneath. Perhaps inevitably, the novel's strengths are closely related to some of its relative weaknesses. One of these comes in the area of characterization. Vonnegut has often been apologetic about this part of his work, perhaps more than he need be. True, many of his characters appear two-dimensional or stereotyped. But that is also true of characters in some major "serious" American novels. Furthermore, Vonnegut has shown the ability, on the one hand, to create some major characters of considerable interest and depth and, on the other, to make a number of the two-dimensional lesser characters sharp and memorable. In *Breakfast of Champions* none of the characters amounts to what would normally be considered a really well-developed characterization. The two major figures, Dwayne Hoover and Kilgore Trout, though clearly defined, immensely amusing, and quite memorable, remain essentially enlarged, two-dimensional secondary characters. Yet that is appropriate. Kurt Vonnegut is the central character of this novel, and Hoover and Trout have supporting roles both in the sense of being secondary to the author-protagonist and in the way they effectively enlarge and complete the central character.

Vonnegut has used the device of having characters represent aspects of himself before. Here he extends what is begun in *Slaughterhouse-Five,* where he also introduces himself. The interjection of self directly as character is much expanded in *Breakfast of Champions*, yet that figure remains far from a complete autobiographical portrait. Vonnegut's own presence in the novel is filled out by Hoover and Trout, each of whom embodies aspects of the author, and even by lesser figures such as Rabo Karabekian, the painter. Dwayne Hoover, the Pontiac dealer who is the focus of action in Midland City until the arrival there of Kilgore Trout and Vonnegut himself, connects with his creator in several ways. Rather like the older Billy Pilgrim, the successful optometrist, Hoover can be seen as a modern Everyman figure, a version of the standard middle-class norm of success. He thus provides a vehicle for one of Vonnegut's favorite themes—the man who attains the stereotyped American goals but is left asking "What is the meaning of life?" or "What are people for?" In Vonnegut, such characters are seldom merely conveniences for social satire: they are treated with sympathy and understanding, embodying much of the Ordinary Man from whom the author never distances himself very far. Not that Hoover is *like* Vonnegut; rather, he incorporates some characteristics which he shares with the author. One of the more obvious of these is the suicide of a close relative: His wife has committed suicide by swallowing Drano, just as, we are told, Vonnegut's mother killed herself with an overdose of sleeping pills. This coincidental biographical detail assumes much importance on two counts: First, it relates to the major theme of human beings viewed as chemically controlled automatons; second, it extends the suggestion that such suicides in near relatives contribute to a person's psychological malaise.

Being the intensely personal novel that it is, *Breakfast of Champions* makes frequent allusion to both of Vonnegut's parents, often in ways which are more profound than they at first appear. Significantly, Vonnegut chooses to discuss the wife's suicide largely from the perspective of the son, Bunny, so that the parallel in the death of a mother receives emphasis (pages 180–182). Yet it is Dwayne who is threatened by the schizophrenia which Vonnegut, more than half seriously, worries about in himself. Like Vonnegut's mother, Hoover's wife feared cameras and would drop to her knees to avoid being photographed (page 181). Vonnegut falls back on an old favorite comic line in describing his mother as "crazy as a bedbug," but obviously that craziness haunts him. In the cocktail lounge of the Midland City Holiday Inn he says to himself, "You're afraid you'll kill yourself the way your mother did" (page 193), and at the novel's close he adds: "My mother stayed far, far away, because she had left me a legacy of suicide" (page 294). This is the most direct statement we find of something to be sensed from much of Vonnegut's work. His father, even his grandfather, are frequently mentioned, obviously revered, and held in close affection; the mother remains a more difficult figure for him to approach, since she is associated with his own deepest fears. Pessimism, despair, and self-doubt abound in Vonnegut's fiction, even as a source of much of his humor, and in *Breakfast of Champions* they are frankly declared, even if answered with apparent resolution. As he says, "I am better now. Word of honor: I am better now" (page 194).

Growing out of the personal experience is the broader theme of human behavior's control by body chemistry. People commit evil acts when "bad chemicals" take over their bodies. Hence, Dwayne Hoover's schizophrenia is caused by "bad chemicals." The connection here is that Vonnegut also speaks of being prone to emotional ill health, particularly depression, which he found could be miraculously lifted by taking pills (page 4). It is hardly likely that Vonnegut's most serious fear was that he would run amok and start biting off people's fingertips, but no doubt the period in his life through which he had passed at the writing of this novel was frightening. The novel might, in fact, be viewed as Vonnegut describes it—as a kind of therapy, as an attempt to clear out his mind ("Good-bye Blue Monday") and reconstruct. In this context, Hoover represents the course of psychological disintegration, which Vonnegut obviously feared as one possibility at this point in his life.

Another traumatic element in Vonnegut's life at this time had obviously been his relatively recent popularity after years of comparative obscurity. This aspect of his experience is portrayed, or lampooned, in his characterization of Kilgore Trout. Significantly, Trout's ultimate acclaim comes not as a writer but when he receives the Nobel Prize for his contributions in the field of mental health: "He advanced his theories disguised as science-fiction" (page 15). This obviously plays on Vonnegut's assertion that science fiction is dubious in its science, as well as on the time-honored problems of the science-fiction writer in being taken at all seriously. It might also make a more than passing allusion to the fact that so much of Vonnegut's popular acclaim came not so much for his fiction as for his ideas and "healthy perspective," making him for many a kind of guru disguised as sci-fi writer. In the characterizations of Trout and Hoover we sense some of the anxieties of a man caught between his own doubts and a popular expectation of him as a man who has the answers. From his first appearance in the novels, Trout has served Vonnegut as a vehicle of self-parody tinged by poignancy, the neglected and misunderstood science-fiction writer condemned to obscurity. Now he finds himself suddenly famous but still misunderstood. Most people still do not know whether to take him seriously, and that, surely, is an audience response Vonnegut has shared and probably, like Trout, even cultivated. Trout also has problems in deciding how to respond to his new fame. His desire to shock his new admirers is something which we sense that Vonnegut may have felt more than a touch of. His whimsical sketches in *Breakfast of Champions* may be one playful expression of that desire. And, as he remarks, "I now make my living by being impolite" (page 2).

Other apparent correspondences between Vonnegut and Trout range from the incidental to the characteristic. On the minor end of the scale, Trout's relationship with his parrot, Bill, resembles that which Vonnegut several times describes as existing between himself and his dog. (And Hoover also has a dog.) The resemblance between them becomes most apparent in their science-fiction stories—inevitably, since after all Trout's stories *are* Vonnegut's—particularly in the way in which Trout's stories usually originate in observation of some pattern in ordinary life and develop as a kind of hyperbolic social commentary. In his portrayal of Trout in *Breakfast of Champions* Vonnegut probably goes further than he has previously in revealing an essential element of his own method. Trout's stories work effectively to assist the thematic direction of the novel; they serve as exemplars, as supportive digressions which illustrate and emphasize the themes implicit in the larger structure. Perhaps the most important interrelating theme is that presented in Trout's *Now It Can Be Told*—the perception of people as robots. Trout's novel is written as a message from the Creator of the Universe to the reader which begins as follows:

> You are an experiment by the Creator of the Universe. You are the only creature in the entire Universe who has free will. You are the only one who has to figure out what to do next—and *why*. Everybody else is a robot, a machine. [page 253]

Obviously, the idea of humans as robots connects with the Dwayne Hoover side of the story, with its theme of human behavior biochemically controlled. The two themes merge when the two characters meet in the bar in Midland City, where Trout gives Hoover a copy of the novel. The general concept and its implications are not new in Vonnegut. People behaving "as it was meant to happen," questions of free will, characters being treated as neither virtuous nor evil because they were simply doing all that was possible to them, have had prominence in Vonnegut's novels at least since *The Sirens of Titan*. But here the twin themes emerge with peculiar force and particular personal relevance.

Hoover takes Trout's "solipsistic whimsy" as literal gospel and proceeds to attack the surrounding "robots" in the conviction that his violence cannot be felt and does not matter. Clearly, in having "bad ideas" transmitted to Hoover through Trout (pages 14–15) Vonnegut expresses some of the anxiety that any writer, particularly one adopted as a visionary, must feel about his responsibilities for the crazy reactions of his readers. One thinks of what Charles Manson did with the Beatles' "Helter Skelter." The same idea recurs when Vonnegut speaks of Americans behaving abominably to each other because that is what they learn from fiction (pages 209–210). So, again, Trout becomes a vehicle for the expression of the author's own misgivings. Yet ultimately the personal significance of the bad-chemicals-and-robots theme finds expression through the unlikely character of Rabo Karabekian. As the character-author himself says, it was through the outburst of the painter that he was reborn (page 219).

It seems typical of Vonnegut that the sympathetic Trout's ideas lead to mayhem while the dubious Karabekian's bring regeneration. And the brash artist *is* unsympathetic: He has a "barbaric face," and character-Vonnegut calls him "a vain and weak and trashy man, no artist at all" (page 220). We may see Karabekian as yet another of Vonnegut's portraits of the artist, a generally unforgiving one which embodies the self-doubts of artist-as-fraud which we have seen before. Yet there is the other side, too: Karabekian's painting, which has been the object only of ridicule, something any five-year-old could do, becomes accepted once the artist explains and defends it. There we have an expression of the defensiveness which Vonnegut sometimes exhibits along with his self-denigration. And ultimately Vonnegut makes Karabekian's defense of his art his own.

The danger comically present in Trout's *Now It Can Be Told* is its "solipsistic whimsy." The story, like many of Trout's, is written solipsistically; Trout develops an idea into a personal fantasy which he then imposes on a vision of the world. That danger becomes explicit when the book falls into the hands of the already solipsistic (being trapped into a distorted vision of reality by his "bad chemicals") Dwayne Hoover; the conception of others as robots becomes a "foma" which accords perfectly with Hoover's psychopathic disposition. The same dangers of solipsism afflict Karabekian's painting if it says only "I am," and may be implicit in Vonnegut's novel if it is only a self-indulgence, a birthday present to himself. And a similar danger is pointed to in the behavior of Americans throughout their history—for example, white Americans seeing 1492 as the first arrival of humans on the continent, or the use of black persons as slaves, as robots. Vonnegut makes this generalization most explicit when speaking of the bad influence of fiction in making people behave as if others were lesser characters in stories who can be manipulated, disregarded, or struck from the plot without a second thought (pages 209–210). But while in this sense the solipsism which leads to treating other humans as robots is obviously decried for its lack of humanity and awareness toward others, it also denies the perception of these same qualities in regard to themselves. We have seen elsewhere in Vonnegut, perhaps especially in *Slaughterhouse-Five,* people doubting their own worth because of a denigration of the worth of people generally. The same appears true in *Breakfast of Champions.* Trout's novel makes "Y-O-U," the reader, not *more* important because he or she is the only human among robots, but *less* important as a mere experiment. Vonnegut even diminishes himself to the doubtful or doubting level of "a writing machine" in the bar episode, in which people-as-robots comes to the fore and he languidly plays with his characters. He sums this up precisely in describing his "pre-earthquake condition":

> As for myself: I had come to the conclusion that there was nothing sacred about myself or about any human being, that we were all machines, doomed to collide and collide and collide. [page 219]

Rabo Karabekian's first remark, the one which has "such thundering consequences," comes when he sees Mary Alice Miller, the swimming champion, and exclaims, "What kind of a man would turn his daughter into an outboard motor?" (page 219). His outburst goes to the heart of the robot-making solipsism Vonnegut is about to expose. Driven to defend his painting, Karabekian says that it "shows everything about life which truly matters, with nothing left out" (page 221). This accords exactly with what Vonnegut has said about his own intentions when he resolves to give up storytelling because it leads Americans to treat each other like characters in fiction. "I would write about life. Every person would be exactly as important as any other. All facts would also be given equal weightiness. Nothing would be left out" (page 210). The "everything about life which matters" which Karabekian paints is "the awareness of every animal. It is the immaterial core of every animal—the 'I am' to which all messages are sent. It is all that is alive in any of us" (page 221). This awareness, which Karabekian portrays as a vertical band of light, is, he says, "all that is alive and maybe sacred in any of us" (page 221). Vonnegut naturally treats all of this with tongue in cheek, as when, a little later, he says:

> My doorbell has just rung in my New York apartment. And I know what I will find when I open my front door: an unwavering band of light.
>
> God bless Rabo Karabekian! [page 225]

But behind the irony resides a serious truth which could effectively counter many of the nightmares of robots, bad chemicals, and solipsism. Recognizing that within each individual being, within the physical "meat machine," lives an immaterial core of awareness entails a recognition of the peculiar individuality, the uniqueness, the "sacredness" of that being. Here Vonnegut perhaps approaches Iris Murdoch, who frequently has her characters struggle through solipsism toward a love which she defines as "the imaginative recognition of, that is respect for, the otherness of another person."[7] Karabekian's "awareness" is sacred in that it implies just such imaginative recognition; in effect, "awareness" is another name for "imaginative recognition," and what is imaginatively recognized and respected in the other person is his or her essential "I am." Such an awareness counters the solipsism which reduces others to robots, by recognizing their "I am," their uniqueness, their individual worth as beings endowed with their own perceptions and feelings. This recognition thus becomes a key to behaving toward others with humaneness. Similarly—and the outward and inward directions of this recognition are coalescent—self-respect also comes from affirming the "I am" within and respecting one's own humanity. Thus, this characteristically simple perception makes possible the reversal of character-Vonnegut's earlier pessimistic conclusion, by arguing that there *is* something "sacred about myself or about any human being" and that we are *not* all merely "machines, doomed to collide and collide and collide." That discovery is Vonnegut's cocktail-lounge epiphany, the cause of his subsequent "rebirth" and "serenity." It explains the epigraph:

> When he hath tried me,
> I shall come forth as gold.
> —Job

The novel's structure effectively serves the elements of characterization and theme which we have just examined. It, too, connects the inner and the outer worlds. The initial pages are concerned with a broad social and historical view of the United States as one piece of real estate on a "dying planet," one nation among a quadrillion in the universe (page 8). The two principal juxtaposed characters, Trout and Hoover, are separated, one in New York, the other in Midland City. As Trout moves toward Midland City, the two can be seen as converging physically, just as the themes converge. Trout's journey permits him to observe inhumanity in, for example, the destruction of West Virginia by mining. Hoover's Midland City shows the similar lack of human awareness in the small town's residents' stereotyped treatment of one another. Wayne Hoobler, the black ex-convict, brings to the Midland City convergence the embodiment of all that has been said about slaves, "niggers," and prisoners as human robots. Karabekian and Vonnegut, himself stepping into and out of the story, also come to Midland City. All narrows to the cocktail lounge of the Holiday Inn for the climactic scene, but at that point is already contracting even further to the consciousness of Vonnegut himself. Thus, the structure roughly resembles that of *Slaughterhouse-Five*, with numerous episodes, separated temporally and spatially, drawing inevitably toward one point of epiphany. One distinctive feature is that at the point where the "spiritual climax" (page 218) begins, a shift in setting and character relationship develops. The characters dwindle as seemingly real independent entities and become increasingly viewed as fictions in Vonnegut's imagination. The setting moves essentially into the author's mind, and the action is made explicitly his manipulation. This internalization complements the thematic relevance of the plot and emphasizes the therapeutic denouement which takes place within the consciousness of the author.

The structure lends itself well to the intentions Vonnegut declares in his preface. It permits him to set his personal emotional state in the context of the state of the country or even of the universe which is partially its cause. The structure even allows him a kind of objectivity in viewing that context; America is described as if to a visitor from another planet, an outsider's perspective which Vonnegut has used before, and much American social behavior is described through the eyes of Trout, Hoover, and others. In these cases Vonnegut's own perspective is always at least implied and often interjected directly. This beginning, with its broad, seemingly detached depiction of nation and world, helps to explain the depressed view of life with which Vonnegut enters the novel. As it proceeds, the structure may appear to be random and fragmented because it is so episodic, and the episodes so scattered in time, place, and subject. Yet it has pattern and cohesion in its moving toward one time and place, in the thematic connections between its episodes, and in its pointing to the final affirmation. There is even pattern in the manipulation of tempo, from the relaxed digressions of the earlier chapters to the hurried conversational style of the later ones, with the colloquial "Listen," "See," and "And so on." We might even apply the cliché "montage" to this technique—the illustrations provide a visual contribution to this effect—except that most of the episodes are more perceptibly related than may be true in the classic montage.

The foregoing discussion of the characters, themes, and structure of the novel, however, tends to make it sound like the kind of solemn and traditional "art novel" it is not. But *Breakfast of Champions* has strengths and makes serious statements which perhaps can be understood best by examining it through the familiar techniques which might be applied to the traditional novel. Above all, the tone must always be kept in mind when discussing Vonnegut. In *Breakfast of Champions* there is plenty of "yin and yang," of taking away what has been offered and undercutting what has been affirmed. There is spoofing; despite the use made of Karabekian's speech, his own personality and his painting of "an unwavering band of light" are surely mocked. The irreverent and the poignant stand side by side—Vonnegut's pathetically psychotic mother is "crazy as a bedbug." And there is the ever-present mix of the joyful and the pessimistic. While Vonnegut says that he finds serenity, and the general tone of the novel is upbeat, gloom remains. After all, the sacred awareness which he discovers continues to be ignored in the world around him. Even Vonnegut's freeing of his slaves, his characters, is ambivalent. Freed from their creator, they cease to have existence. Of course, the freeing of characters is a comic conception, as the ironic reference to Jefferson's freeing of his slaves emphasizes. And there is a sense in which, ultimately, Vonnegut can be no more freed from these his children than he can be from the parents he so constantly recalls. Trout embodies much of the father—even his shins, his feet, and his voice—but he is also father to Vonnegut, in part the obscure writer he once was, in part the man he might have become, and in part the often bemused but patiently cheerful person he remains. So, while *Breakfast of Champions* celebrates a birthday, discarding old trappings and offering new beginnings, the happy anniversary is not wholly joyous. It is, after all, his fiftieth. Vonnegut's last words might echo Trout's—"Make me young, make me young, make me young"—and the final portrait shows him with a tear in his eye.

Slapstick returns our attention to the questions raised earlier about the presentation of the autobiographical element in Vonnegut's fiction. He declares in the first sentence: "This is the closest I will ever come to writing an autobiography." In narrative method it differs dramatically from the previous novels, which were framed by authorial discourse, while the new novel ends with the author-character speaking. After the usual Vonnegut prologue, *Slapstick* employs a fictional first-person narrator but ends with the third-person omniscient point of view. Vonnegut's shift from such a personal narrative perspective to one which involves, at the least, the distancing of speaking through a persona is an interesting change for a book which he calls autobiographical. But then, the sense in which he intends this as autobiography is qualified: "It is," he says, "about what life *feels* like to me" (page 1). While events in the novel may be traced to biographical fact, it would appear that as autobiography *Slapstick* has more psychological than literal veracity.

Throughout his novels Vonnegut has drawn on personal experience, as might be expected. *Player Piano*, for example, transposes into the Ilium Works the General Electric plant in Schenectady where the author had once worked. Paul Proteus and Ed Finnerty probably both serve to voice various of Vonnegut's reactions to that employment. This was the technique which Vonnegut was to use in most of his novels, to varying degrees. Sometimes, as in *The Sirens of Titan* and *God Bless You, Mr. Rosewater,* the amount of factual biographical correspondence seems limited, although both novels might be autobiographical in the sense of projecting states of mind, raising questions, expressing doubts, or presenting thoughts which preoccupied Vonnegut at the time. In other works, such as *Cat's Cradle,* there appears a more factual autobiographical element. John/Jonah, for example, is—like Vonnegut—a writer who sees and writes of "the end of the world." The Hoenikker family approximates Vonnegut's own: Frank, the older brother, a scientist like his own, Angela a tall substitute mother like his own sister, and Newton, the midget younger brother, corresponding in some respects to the author himself. In both of these forms Vonnegut does indeed "include myself . . . slyly."

In *Slapstick* Vonnegut returns to this successful earlier technique, discarding the direct inclusion of self used in *Slaughterhouse-Five* and, more emphatically, in *Breakfast of Champions.* This newest novel perhaps resembles most closely *Cat's Cradle* in its use of the autobiographical, except that the author is more positively included, this time through a single narrator-protagonist rather than through characters who might combine to represent him. The tall sister appears again, there is no obvious counterpart to the older brother, and the parents seem to have limited biographical basis even as vehicles for the reconstruction of childhood emotions.

Vonnegut's prologue explains the way in which the novel illustrates "what life *feels* like to me." It speaks at length of the dissolution of the once tight-knit and proud Vonnegut family in Indianapolis and of the similar loss of roots and family in America generally. Vonnegut writes tenderly of his sister, his closest sibling temporally and emotionally, who died of cancer two days after her husband was killed. She, he says, had served as the audience to whom he had written his books. He speaks of his late Uncle Alex, who may have joined Alcoholics Anonymous as much out of loneliness as from any "dread of alcoholic poisoning." He tells of flying to Uncle Alex's funeral with his brother, and mentions family children, including his own and those of his sister whom he took in. The children, he finds, tend blessedly to forget sad things and even to lose memories of loved ones, as he has to a degree himself.

Thus, the prologue speaks of such loneliness, separation, and sadness as might presage a singularly "dark" novel even for Vonnegut. But in explaining what life feels like to him, Vonnegut evokes a parallel with the Laurel and Hardy comedy films. "There are all these tests of my limited agility and intelligence. They go on and on" (page 1). And he continues:

> The fundamental joke with Laurel and Hardy, it seems to me, was that they did their best with every test.
>
> They never failed to bargain in good faith with their destinies, and were screamingly adorable and funny on that account. [page 1]

In commenting on the fact that love has a small role in Laurel and Hardy films, he goes some way toward explaining its infrequency in his own novels. Love, he feels, is less important than "bargaining in good faith with destiny" and treating other people with what might be described as "common decency." Otherwise, he finds the love he has shared with people indistinguishable from the uncritical affection he has enjoyed with dogs, and seems to suspect romantic love as coercive.

What remains, then, is a view of life as being as his dying sister described it: "Slapstick." Given the conditions he has described—of isolation, of inevitable death, of bargaining in good faith with a meaningless universe—one might choose another word: "Absurd." Except that Vonnegut's word typically emphasizes the comic (or comical) potentialities so often overlooked by the existentialists. He says that he daydreamed the book while flying to his uncle's funeral and reflecting on the tragic death of his sister, which is why it "is about desolated cities and spiritual cannibalism and incest and loneliness and lovelessness and death, and so on" (pages 18–19). Yet just as the prologue, which reflects on many such occurrences in Vonnegut's own life, does not seem depressed, so the novel's tone transcends the gloom inherent in much of its content. And, for the same reason. Vonnegut himself seems steadier, more composed, more at terms with life in this prologue than in those which immediately precede it. Likewise, his narrator in *Slapstick*, though wearied and in some senses disillusioned, seems calm and resigned.

In casting himself as Wilbur Swain and his sister as Eliza Swain, Vonnegut has made both "monsters." This may seem perverse or whimsical, yet remains characteristic of Vonnegut. He is consistently self-denigrating in his fiction and the prefaces. Some of the characters with whom he might be most nearly identified and some of the "heroes" of his fiction are abnormal physically or psychologically, and when he approaches self in portraying artists and writers he typically undercuts. One senses a degree of embarrassment here in a writer who nevertheless feels compelled to be direct and personal. It is as if he needs the protection of irony and whimsy after having come so close to the nerve. Usually the protection serves well, saving him in tricky spots from what might otherwise become sentimental self-pity, didacticism, or plain morbidity. In *Slapstick* the character of Wilbur Swain works effectively as such a mask, but more importantly helps to advance thematic content. Most notably, casting the young Swains as seven-foot freaks gives comically dramatic emphasis to the notions of "common decency" in human relations and "bargaining in good faith with destiny."

Those two themes intertwine in the accounts of the childhood years of Wilbur and Eliza. Having been diagnosed as incapable of intellectual development, the children bargain in good faith with their destinies by acting as idiots and show common decency in thus performing according to what is expected of them. They are innocently eager to please. Inevitably this changes when, on their fifteenth birthday, they discover that their parents are horrified not just by their appearance but by their idiocy. Then, of course, they blunder by again bargaining in good faith and revealing their sophistication. At this point the frailty of love emerges. Their parents had felt free not to love them since they were so totally unlovable. Now it is the parents' *duty* to love the children, and they feel incapable of so doing (page 75). Later Eliza expresses her skepticism about love when Wilbur, having read that love is "the most important thing of all," suggests he should declare his love of her. She thinks not.

> "It's as though you were pointing a gun at my head," she said. "It's just a way of getting somebody to say something they probably don't mean. What else can I say, or *anybody* say, but, 'I love you too'?" [page 108]

The echo of Vonnegut's first novel, *Player Piano*, where Paul and Anita Proteus repeat the ritual—

"I love you, Paul."
"I love *you*, Anita."

—rings loud, and reminds us again how much *Slapstick* resembles earlier work.

Where the autobiography lies in all of this (and one should not take the novel as some kind of psychological *roman à clef*) perhaps only Vonnegut can answer. His sister, Alice, was tall, embarrassed by her height, and developed bad posture—all hyperbolically reproduced in Eliza. Vonnegut felt especially close to her, claims that she was the only person he had written for, and adds:

> She was the secret of whatever artistic unity I had ever achieved. She was the secret of my technique. Any creation which has any wholeness and harmoniousness, I suspect, was made by an artist or inventor with an audience of one in mind. [page 15]

The parallel to that obviously emerges in Wilbur and Eliza's joining to form one genius, and in the Chinese system of bringing together harmonious pairs of thinkers. Alice dies "among strangers" in a hospital; Eliza dies among Chinese on the moon. Alice's children find that they cannot recall their parents; the young Wilbur comfortably forgets Eliza when they are separated. But Vonnegut does not forget his sister, and the older Wilbur says he is "dying to meet" Eliza in the afterlife.

There are many such correspondences. But again the emphasis should remain on "what life *feels* like to me." And what is felt here is the never-equaled closeness with a sibling in childhood, the pain of loss, the difficulties of growth and of love. All the confusions of childhood, of trying to behave according to expectations, to apply to life the "wisdom" of literature (as in their encounters with Darwin and the story of the ugly duckling), can be seen as expressions of what "life feels like" to the child. But a further purpose is to comment on family life. After her release from the mental institution where she has been abandoned, Eliza says, "What civilized country could be interested in a hell-hole like America . . . where everybody takes such lousy care of their own relatives?" (page 118).

Relatives, family, taking care of one's own, home, a place where one belongs—Vonnegut speaks of these things repeatedly in the prologue, primarily in connection with the Vonnegut family. His personal concern is obvious as he mourns the decline of his family's unity and its ties with Indianapolis, treasures relationships with brother and sister, and regrets the loneliness and rootlessness which accompany modern American transience.

> When we were children in Indianapolis, Indiana, it appeared that we would always have an extended family of genuine relatives there. Our parents and grandparents, after all, had grown up there with shoals of siblings and cousins and uncles and aunts. Yes, and their relatives were all cultivated and gentle and prosperous, and spoke German and English gracefully. [pages 5–6]

This need for "family" becomes the major theme of the novel, expressed personally as part of what life feels like to Vonnegut, and more broadly as a universal human requirement. As he says, "human beings need all the relatives they can get—as possible donors or receivers not necessarily of love, but of common decency" (page 5). Vonnegut originally worked with the title *The Relatives* for this novel,[8] and his present subtitle, *Lonesome No More!*, gives similar emphasis to the family theme. In the *Playboy* interview, reprinted in

Wampeters, Foma & Granfalloons, Vonnegut says that he once suggested to the 1972 McGovern campaign that Sargent Shriver stress the need to recreate a spirit of closeness among the American people with the slogan "Lonesome no more!" (page 274). In *Slapstick* that war cry brings Wilbur Swain election to the White House, and becomes the motto of his program to create artificial families to include everyone.

The genesis of the artificial families President Swain creates in *Slapstick* can be traced in earlier Vonnegut writings. As far back as *Player Piano* there are Shriners and Ghost Shirters and management retreats, where people with some common bond draw together. But the extended family itself features prominently in two segments of *Wampeters, Foma & Granfalloons*: the essay "Biafra: A People Betrayed" and the *Playboy* interview. In the former he speaks with awe of the large Biafran families who cared for their disparate members through the horrors of that war. In the latter he begins by explaining the appeal of Charles Manson as his willingness to be father to homeless sixteen-year-olds and give them a sense of permanence. Then he tells of writing "a Kilgore Trout story" in which the government assigns people to random families on the basis of middle names such as Daffodil. Pressed by the skeptical *Playboy* interviewer, Vonnegut seems to hold firm to his idea, saying that the extended-family members would be "like regular relatives," with their deadbeats and panhandlers and insular pride, but also with the likelihood of being glad to meet and help each other. The essence of what appears in *Slapstick* is outlined in the interview.

Inevitably, the extended-family idea raises the sort of questions that get asked about most of the ideas Vonnegut advances through his fiction—the big one being, is he serious? That, of course, takes us right back to Kilgore Trout in *Breakfast of Champions*. The portrayal of the extended-family plan in *Slapstick* is hedged about with ironical—and farcical—undercutting. It also gives expression to some of the "serious" objections that might be raised to such a scheme. Predictably there are some who object to any such "Federal interference" in their lives or who hate being lumped together with segments of the great unwashed. Some wear buttons reading "Lonesome Thank God!" (page 173). Wilbur's wife, Sophie, would rather remain a Rothschild than become a Peanut-3. Assorted misfits converge on the White House to claim kinship with the President. Even Wilbur has to admit that he can barely tolerate his "brother" Carlos Daffodil-11 Villavicencio. Wilbur describes Richard Nixon and his associates as being "unbalanced by loneliness of an especially virulent sort."

> "They were not basically criminals," I said. "But they yearned to partake of the brotherhood they saw in Organized Crime." [page 166]

Through all of the slapstick mocking of the idea, however, some reasonably serious defense of extended families survives. To Sophie's repulsion with the "freak show" outside the White House, Wilbur counters:

> "And you are not mistaken when you say that they have crawled out from under damp rocks—like centipedes and earwigs and worms. They have never had a friend or a relative. They have had to believe all their lives that they were perhaps sent to the wrong Universe, since no one has ever bid them welcome or given them anything to do." [page 176]

The unloved, it seems, would have the chance of at least finding one another. Family newspapers and meetings provide warnings of exploitative, dangerous, or criminal members, and offer advice and services. One paper suggests that family concern may make police forces obsolete; if a criminal relative is found, "don't call the police. Call ten more relatives" (page 180). The Daffodil meeting which Wilbur attends is such a model of decorum and decency that it suggests parody, yet even this contains some reminders of what such a sense of community might achieve.

By the end of the novel the artificial families still function, though they have been partially displaced by other confederations as the national structure collapses. The potential for families to band together against others is recognized when a Hatfield, who "never was big for them new-fangled names," emerges, still feuding with McCoys. Across the land regional tribes and armies war with each other under group labels such as "Hoosier" and "Sooner," led by the likes of the King of Michigan and the Duke of Oklahoma. This might suggest a dangerous progression of family to clan to tribe to petty kingdom, except that extended-family relatives on opposing sides tend to shelter one another. Perhaps it serves to contrast the extended family to such falsely based social groups, which in *Cat's Cradle* he calls "granfalloons." On "The Island of Death" (Manhattan) families continue as the sole social structure. The Raspberries are delvers and hoarders, a colony of human ants. Vera Chipmunk-5 Zappa runs her model farm with voluntary slaves—all Chipmunks, of course. There may be an implied warning here of submission for the sake of belonging, an old danger to would-be joiners, yet the benevolent Vera seems nothing like a Charles Manson.

So, while Vonnegut laughs at the craziness likely to come with such a scheme, and recognizes limits to its effectiveness, he seems serious about some of the benefits it might achieve. Above all, he remains deadly serious about the psychological and social ills which the extended families are intended to alleviate. He uses a "modest proposal" to expose the nature of the malady which needs cure. Between prologue and novel Vonnegut emphasizes what family and roots could, and perhaps once did, provide. Once, he says, there were uncles and aunts, cousins and grandparents, and a home town from which one might wander but to which one ultimately returned. Family offered a mix of sexes, generations, and personalities, yet had unity along with the virtue of diversity. Vonnegut comments on this conception in the *Playboy* interview:

> Until recent times, you know, human beings usually had a permanent community of relatives. They had dozens of homes to go to. So when a married couple had a fight, one or the other could go to a house three doors down and stay with a close relative until he was feeling tender again. Or if a kid got so fed up with his parents that he couldn't stand it, he could march over to his uncle's for a while. And this is no longer possible. Each family is locked into its little box. The neighbors aren't relatives. There aren't other houses where people can go and be cared for. . . . We're lonesome. We don't have enough friends or relatives anymore. And we would if we lived in real communities. [*Wampeters*, pages 242–243]

One counter to such loneliness which Vonnegut posits is the larger "extended family" of people connected by common interests, such as the professional coterie. He cherishes his own connection with other writers, for example, and approves of Uncle Alex's joining Alcoholics Anonymous more from fear of loneliness than of drink. These groups, however, lack some of the diversity and the emotional and geographical community of the family. There remains, then, the modern family "locked into its little box." That sounds rather like the Hagstrohms of Homestead in *Player Piano,* or the various "nations of two" throughout Vonnegut's fiction. His marriages seldom seem to work well, and frequently they tend to lock out other associations. Vonnegut implies that the modern model mini-family of Mom, Dad, Dick, Jane, and Spot fails where the larger family unit once succeeded. Mom and Dad may have a strained relationship, Dick and Jane may be cut off from the parents, and only Spot remains capable of uncritical affection.

That failure of the modern family emerges again in *Slapstick* with the Swains. Not that any of them is really *blamed* for the failure. Parents and children try to act for the best, at least most of the time. Perhaps Dr. Cordelia Swain Cordiner stands as the closest thing to a villain of the piece. (One whose name is a superb piece of irony, incidentally.) Her "basic rule of life" is "Paddle your own canoe" (page 93). And, as her motto promises, she becomes the initiator of separation, both of the children from the parents and of the children from each other. Those separations condemn the children to loneliness and lovelessness, and to being forever "Betty and Bobby Brown," as they name their dull separated selves. If one were to compare the novel with Coleridge's *The Rime of the Ancient Mariner*, this separation would be the equivalent of the shooting of the albatross. From this point on, things disintegrate, stayed only by moments of reintegration, which generally involve at least a symbolic connection between Wilbur and Eliza. Most such moments are hilariously, grotesquely undercut—as with the five-day orgy in Back Bay, the communication via the Hooligan—yet they produce harmonious, humane results like the book on pediatrics and the artificial-families program. For Wilbur, one of the happiest moments comes while he is President and receives a letter from himself informing him of his membership in the Daffodil family. Vonnegut integrates that joyous time in the "past" with another in the "present" of Wilbur's writing: the preparation for Wilbur's birthday party. And in that present Isadore, lover of Wilbur's granddaughter Melody, living harmoniously with the girl and the old man and Vera's happy slaves, sings an answer to Cordelia's "basic rule of life":

> "Row, row, row your boat . . .
> Gently down the stream.
> Merrily, merrily, merrily, merrily—
> Life is but a dream." [page 169]

Some of the other major motifs in *Slapstick* serve the theme of relationship. The variation of gravity, while certainly "slapstick" and likely to turn *anyone's* bargaining in good faith with destiny into Laurel and Hardy, becomes a device for accelerating the social disintegration the novel warns against. The Albanian influenza and the Green Death decimate the population and bring further social disintegration. Even the fact that the one is caused by the ingestion of microscopic Chinese and the other by the inhalation of invading Martians seems relevant—the interlopers disrupt the cellular family of the body. (Vonnegut's discussion of "nucleation" in the *Playboy* interview, in which he speaks of cancer cells along with nuclear families, bears on this subject [*Wampeters*, page 245].) The subtheme of the Chinese, while mainly a brilliant satire of the mystery and near-superstitious awe in which they are currently regarded, also relates thematically. The Chinese are presented as a kind of super-family, totally withdrawn into themselves, with concern for the larger community welfare carried to an extreme. That other outrageous parody of a current social phenomenon, the Church of Jesus Christ the Kidnapped, also serves. The sect perhaps shows a continuing need for other extended families, or for a family which transcends terrestrial limits and provides a sense of belonging in the universe and continuity beyond death. "The Turkey Farm," *Slapstick's* jaundiced view of Eternity, provides the last word on that line of thought.

Typically, then, Vonnegut's plot is more artfully structured than it appears at first glance. The interweaving of the present in which Wilbur writes and the past which he recalls proves effective, the two working simultaneously toward denouement. The sudden death of Wilbur and the concluding of his story by an omniscient narrator surprises, and may at first seem a weakness, suggesting almost that Vonnegut grew tired of the first-person method or was not sure how to draw it to a close. But Wilbur's death, the narrative shift, and the ending all contribute to Vonnegut's theme. Wilbur dies following his birthday party, coming to his end in his beginning, as it were. Birthdays are made much of in the story, from the childhood "Fuff-bay" on, seemingly as one of the "ancient games" that continue endlessly and give pleasure to the daily round, and as family ritual. Wilbur's last birthday party is a happy one for all. A thousand candles are lighted on the floor, and Wilbur's narrative ends with this impression:

> Standing among all those tiny, wavering lights, I felt as though I were God, up to my knees in the Milky Way. [page 228]

Our narrator makes a charming exit—and a necessary one. The account that follows of his communication via Hooligan with his sister, the dreary picture of "The Turkey Farm" of the hereafter, and his heading for "The Island of Death" as an act of suicide would make the grace of his death more difficult to sustain. But, more important, by having Wilbur's death occur at this point Vonnegut can achieve an ending which brings affirmation out of the bleakest point in the novel. The switch to omniscient third-person narration which follows also assists. Moving to an objective perspective makes possible an apparent detachment which, while avoiding the sentimentalism that might emerge in first-person narration of the same events, actually serves to heighten emotion. William Golding has employed the same device with great effectiveness in the endings of *Lord of the Flies* and *The Inheritors*.

In this last important section of the book, we see Wilbur devastated by his communication with his sister and his withdrawal from tri-benzo-Deportamil, ready for death, but then finding some basis for going on in helping, and being helped by, the Raspberries. Then comes Vera to nurse him, and later his granddaughter Melody. From this point we go back to the beginning and the story Wilbur has just told. And that is a story told by a weary and resigned man, yet one still finding happiness in remembrance and dreams, still with a sense of humor, and still "proud of what he and his sister had done to reform their society" (page 229). But the novel concludes with Melody's story, which is full of barbarity and pain, yet tells of a girl setting off in search of her blood relative, aided by artificial relatives.

> They would feed her and point the way.
>
> One would give her a raincoat. Another would give her a sweater and a magnetic compass. Another would give her a baby carriage. Another would give her an alarm clock.
>
> Another would give her a needle and thread, and a gold thimble, too.
>
> Another would row her across the Harlem River to the Island of Death, at the risk of his own life. [page 243]

Thus the novel ends with affirmation in terms of its major theme. Caring relatives behave with decency, and the bargaining in good faith with destiny goes on. And this affirmation arises out of a view of life bleak enough to contradict any suggestions of bland optimism. The last words—"Das

Ende"—also nod toward relatives: those Vonneguts who "were all cultivated and gentle and prosperous, and spoke German and English gracefully" (pages 5–6).

This, then, is the slapstick of life as Vonnegut feels it. Much of that experience seems painful. Wilbur's pill-popping, his birthdays, his father-son relationships, his loss of a sister, all echo phases in the author's life. Often the comical coexists with the painful, as agility and intelligence are sorely tested. Like a Laurel and Hardy film, Vonnegut's fictional world is "funny and adorable" but also poignant. In the *Playboy* interview Vonnegut says, in an apparent non sequitur, "People are too good for this world" (*Wampeters*, page 244). For a moment this almost startles us, because although Vonnegut claims not to create villains or heroes, he portrays some rather nasty people and shows plenty of suffering caused by human action. Yet his prevailing attitude remains one of sympathy for the human lot. The destiny with which humans gamble does not always keep good faith; if gravity is not unpredictable, the weather certainly is. The best that humans can do is often not good enough, and Vonnegut breathes another "Hi ho," bespeaking a weary resignation but not, ultimately, rejection. He sees humans generally as limited in the same ways as himself, and that gives rise to one of the major strengths of *Slapstick* and of his other fiction: the ability to interconnect the intensely personal with the universally human.

Slapstick brings Vonnegut back closer to the direction of his first five novels. *Slaughterhouse-Five* represents a thematic culmination but a stylistic departure. In content and narration it is more directly autobiographical than the novels which precede it. *Breakfast of Champions* takes the autobiographical element a stage further in introducing the author into his own fictional world, and in its intensely personal subject matter, embodying the author's artistic and social uncertainties. *Slapstick*, too, is autobiographical, but, as we have seen, in a perhaps less private way, and in a manner closer to the sense in which the earlier fiction was autobiographical. Again, much in this newest novel seems reminiscent of the *Cat's Cradle–Mother Night–God Bless You, Mr. Rosewater* era. There are differences, of course: Apart from Bernard O'Hare and Norman Mushari, the old familiar characters are gone; the injunctions to "Listen" and the choric "Hi ho" grow out of *Slaughterhouse-Five*'s "So it goes" and *Breakfast of Champions*; and the short, clipped paragraphs are characteristic of the later work. The author's prologue is more than ever integral to the novel. That prologue helps signal one of the more subtle evolutions in Vonnegut's work—that of tone. The change is subtle simply because so much remains constant. But there is, for example, something approaching bitterness in *Player Piano* and pessimistic fatalism in *Slaughterhouse-Five*. *Slapstick*, for all the bleakness of content, exudes an affirmative assurance. That tone is surely not born simply out of a belief in the powers of artificial extended families. It derives less from the content than from the author's attitude. Vonnegut appears more confident, more comfortable with the world and himself in *Slapstick* than in *Breakfast of Champions*, where self-doubts emerge and the laughter sometimes seems forced. So, while it retains echoes of the earlier works, *Slapstick* evolves out of the experimentation of the two previous novels. Yet whereas they each involved a "sweeping away," a termination—*Slaughterhouse-Five* of the Dresden experience and *Breakfast* of the old characters—which seemed hard to follow, *Slapstick* appears to promise continuation.

NOTES

1. Kurt Vonnegut, "*Playboy* Interview," in *Wampeters, Foma & Granfalloons*, p. 281.
2. Iwao Iwamoto, "A Clown's Say—A Study of Kurt Vonnegut, Jr.'s *Slaughterhouse-Five*," *Studies in English Literature* (Tokyo), English Number 1975, pp. 21–23.
3. Peter J. Reed, *Writers for the Seventies: Kurt Vonnegut, Jr.* (New York: Warner Paperback Library, 1972), pp. 172–203.
4. Leslie Fiedler in "Democratic Culture," transcript of interview with William F. Buckley, Jr., broadcast on PBS on December 1, 1974 (Columbia, S.C.: Southern Educational Communications Association), p. 11.
5. Leslie Fiedler, "The Divine Stupidity of Kurt Vonnegut," *Esquire*, 74 (September 1970), 195–204.
6. Clinton S. Burhans, Jr., says that in entering the narrative as himself to talk to his characters Vonnegut "erases the distinction between fact and fiction and implies that 'real' people are as much a product of their own imaginations as fictional characters are the product of the writer's imagination." "Hemingway and Vonnegut: Diminishing Vision in a Dying Age," *Modern Fiction Studies*, 21 (Summer 1975), 185.
7. Iris Murdoch, "The Sublime and the Good," *Chicago Review*, 13 (No. 3, 1959), 52.
8. Jerome Klinkowitz, review of *Slapstick*, *New Republic*, 175 (September 25, 1976), 40–41.

Donald L. Lawler

Vonnegut in Academe (II)

At the Vonnegut seminar, the panelists first described the purpose of their papers, and then joined with the audience in the following discussion.

LAWLER: Our first speaker is Jerome Klinkowitz. Jerry is Professor of English at the University of Northern Iowa, and is co-author of *The Vonnegut Statement*. His book *Literary Disruptions* (University of Illinois Press, 1975) also has a chapter on Kurt Vonnegut. His subject today is Vonnegut's early short stories.

KLINKOWITZ: I was drawn to these short stories for two reasons, both of which are important for understanding Vonnegut's later work. For the first, these early stories from *Collier's* and the *Saturday Evening Post* are Vonnegut's raw beginnings as a literary artist. In such rudimentary work it is often easier to see the artist's hand at work; the brush strokes are more prominent, and they give us a clue to his later subtleties. Secondly, these stories are very accessible; if the later Vonnegut becomes complex, in these earlier works he is amazingly simple and direct. But it should be no surprise that the same attitudes carry over into his mature novels—only you have to dig a bit to find them. So many of us, as we'll all admit, have had trouble when we first look at Vonnegut's novels; it's very hard to analyze Vonnegut's art in a novel like *Slaughterhouse-Five* because, in terms of mainstream literature, he's such a radical innovator. His stories, however, give us the materials for a track record. They are the trail Vonnegut left as he worked his way toward becoming an innovative writer. The novels themselves are indeed perplexing. We admire them, but are often speechless when asked, what's the technique? It's hard to point out anything, beyond the obviously short sentences and the short paragraphs. But if you look at his essays from many of the same popular magazines, you can use traditional rhetorical techniques to spot exactly what he is doing . . . really trace out the discontinuities and find some of the marvelous things that he accomplishes.

So, I have been looking at the stories from that point of view. I find a consistent middle-class perspective which becomes represented in most of the latter novels. Vonnegut will take a simple, common, good, middle-class hero and infiltrate him into the upper classes—either into their money or their affectations—really, most importantly, into their values. The key story, the model story, of this technique would be the piece Vonnegut wrote in 1963 for the *Saturday Evening Post* but which never ran, called "The Hyannis Port Story," where he has his storm-window salesman dropped into Hyannis Port with not only all of the money but also a lot of the craziness of the Kennedy hysteria: the P.T. 109 Cocktail Lounge, the First Family Waffle Shop, and so on. You can take this story and trace out a pattern which then becomes like an overlay not only for the other stories but also, I think, for the novels as well. Vonnegut's rejected Master's thesis at the University of Chicago Anthropology Department, "Fluctuation Between Good and Evil in Simple Tales," studied exactly that technique. Vonnegut analyzed Kentucky folk ballads, Russian folk tales, *Esquire* stories, *New Yorker* stories, radio soap operas, and found there was a distinctive pattern for each kind of story. Fifteen years of writing for the slicks taught him to perfect a contemporary pattern of fantasy which, I think, finally triumphs in novels like *God Bless You, Mr. Rosewater* and *Slaughterhouse-Five.*

LAWLER: Thanks, Jerry.

My own interest in Vonnegut focuses on *The Sirens of Titan*, and I approach the novel by asking myself if Vonnegut really is a science-fiction writer or whether he is perhaps a science-fiction writer in sheep's clothing. I opt for the sheep's clothing. My argument is that *The Sirens of Titan*, being generally agreed upon as the one SF novel Vonnegut has written if he ever wrote any at all, is SF *in fact*, not simply by virtue of having a few elements—that its basic organization, its basic assumptions, its basic probabilities are SF; and, really, without the SF there isn't a novel. It's not something added on like a lacquer finish. And yet when I look at the novel closely, I find that the techniques of SF are being used not for what I would call SF ends—SF for SF's sake—but for other purposes which I try to define in my paper. I won't overwhelm you now with an analysis of those areas where I find relevance, but basically SF in *The Sirens of Titan* is what I call "enabling form," a vehicle which permits Vonnegut to do certain other things. First of all, he wants to make a criticism of ideas—ideas basically taken from metaphysics and theology, ideas related to some of the basic and profound questions about the meaning of life and the direction of history. Now, Vonnegut will not ask these questions directly or earnestly; he will undercut his question; he will cloak it with irony; he will present it in a burlesque fashion. I have come to the conclusion that the choice of the space opera as the basic SF form for this story was made because it enabled Vonnegut to do that kind of burlesquing, to make that kind of parody most effectively, not because he wants to write space opera. In fact, in the *Playboy* interview he says the space opera is a form of SF that is obviously of "a kidding sort," which means that it is obviously exaggerated, obviously extreme. In Vonnegut's view it's obviously absurd. And a part of the fun of the novel is that, in a sense, Vonnegut is hoaxing the reader. It is, in effect, then, a booby-trapped novel, and we're the boobies. He is always leading us on, for example in the space opera, asking us to accept it as though it were a kind of straight SF novel; and as soon as we turn up the last bit of paper, something blows up in our face. If we accept the space opera, we're led to Salo's "Greetings" after three hundred pages.

This formula, incidentally, is one that tickled my fancy. The more I thought about it, the more it reminded me of the shaggy-dog story. It seemed pretty farfetched at first, until I began to look more closely at the novel. Then I reread that *Playboy* interview, where Vonnegut said that he was really dealing with jokes. His novels are put together as though they were a series of jokes; the jokes were like traps set for the reader and sprung at important parts. And as I looked at *The Sirens of Titan* I said to myself, this is exactly what Vonnegut is doing. He is setting traps in a hoaxing, punning fashion, inviting the reader, as it were, as part of the joke, to be hoaxed along with the characters. I think he does this for several reasons. One of them is that he has to establish a kind of alienation, a distance between his audience and his topic; otherwise, he can't make his characters behave as robots and still make us responsive to them. We're not really intended to identify with those characters. We're supposed to see them turning into automatons, to watch them being controlled by Tralfamadorian robots or by Rumfoord; and I think we're supposed to react to them the way we react to characters in satire or in serious comedy. In any case, the booby traps certainly do work. The shaggy-dog analogy is not perhaps as farfetched as it may seem. In fact, if you look at the plot lines in *The Sirens of Titan*, each one of them turns out to follow one of the better-known shaggy-dog formulas: either the catch tale or the hoax tale, rather than the more famous punning shaggy-dog stories.

So, my conclusion was that if Vonnegut is a science-fiction writer, he is a science-fiction writer of a very definite, and I might say traditional, sort. But the tradition is that of Swift, Voltaire, and Twain rather than the tradition of Heinlein, John W. Campbell, and some of the other SF writers who are better known to the present generation, like Ellison and Delaney.

Our next speaker is Willis McNelly, who comes to us from California State University at Fullerton. Willis is a member of the Science Fiction Writers Association. He has edited several anthologies: *Above the Human Landscape* and *Science Fiction: The Academic Awakening*, a chapbook, [which] is probably well known to you. He teaches science fiction, courses on Joyce and Yeats; and I guess I could go on and on. He was, incidentally, the first academic asked by the Science Fiction Writers Association to Contribute to the Nebula Award. He is on the panel of the John W. Campbell Award.

MCNELLY: I guess I am defending Vonnegut as a science-fiction writer. Eliot Rosewater once said, "I love you sons of bitches, you are all I read any more." (He'd invaded the famous science-fiction writers conference at Milford, which was an actual one founded by Damon Knight.) He then went on to say,

> You're the only ones who'll talk about the *really* terrific changes going on, the only ones crazy enough to know that life is a space voyage, and not a short one, either, but one that'll last for billions of years. You're the only one with guts enough to *really* care about the future, who *really* notice what machines do to us, what wars do to us, what cities do to us. . . . You're the only ones zany enough to agonize over time and distances without limit, over mysteries that will never die, over the fact that we are right now determining whether the space voyage for the next billion years or so is going to be Heaven or Hell. [*God Bless You, Mr. Rosewater*, page 27]

Fine, a paean of praise for SF! And then on the dust jacket of the hardcover edition of *Slaughterhouse-Five* I read, "Once mistakenly typed as a science-fiction writer, Vonnegut is now recognized as a mainstream storyteller, often fascinated by the tragic and comic possibilities of the machines." Well what's the truth? Is he or isn't he? Does he or doesn't he?—Well, somewhere between the two. What I am objecting to, I think, is the notion that if it's good, it can't be SF; and if it is SF, it can't be good. For heaven's sake, let us all realize that Buck Rogers is dead and what is going on in SF today at the hands of writers, perhaps not Heinlein but certainly writers like Brian Aldiss, John Boyd, Arthur C. Clarke, Bradbury, Vonnegut himself, Robert Silverberg, Philip K. Dick, and a dozen others that I could name if I were going into it at any length, is a new kind of fiction. May I refer you, incidentially, to an article of mine published in the Jesuit weekly *America* back in early November [1975] for a general assessment of what has been going on in SF the last twenty or twenty-five years for that coverage.

But I suspect that what Vonnegut is doing is using SF as an "objective correlative"—a sort of literary Pavlovian response where a writer such as Eliot says "Hamlet," and we all salivate, and put outselves in the emotional condition in which we first read *Hamlet*, and then he takes us from there. Well, I think, that Vonnegut is doing much the same thing—he is using SF to enable us to distance ourselves from some kind of present reality. It was also Eliot, in "East Coker," I believe, who said "human beings cannot stand very much reality." And so, if we were to examine in some detail how Vonnegut utilizes SF devices as a commentary, a social commentary of placing us, in the words of Rasselas, "above the human landscape," it might indicate then that Vonnegut uses these devices, these SF techniques, for purposes which cannot necessarily be reached in so-called mainstream fiction. SF, he indicates in *Slaughterhouse-Five*, is a help in reinventing ourselves and understanding the world better. Tralfamadore, Kilgore Trout, and all the rest of the SF "impedimenta," if I may use the word, are radically discontinuous, in Robert Scholes's phrase, from the world that we know, and yet they circle about to look at that world again in a certain cognitive way. In Vonnegut's view, mission and futility seem to brother each other, but the cyclic vision of a spring bird singing "Po-too-weet" augurs some kind of a rebirth. Vonnegut then perhaps uses SF as a counterthrust to his own mordant humor, and with his comedic vision provides some kind of a final affirmation. If it takes SF to give some kind of affirmation or hope, then—well, so it goes.

LAWLER: Our next panelist is Professor Conrad Festa, a friend from Old Dominion University and a fellow displaced Victorian. He is the editor of the *Victorians Institute Journal*, and the author of articles on Victorian poets, prose writers, and otherwise. He is a man with a deep interest in Vonnegut's satire.

FESTA: I experienced the same problems of interpretation and classification that have been expressed thus far. In addition to that bit of tension, I've also felt confused at the reactions that some of my friends and students have had to Vonnegut novels. They either take them very, very seriously (in the Arnoldian sense of high seriousness) or they take them as such hairbrain things that the works become camp. Students especially react in strange ways—they become Bokononists—you know, the religion and the whole business. It confused me, it bothered me somewhat, and, being a traditionalist, I looked for answers in the way I had been trained. I tried to classify Vonnegut, recognizing fully that classifying any artist is a foolish endeavor in itself, but a helpful place to start. What I began to see was that, yes, indeed, he does have elements in some of his works which are in the science-fiction mode, and there are elements in other of his works which are clearly in the confessional mode—but it seemed to me that what he was doing was using those modes as springboards for moral and ethical comments. It is the satirist's favorite technique.

Let's take Jonathan Swift, for instance. Jonathan Swift selected the most popular form of literature of his day in which to write *Gulliver's Travels*, you understand. It's the travel book, and that was an extraordinarily popular kind of literature in the early eighteenth century. He picked it up, and wrote *Gulliver's Travels* right on top of it. Now this is, as I see it, precisely what Vonnegut does—he picks up two of our most popular forms: SF and the confessional (especially in the case of *Mother Night*—that *Portnoy's Complaint*). He uses those forms as springboards to say something important, serious about the modern human condition. And I don't feel, as some people feel, that he doesn't really have anything to say—that all he is doing is asking questions. Nor do I feel that what he has to say is ultimately negative. If, indeed, his work is essentially satire, he of necessity will be pointing out a lot of negative things about our behavior; ultimately his message is positive, since all satirists must feel that some change for the better is possible. Furthermore, if we enter Vonnegut's works by way of satire, they seem to make sense and seem not to contradict each other or to be self-contradictory. But satire is a difficult mode to talk about, because to certain eyes everything becomes satire. Nevertheless, we can tell by tone, by the use of certain devices, what is meant to be satirical. In Vonnegut's case the problem of identification is complicated by the subtlety of his technique. Vonnegut doesn't write the kind of satire that we find in "A Modest Proposal," for instance. I mean, we know immediately we're being put on there—right—and it just becomes more and more horrible as we go along. But he is writing more in the fashion in the Fourth Book of *Gulliver*—unless you're careful, you are going to find yourself admiring the Houyhnhnms, which is a very dangerous thing to do, as you all know. Unless you are careful, you identify with Gulliver, who is a damned fool and shows it by sitting in stables with horses and enjoying the smell of horse manure. We find that Swift has put in some norms, but they're not very obtrusive: Gulliver's wife and children and the Portuguese sea captain. These become the norms to which we look and find positive values—not Gulliver, and of course not the Yahoos and not the Houyhnhnms. Willian Blake is another example. If we go into *The Marriage of Heaven and Hell* with high seriousness and the prophetic vision, we're going to run into all sorts of difficulties with that book. It's a satirical book.

Now, when we come to look at one of the novels that's normally seen as his most dark, *Cat's Cradle*—along with *Mother Night*—without a consciousness of the satire you might mistake Bokonon as the hero. He is not; he is just as much an evil creature as is Papa Doc. And you can see also that the ambassador and his wife, who have a very lovely relationship—but who are also an island unto themselves, completely devoid of a feeling for the real world—go down together in their own lovely little romantic escape. But these events, which have been explained as black humor, began to make sense to me when I saw that what Vonnegut is looking at is a world that is schizophrenic; and when he said that schizophrenia is the greatest boon to mankind, he has said it in an ironic way. We avoid reality in all sorts of ways, and if we do not look at reality, we don't have to solve our problems. And so for Vonnegut, it is not our pride which is the thing to be satirized (which is the human trait most consistently satirized by all the traditional satirists), it is our ability to evade reality; and as we look through a novel such as *Slaughterhouse-Five*, we see time and time again rationalizations for the evasion of reality—Tralfamadore isn't real, you know; you know damned well that Billy Pilgrim got the idea from reading Kilgore Trout. The bastardized Oriental philosophy of passivity preached by those plumber's helpers is a perfect excuse to give up, surrender, dream on.

At any rate, I see that an approach to Vonnegut's novels through satire yields a consistent kind of interpretation.

We must remember, too, that if we go into his work this way, we must apply different kinds of criteria in order to judge the quality of the work than we would if we were going to judge it as SF or confessional or any other type of prose fiction. And even here there are benefits for those of us who really like Vonnegut, since he scores very highly as a satirist, and we now have nice safe rational reasons for admiring his work.

LAWLER: Our next speaker is from the University of Chicago, Bill Veeder, who teaches nineteenth- and twentieth-century American literature, who has books on Yeats, James, and Victorian feminism, and who has a point of view on Vonnegut that we will all be interested in hearing.

VEEDER: I very much agree with Conrad that the issue of what *kind* (in the literary sense, of genre) we're dealing with here is important, and I agree with him also about the confusion that I feel at times reading Vonnegut and that friends and students of mine have. I think where I would disagree probably is in the belief that we can find a consistent kind of reaction if we take the proper point of view. My paper was a comparison of Nabokov and Vonnegut. Since this is a Vonnegut seminar, let me focus on what was the real issue of the paper, which is the nature of ambiguity. What kind of artistic control is needed to achieve effective ambiguity?

Wayne Booth has demonstrated how substantial a difference there is between ambiguity and confusion. Kurt Vonnegut sets up an ambiguous world in the first sentences of the Editor's Note to *Mother Night*, and at times throughout the novel the ambiguity is effective—for example, the emotions which Kraft and Resi feel, Vonnegut's use of the Israeli guards, his great humane theme of the brotherhood of guilt. These are effective in *Mother Night*. But the book does not work this way consistently.

There is a tension between contradictory tendencies in Vonnegut—the need to affirm mystery and ambiguity on the one hand and the need to offer truths on the other: Vonnegut as artist and Vonnegut as guru. *Mother Night* is an uneasy mixture of these two Vonneguts. The book is at times a novel and at other times an apologue. Some scenes are complexly ambiguous, others reveal a fairly schematic moralism. What we experience is not the oscillation of controlled ambiguity, as we do in a Shakespeare sonnet or at the end of *As I Lay Dying*, but a wobble that leaves us unsure of Vonnegut's intentions and meaning.

Let me quickly give an example of each of these tendencies—first apologue, then novel. In the scene with the G-men and the American Nazis, Jones the American Nazi is talking about people who are ruining America. He says, "Haven't you found out in the course of your work the Jews, the G-men, the Catholics, the Negroes, the Orientals, the Unitarians, the Foreign-born who don't have any understanding of democracy, who play right into the hands of the socialists, the communists, the anarchists, the anti-Christs, and the Jews!" The narrator concludes, "I have never seen a more sublime demonstration of the totalitarian mind. . . ." Campbell here is making his moralistic point inescapable. He opposes "the" totalitarian mind. He refers soon to "the classic totalitarian mind." So we get the point. The question is, where is Vonnegut? Does he dissent from the dehumanizing categorization of "the" totalitarian mind? For sure there is the clear fact of the dialogue itself—which Kurt Vonnegut, and not Howard Campbell, is ultimately responsible for. Jones's words are indeed the words of a cardboard figure made to justify Campbell's phrase "the classic totalitarian mind." Our laughter at Jones does not humanize the scene; we laugh derisively, because our political antagonists are shown to be as simplistic and vicious as we want to imagine they are.

In the scenes with the American Nazis, the G-men, and the policeman, Vonnegut's moral seems so schematic that it runs counter to the theme of common humanity which the book teaches elsewhere. At such moments, *Mother Night* seems much closer to an apologue than to a novel, and Vonnegut is indeed the guru teaching us to be good left-wingers. Or, if he is not, if he is indeed distanced from Campbell's moralism here, how are we to know with reasonable certainty?

On the other hand, Vonnegut at times is so novelistic in his refusal to enter Campbell's scenes that we are not sure what to think. In *Mother Night,* Howard Campbell looks out upon the children playing and is very moved by the call "Olly-olly-ox-in-free." As a reader, I'm not much moved here. The scene seems sentimental to the point of bathos (as I try to explain in the paper). The point that I want to make now, however, is that Vonnegut has not provided a signal, as he did in *The Sirens of Titan.* Granted that Campbell is sentimental, but what does Vonnegut think? What are we to think? If Vonnegut is himself distanced from Campbell's sentimentality, and if Vonnegut distances us with controlling techniques, then the scene could be complexly ambiguous. But, as it is, we're not certain how to react. Instead of ambiguity, we are left with confusion. I feel the same way about Campbell's suicide. Is it supposed to be a very sad fact? I don't experience it that way. But I'm not at all sure that Vonnegut intends the end of the book to be as flat as I feel it. Again I experience not ambiguity but confusion.

Now, I am not looking for clear, easy answers. But great books give us the tools with which to understand them.

The tools define and control the fictional world. *Mother Night* does not provide us sufficiently with these tools. Many readers of the novel, among them Peter Reed and most of the people I know, feel that Vonnegut intends us to be deeply moved by Campbell's final plight. Other readers, like Donald Lawler, feel that Vonnegut is quite emphatically distanced from Campbell throughout the book. Disagreement this substantial among Vonnegut's partisans is caused by Vonnegut's failure to control effectively the contradictory impulses that lie behind his art.

LAWLER: Thank you, Bill. The next panelist is Professor Peter Reed from the University of Minnesota. Peter, a scholar-athlete, was a long-distance runner. He is the author of a study of Kurt Vonnegut, in the Writers for the Seventies series. It was the best thing done on Vonnegut at the time and remains the best that has been thought and said on the subject to this day. Professor Reed's attention is directed today at the later work of Vonnegut.

REED: As I explained in my paper, and in the summary handed out here, I used *Slaughterhouse-Five* as a cutoff point. *Between Time and Timbuktu* is a teleplay script drawn largely from earlier Vonnegut. *Wampeters, Foma & Granfalloons* is a collection of speeches and essays which I think very useful but which is not actually new in content. *Happy Birthday, Wanda June* is based on another play, *Penelope*, drafted earlier. *Breakfast of Champions* is thus the first entirely new work since *Slaughterhouse-Five*.

One thing I might emphasize is the word "solipsism." There's a great deal about solipsism in the novel, and I think it is an important theme—one which is at the heart of what the book has to say and through which Vonnegut says a lot about his own method. Remember that in *Breakfast of Champions* Trout's novel *Now It Can Be Told* is described as "solipsistic whimsy." Hoover takes it as gospel, and the result, for him, is catastrophic. Vonnegut may be saying something about his own position in being treated as a "guru," having at least part of his audience take his writing as gospel. At the same time, he's called this book a birthday present to himself; it appears on the surface a kind of self-indulgence, and many people have taken it for that—"solipsistic whimsy," in fact. I found the novel looks rather like that at first, but the more one reads it, the more it becomes clear that it isn't. I'm not going to repeat what's in the paper, but I do believe that the solipsism theme is what makes *Breakfast* a worthwhile book.

Breakfast of Champions has drawn mainly negative responses in reviews. That may be largely because many reviewers have failed to see that thematic unity I've alluded to. Another thing which may disturb readers, and which disturbed me, is the manner of intrusion of self in this novel—the way in which Vonnegut enters the fictional world of the novel, is at once character, narrator, and author. He has done something similar before but on a smaller scale. In *Slaughterhouse-Five,* he frames the story with first and last chapters where he speaks autobiographically from the present of writing the novel, and enters the narrative intermittently as a minor character saying, "that was me." That seems natural and enables Vonnegut to blend the perspectives of participant and observer, to combine immediacy and reflection. In *Breakfast of Champions,* the intensely personal intrusion remains less comfortable—it seems rather too self-conscious or posed. Whereas in earlier works we sense the presence of the author, hear his voice, and enjoy the kind of personal warmth that imparts, here we may actually feel excluded.

In considering Vonnegut's later work, I found it hard to reach sure conclusions about the direction he is taking. I sense that he might be uncertain, too. His work with drama after saying he was "through with spooks in novels" might suggest that. The apparent uncertainty he expresses about his public role, about speaking at colleges, for example, suggests the same self-consciousness and uncertainty. And similar doubts seem to exist among those of our profession about Vonnegut's direction and his place. For instance, I find that in my own department the American-literature people tend not to pay him much heed, if they even read him. Curiously, the colleagues I've found most interested and knowledgeable in Vonnegut are a medievalist and a Renaissance scholar.

Part of the difficulty with placing Vonnegut is one that has been evident here—the difficulty of categorizing him. The problem with determining the direction he is going is that, to me at least, *Slaughterhouse-Five* did seem to mark the end of a movement, taking the first six novels as an organic whole. The switch to a play, then the publication of *Breakfast of Champions*, which is in many respects different from the other novels and looks almost like something of an appendage, makes tracing the direction hard. Is this a lull, or is, as at least one critic has suggested, Vonnegut losing his powers, like Hemingway in his later years? I prefer to opt for the former, but we'll have to wait and see. The direction I would like to see Vonnegut take is along the lines of *The Sirens of Titan*. But I can't think of a worse mistake than for a successful novelist to follow the recommendations of an academic like me!

We *can* see certain directions being followed by Vonnegut. The autobiographical element continues and grows. The science-fiction component remains important. The social satire, the dark humor, the concern with "man's inhumanity to man," the underlying compassion, and the surface cynicism all carry through. But beyond observing these sorts of continuity in the fiction, I think it is difficult to speculate at this point on direction. *Slaughterhouse-Five,* which at last confronted the Dresden experience and seemed to pull together so many of his themes, left us asking, where next? And I think we are still left at that point.

LAWLER: Thank you, Peter. That concludes the initial remarks of our panelists. I see that we have several questions, so let's begin with this gentleman on the left.

QUESTION: My question is to Mr. Reed. You've said that you aren't happy with the appearance of Kurt Vonnegut as himself in *Breakfast of Champions,* but you've also said that there is an autobiographical element in most of his work. Would you talk about that a little more?

REED: Yes. I think Vonnegut does, as he says, put himself into most of his fiction. He does this not always through one character. In *Player Piano,* for example, there may be much Vonnegut in Paul Proteus, whose break with the Ilium Works may be one form of expression of Vonnegut's own break with General Electric in Schenectady. There is also a lot of Vonnegut in Ed Finnerty and in various other characters as well. In *Breakfast of Champions,* there's that same sort of middle-class narrator figure Jerry has talked about in Hoover. Kilgore Trout is obviously another aspect of the author. Hoover is Vonnegut, who is, was, remains something of a middle-class ordinary Joe. Trout is another aspect that Vonnegut introduced, and I think through the interaction of these characters he presents the various aspects of himself. There is also, of course, the presence of Kurt Vonnegut conveyed through the narrative voice. We always sense the presence of Vonnegut in his fiction through the tone, the implied attitudes, even without direct intrusion or the more obvious devices like the repeated catch phrases.

Vonnegut says he puts himself into his novels "slyly," and there's some truth to that. In *Breakfast of Champions* it does not appear to be quite so true, because he is there as character (who is also author), and the interjection of self *seems* direct and obvious. But I think this interjection remains tricky—can the Kurt Vonnegut in the novel be taken at face value, as wholly and consistently Kurt Vonnegut the author? I'm not sure we trust that. Some of the "real" Kurt Vonnegut continues to reside in Trout and Hoover. I think we have to put the three together to come closer to a portrait of the man himself. In the other novels, the presentation of self is also sly enough to require cautious handling. No doubt there's a good deal of Vonnegut's compassion—and neurosis—in Eliot Rosewater, but one obviously would be wrong to take all that Rosewater says as representing Vonnegut's own thinking. On the other end of the scale, there's Campbell. Through Campbell, Vonnegut seems to address some of the doubts he feels as a writer. Perhaps he also voices other uncertainties through Campbell—for example, the ambiguity of his position in Dresden, being bombed by his own side, or the things that he has said about being of German extraction and that if he were still German he might have been on the other side in the war. But Campbell remains a rather puzzling figure: part Eichmann, part modern Everyman victim, part writer—even "guru"—facing some of the same questions as his creator. There is some ambiguity about his role, which remains one of the problems with that novel. And it isn't, as Bill has suggested, Vonnegut's best novel—not by a long shot! If that novel is to work, I think there has to be something of Vonnegut in Campbell. That is where I think Bill's got a good question. How clearly do we see any of Vonnegut in Campbell?

VEEDER: Could I speak to this: I think where we would find it is in the sense, maybe, of *self-pity*, or at least the sense of the isolated individual alone in the hostile world. In other words, as you were saying last night, Will, that there are aspects about him taken from this other Campbell [John W. Campbell] that aren't going to be Vonnegut. So it is not a one hundred percent connection with Vonnegut by any matter of means. But if I were trying to sift through the various aspects of this personality, *that* is where I find Vonnegut is feeling himself in the character.

KLINKOWITZ: I think the whole key would be finding correlations between Vonnegut and Campbell. That is where this whole argument will make or break. Simply on a circumstantial level, think of Vonnegut's life, sitting in West Barnstable being a writer. That's like being a counterspy while everybody else is storm-window salesman or a crab fisherman. Also, the idea of simultaneously writing stories for *Fantasy and Science Fiction* and *Better Homes and Gardens* (where, honest-to-goodness, one play of his appeared). That's certainly the idea of a counterspy. The whole schizophrenic existence which Vonnegut talks about. Starting from there we could go somewhere.

REED: I don't think he's at all happy with this first-person intrusion. Or at least it doesn't work very happily, to my mind. I think in *Breakfast of Champions* he intends to include us more directly than in any of his work, and it doesn't work. We feel somehow excluded. He's telling us what he is going to do with his characters; he's sharing that whole creative process with us, and yet somehow I think he's alienating us. We're let in, and yet we're not let in. He is still making the decisions: He is telling us what he is doing. But he is doing it, and we're on the outside looking in. It doesn't include us more. He talks so much there and in the [*Playboy*] interview about the fact that he has been thrust into his novels, in a way, by his stature as a popular guru. I think he is very troubled by that; I don't think he is at all happy with it, and it shows something in the way the first person appears—that somehow this man is expected to emerge. He knows he has readers sitting there waiting to hear what Vonnegut says. It's like an additional gospel. I don't know if this really happens. It's a strange thing to me. I think that a lot of the academic resistance to Vonnegut comes from people who suspect there are a lot of Vonnegut freaks around, and they don't like Vonnegut freaks. That's true—I had resisted writing a book on Vonnegut. I waited a long time before offering a course on Vonnegut, because I didn't want to teach a course to a classful of Vonnegut freaks.

MCNELLY: You're sort of glad you're not in their karass.

REED: You open the doors and you wait for the Earth-Shoes-and-granola set to arrive. I got to the course, and a lot of students came very tentatively: Is this going to be full of Vonnegut freaks? It's everywhere. I think, thank God, it's passing, and we have come out of that. I am firmly convinced that he is going to emerge as the dominant serious novelist of the last decade. I did not believe that at all at one time. But that problem shows in that whole first-person business.

LAWLER: I think it does, and it centers around the business of alienation. Is it a deliberate technique? In my paper I argue, yes, it is; he knows what he is doing. After all, alienation is necessary if a satirist is going to attack certain basic ideas with which the reader must not be actively sympathetic as he is reading the book. Because if he is, then the satirist winds up assaulting allegiances, and the reader is going to resist. Vonnegut knows he cannot afford that. No satirist can afford to have the reader put in that position. So I think the alienation is deliberate. Look at *The Sirens of Titan*, at the introduction and what he does there. He launches us about a hundred years into the future, when the secret of existence happily is known to us and the portals of the soul are open and so on. He then flashes back to the immediate future, when four benighted souls were wandering in pretty much our present, wondering what the meaning of life was all about and asking those questions that Vonnegut wants to demonstrate are absurd and meaningless because they cannot be answered. And to demonstrate that, he tells us the shaggy-dog story about the meaning of human life, which turns out to be the delivery of a spare part to a stranded robot on Titan so that he can send a message across the universe that says "Greetings." I think such alienation is a deliberate comic device that seems to work in *The Sirens of Titan.* I'm not so confident about what he is doing in the later novels as he becomes more and more a part of his own scenario. But let me just drop this in from the *Playboy* interview, where he said this: "Writers are specialized cells in the social organism. They are evolutionary cells. Mankind is trying to become something else. It is experimenting with new ideas all the time, and writers are a means of introducing new ideas to society and also a means of responding symbolically to life." I don't know whether this is a key, but if Vonnegut is really doing that, then it would apply both to himself as a writer and, I think, to himself as a representative man. He is responding symbolically to life, and maybe he felt that unless he was there as a character in the book, that kind of symbolic response would not be visible.

MCNELLY: I wonder if one of the problems we are all having in trying to fit Vonnegut into some sort of category and to come up with some kind of answer about him doesn't stem from the fact that essentially Vonnegut is, as we remarked last night, perhaps dealing with aspects of the Tao. Perhaps in a certain sense he's concerned with the Manichean aspect of the creativity of good and the possible creativity of evil working simultaneously in our universe, and to come up with an assertion that any one thing in Vonnegut is the answer is to ignore the black/white, right/wrong, either/or, yes/no aspects of everything that he is doing. For example, much of the character of Howard W. Campbell, Jr., may be derived from John W. Campbell, Jr., the editor of *Astounding,* later *Analog Science Fact Science Fiction Magazine,* for many, many years. Vonnegut submitted to Campbell and was rejected, and so it's a little in-joke among SF writers that he put the Campbell name into his works as a quasi-Nazi to sort of even the score. At the same time, if one has read John W. Campbell's editorials in *Analog* for many years, one realizes where many of Howard Campbell's ideas are derived from. For instance, John Campbell once wrote an editorial in which he argued that slavery was a pretty good idea on occasion—that kind of thing. And yet the ambiguities in the character of John Campbell, which were great, also show up in the character of Howard Campbell, and so you can't say that Howard Campbell is this or is that or Vonnegut is this or is that. To try to reconcile these opposites is, I think, almost fruitless. We have to say that they exist there, and that he is trying to deal with them in a Taoist way or a Manichean way.

QUESTION: I wonder if Mr. Reed would comment on the prologue to his forthcoming work on Vonnegut as a dramatist and Vonnegut as a producer of film. How does that fit in with the later fiction?

REED: I'm not sure. I'm inclined to see it as Vonnegut at sea, finding *Slaughterhouse-Five* in film, oh, very beautiful, and finding that tempting. He makes the comment, and I think it may be in the *Playboy* interview, that he doesn't like film because writers always put themselves into their work (and he does particularly) and he can't do that in film. I would feel that perhaps the same applies to drama.

I think in *Wanda June* perhaps he is looking for a place to go at the end of the novels, and, looking for a new outlet, he revised *Penelope*. (*Happy Birthday, Wanda June* is based on a play, *Penelope*, that he had written fifteen years before.) I don't know how close the relationship is, but he certainly seems to be looking for another direction. Perhaps he had found the same sort of limitation there that he did in film. Jerry might know something more.

KLINKOWITZ: I did a paper once on *Wanda June* for a journal called *Players*. And there are all sorts of interviews here you can look at. Vonnegut says he went to the theater because he wanted a community; he was too lonely sitting alone with his typewriter. But also there is an interesting thing: His entire vision changes when it gets transformed from fiction into drama. Now, in fiction, in most of his novels, he would have a protagonist who's way out ahead of society, with society, time, space, and everything else riding behind. In *Wanda June* it is just the opposite: Society is way ahead. His Hemingway-type character comes out of the jungle and has to fight to update himself, and Vonnegut found this a dead end for his own vision; therefore, he went back into narrative fiction. The thing that Peter's noting about not being able to put yourself into film is in the preface Vonnegut wrote to *Between Time and Timbuktu*. He mentions it in several places, but I think the best statement of it is there. Really, in terms of theme and technique, leaving narrative fiction turned out to be a blind alley for Vonnegut.

REED: I think *Wanda June* gets into trouble because Penelope should be the heroine. Penelope should be coming through at the end as dominant; instead, he has got this other bloke going on shooting himself and then not shooting himself.

AUDIENCE COMMENT: I was going to comment on the play:

They made him rewrite away from a black ending so that it would become a salable commodity. That is another reason it didn't do so well. In the first ending the hero gets killed. The funeral scene was changed.

LAWLER: Satirists are always running into that kind of problem. Here is another question.

QUESTION: As near as I can tell, all the panelists, and I think all of us who are interested in Vonnegut, like him because we think of him as being innovative and experimental. Yet the panelists seem to have fallen back on essentially traditional although not necessarily academic categories to describe their understanding of Vonnegut. Now, what I would like to find out is whether any of you ever felt compelled to construct a new language or new concepts in order to interpret Vonnegut. How experimental is he?

FESTA: Let me answer that. No, I haven't felt compelled at all. I find the new language jargony and not very helpful to me. I shied away from "black humor," for instance, and all of the terms that have grown out of that, because it really doesn't clarify anything for me; and I don't feel compelled at all to create or discover a new language. The language was already there for me, and it was meaningful. Traditional critical language hasn't died for me, and I can use it as a means of getting into his fiction. I don't see him as one of the great experimental novelists. He is doing what has often been done before—what gives it the sense of newness is that he does those things so awfully well.

REED: I think your question implies that you are seeing, say, "black humor" as one of the terms around.

QUESTIONER: No. I'm thinking of whether we may not need to go beyond what we think of as contemporary critical terms.

REED: I haven't, of course, come to that conclusion, but I think there might be a need for such language, because it is interesting to talk about him as an SF writer but he is not simply that. You can't hook the rest of SF onto him. I think that Willis's "objective correlative" idea may be close. Vonnegut writes satire, yes, but he is larger than that. I really thought that *The Sirens of Titan* was a good direction for him to be going. SF serves, I think, to enable him to—I think he is reaching for a mode of expression that fits his fiction to the post–second industrial revolution, the post–computer revolution era, in the same way that the novel traditionally is fitted to post–industrial revolution society—Ian Watt's idea of the rise of the individual and that sort of thing. I think that is what he is reaching for. This combination of forms may be achieving it, and that may call for a new language. I think that is a good question. I haven't got very far with it.

KLINKOWITZ: It is a very good question. Because the only answer will wind up being complex. We really have to write about Vonnegut in four ways to cover everything. You have to write about him traditionally, because it is important to emphasize the continuity of Vonnegut in the development of American fiction. Second, you have to use SF critical techniques in order to do justice to his variety and range of treatment there. Third, you have to introduce criteria from popular culture, something that academics are horrible at doing. They're too snobbish to do that. But you have to start talking about the hardware store on Saturday morning to understand a lot of what is behind Vonnegut. Finally, there is this new paracritical technique. I have done a few pieces, I call them "super-fiction essays," where we make Max Ernst–style collages which we print ourselves. *Critique* let us do one on Barthelme, for which we set the print and sent them camera-ready pages. The whole technique uses spatial juxtaposition rather than a linear discursiveness. The University of Illinois Press will publish them all in a book entitled *The Life of Fiction*. Ihab Hassan published a book with Illinois Press called *Paracriticisms*, in which I think he is working toward the kind of technique appropriate to Vonnegut's experimentalism. So people are working at this. It is just that you can't do all four at once.

LAWLER: I think that what happens often when we do is that we find ourselves repeating what critics of the past have already said. Oscar Wilde in a sense anticipated the paracritical approach (maybe not specifically those techniques but that kind of approach) in "The Critic as Artist."

I've tried to do two things in my paper. One was to include in my field of vision what I thought was a very considerable aspect of surrealism in *The Sirens of Titan*, and not only in that book but in almost all the major novels of Vonnegut, with one notable exception, and that's *Player Piano*, the first novel. In fact, I started making up a list once, thinking somebody would surely ask me about surrealism and I'd better be ready. Well, I just ran out of paper and patience—the list got so long and cumbersome that I thought nobody would believe it even if I read it like a favorite recipe. It's astonishing. And yet when I ask myself, does that make Vonnegut a surrealist, I feel I have to say "no," despite the fact that he seems to meet many of the tests. I don't believe he has that surrealist faith in the power of imagination.

The point of distinction comes when the moralist in Vonnegut resists the notion that the world is going to be transformed by man's willing it. If you are a real moralist, and I think Vonnegut is, you just don't believe that. I did work up a new term, . . . "enabling form," a very modest effort indeed, which probably needs more explanation than it deserves. But I was trying to suggest that Vonnegut uses space opera in *The Sirens of Titan* as a way of executing certain strategies he otherwise would never be able to introduce, given his critical position, given his position as satirist, as a moralist, and so on. It enables him to be a satirist and a parodist. Space opera enables him to introduce cosmic questions which otherwise he could never develop in the right frame. It enables him to produce the surrealist effects of the shaggy-dog story, for instance.

LAWLER: Here's another question. Yes, Al.

ALAN LEFKOWITZ (U.S. Naval Academy): Don, wouldn't your concept of enabling form, which I'm very interested in, indicate something about Vonnegut? In fact, isn't he an experimenter in the same sense that Joyce is an experimenter and that's why he is so acceptable to our students? He's using a grouping of forms that they already know. If he were truly experimenting, such as Barth, he wouldn't be as accessible to them.

LAWLER: Yes, that's a good point, Al.

LEFKOWITZ: It seems to me, too, that some analogy may be drawn to what C. S. Lewis would do in *Out of the Silent Planet*, using SF as an enabling form in order to get across the particular theology of Christianity.

LAWLER: Right. And I'm not so sure that Lewis's intentions were all that different from Vonnegut's when you really get down to the basic ideas, to the bedrock of what each man is saying. We have time, maybe, for one last question.

QUESTION: Is it true that for the panelists, you see him as more of a moralist using particular forms than someone who is trying to experiment with both perceptions? Is my question clear?

VEEDER: It's clear to me. It's a good question.

FESTA: I don't want to be pushed too far over in that direction—that he is a *moralist* with a capital "M" and that he is just interested in moral questions alone—because I do feel that he is a conscious artist, working with the tools of his trade, and he is consciously developing these things. But yes, I would tilt the balance toward moral rather than experimental.

MCNELLY: But have we really needed a new critical language since *Finnegans Wake?* I ask that because I suspect that many other SF writers, such as Ellison, Silverberg, Aldiss, Delaney, and others I could name, have done far more experimentation in both ideas and forms than Vonnegut has. The entire thrust of the New Wave, for example, in SF is very experimental, and it does use SF as an enabling form, to use your term, Don. I don't think it's really necessary to invent a new critical language, because Vonnegut himself has not, in that sense, invented anything new of comparable thrust or originality of perception.

LAWLER: Well, maybe we can't really see him in proper perspective because of the critical isolation we've imposed upon his work today, of necessity, in this seminar. If we're going to need a new critical language to account for what's going on in the fictions of New Wave SF writers along with Vonnegut, Barthelme, Barth, and their cohorts, perhaps we may think of this as a beginning rather than an ending, as our clock seems to be telling us. That's all we have time for this morning. Thank you all for coming and for your interest in our work.

PART 3

THE VONNEGUT BIBLIOGRAPHY

Jerome Klinkowitz

The Vonnegut Bibliography

I. NOVELS

Player Piano

New York: Charles Scribner's Sons, 1952.
New York: Doubleday Science Fiction Book Club, 1953.
New York: Bantam, 1954 (retitled *Utopia 14*).
New York: Holt, Rinehart & Winston, 1966.
New York: Avon, 1967.
New York: Delacorte Press/Seymour Lawrence, 1971.
New York: Book-of-the-Month Club, 1971.
New York: Dell/Delta, 1972.
New York: Literary Guild, 1973.
New York: Dell, 1974.
London: Macmillan, 1953, 1967.
London: Mayflower, 1955, 1962.

London: Panther, 1969.
Munich: Heyne, 1964.
Piacenza, Italy: La tribuna editrice-C.E.L.T., 1966.
Moscow: Molodaia gvardiia, 1968.
Amsterdam: Meulenhoff, 1970.
Budapest: Artijus, 1971.
Rio de Janeiro: Artenova, 1973.

The Sirens of Titan

New York: Dell, 1959, 1966, 1970.
Boston: Houghton Mifflin, 1961.
New York: Dell/Delta, 1971.
New York: Delacorte Press/Seymour Lawrence, 1971.
New York: Literary Guild, 1975.
London: Gollancz, 1962.
London: Hodder & Stoughton, 1967.
London: Coronet, 1967.
Paris: DeNoël, 1962.
Amsterdam: Uitgevrij de Bezige Bij, 1968.
Copenhagen: Stig Vendelkaers, 1971.

Mother Night

Greenwich, Conn.: Fawcett, 1962.
New York: Harper & Row, 1966 (including a new introduction incorporated in subsequent editions).
New York: Avon, 1967.
New York: Delacorte Press/Seymour Lawrence, 1971.
New York: Dell/Delta, 1972.
New York: Dell, 1974.
London: Jonathan Cape, 1968.
Milan: Rizzoli, 1968.
Stockholm: Norstedt, 1971.
Rio de Janeiro: Artenova, 1971.

Cat's Cradle

New York: Holt, Rinehart & Winston, 1963.
New York: Doubleday Book Club, 1963.

New York: Dell, 1965, 1970.
New York: Dell/Delta, 1967.
New York: Delacorte Press/Seymour Lawrence, 1971.
New York: Book-of-the-Month Club, 1971.
New York: Literary Guild, 1973.
London: Gollancz, 1963.
London: Penguin, 1965.
Milan: Rizzoli, 1966.
Tokyo: Hayakawa Shobo, 1968.
Copenhagen: Stig Vendelkaers, 1969.
Hamburg: Hoffman & Campe, 1969.
Prague: Mlada fronta, 1970.
Barcelona: Editorial Novaro, 1970.
Moscow: Molodaia gvardiia, 1970.
Amsterdam: Meulenhoff, 1971.
Paris: Éditions du Seuil, 1972.
Warsaw: Panstwowy Instytut Wydawniczy, 1972.
Riga, Latvia: Liesma, 1973.

God Bless You, Mr. Rosewater

New York: Holt, Rinehart & Winston, 1965.
New York: Dell, 1966, 1970.
New York: Dell/Delta, 1968.
New York: Delacorte Press/Seymour Lawrence, 1971.
New York: Book-of-the-Month Club, 1971.
New York: Literary Guild, 1973.
London: Jonathan Cape, 1965.
London: Panther, 1967, 1972.
Barcelona: Grijalbo, 1966, 1972.
Gutersloh, West Germany: Bertelsmann, 1968.
Hamburg: Rowohlt, 1968.
Oslo: Gyldendal, 1971.
Stockholm: Norstedt, 1972.
Rome: Mondadori, 1973.
Budapest: Európa Könyvkiado, 1973.
Warsaw: Ksiazka i Wiedza, 1976.
Moscow: *Avrora*, 3 and 4 (1976) (serialized).

Slaughterhouse-Five

New York: Delacorte Press/Seymour Lawrence, 1969.
New York: Literary Guild, 1969, 1975.
New York: Doubleday Bargain Book Club and Science Fiction Book Club, 1969.
New York: Dell/Delta, 1970.
New York: Dell, 1971.
London: Jonathan Cape, 1970.
London: Panther, 1970.
Hong Kong: pirated edition, 1970.
Barcelona: Grijalbo, 1970.
Copenhagen: Gylendal, 1970.
Oslo: Gylendal, 1970.
Hamburg: Hoffman & Campe, 1970.
Amsterdam: Meulenhoff, 1970.
Stockholm: Norstedt, 1970, 1971.
Moscow: *Novyi Mir*, 3 (1970), 78–132, and 4 (1970), 148–178 (serialized).
Warsaw: Panstwowy Instytut Wydawniczy, 1972.
Paris: Éditions du Seuil, 1971.
Rio de Janeiro: Artenova, 1973.
Hamburg: Rowohlt, 1972.
Bratislava, Czechoslovakia: Tatran, 1973.
Budapest: Európa Könyvkiado, 1973.
Tallinn, Estonia: Eesti Raamat, 1971.

Breakfast of Champions

New York: Delacorte Press/Seymour Lawrence, 1973.
New York: Saturday Review Book Club, 1973.
New York: Literary Guild, 1973, 1975.
London: Jonathan Cape, 1974.
London: Panther, 1975.
Hamburg: Hoffman & Campe, 1974.
Moscow: *Inostrannaia literatura*, 1 (1975), 154–200, and 2 (1975), 148–209 (serialized).

Slapstick

New York: Delacorte Press/Seymour Lawrence, 1976.
New York: Dell/Delta, 1977.
New York: Dell, 1978.
London: Jonathan Cape, 1977.

II. COLLECTIONS OF SHORT STORIES

Canary in a Cat House

Greenwich, Conn.: Fawcett, 1961.
Contents and where originally published:

"Report on the Barnhouse Effect." *Collier's*, 125 (February 11, 1950), 18–19, 63–65.

"All the King's Horses." *Collier's*, 127 (February 10, 1951), 14–15, 46–48, 50.

"D.P." *Ladies' Home Journal*, 70 (August 1953), 42–43, 80–81, 84.

"The Manned Missiles." *Cosmopolitan*, 145 (July 1958), 83–88.

"The Euphio Question." *Collier's*, 127 (May 12, 1951), 22–23, 52–54, 56.

"More Stately Mansions." *Collier's*, 128 (December 22, 1951), 24–25, 62–63.

"The Foster Portfolio." *Collier's*, 128 (September 8, 1951), 18–19, 72–73.

"Deer in the Works." *Esquire*, 43 (April 1955), 78–79, 112, 114, 116, 118.

"Hal Irwin's Magic Lamp." *Cosmopolitan*, 142 (June 1957), 92–95.

"Tom Edison's Shaggy Dog." *Collier's*, 131 (March 14, 1953), 46, 48–49.

"Unready to Wear." *Galaxy Science Fiction*, 6 (April 1953), 98–111.

"Tomorrow and Tomorrow and Tomorrow" (originally "The Big Trip Up Yonder"). *Galaxy Science Fiction*, 7 (January 1954), 100–110.

Welcome to the Monkey House

New York: Delacorte Press/Seymour Lawrence, 1968.
New York: Dell, 1970.
New York: Dell/Delta, 1970.
Hamburg: Hoffman & Campe, 1971.
Toyko: Hayakawa Shobo, 1970.
Stockholm: Norstedt, 1971.
Prague: Odeon Natodni, 1970.
Amsterdam: Meulenhoff, 1970.

Contents and where originally published:

"Preface." Not previously published.
"Where I Live" (originally "You've Never Been to Barnstable?"). *Venture–Traveler's World*, 1 (October 1964), 145, 147–149.
"Harrison Bergeron." *Magazine of Fantasy and Science Fiction*, 21 (October 1961), 5–10.
"Who Am I This Time?" (originally "My Name Is Everyone"). *Saturday Evening Post*, 234 (December 16, 1961), 20–21, 62, 64, 66–67.
"Welcome to the Monkey House," *Playboy*, 15 (January 1968), 95, 156, 196, 198, 200–201.
"Long Walk to Forever." *Ladies' Home Journal*, 77 (August 1960), 42–43, 108.
"The Foster Portfolio." In *Canary in a Cat House* (*CCH*, above).
"Miss Temptation." *Saturday Evening Post*, 228 (April 21, 1956), 30, 57, 60, 62, 64.
"All the King's Horses." In *CCH*.
"Tom Edison's Shaggy Dog." In *CCH*.
"New Dictionary" (originally "The Latest Word"). *New York Times Book Review*, October 30, 1966, pp. 1, 56.
"Next Door." *Cosmopolitan*, 138 (April 1955), 80–85.
"More Stately Mansions." In *CCH*.
"The Hyannis Port Story." Written 1963, not previously published.
"D. P." In *CCH*.
"Report on the Barnhouse Effect." in *CCH*.
"The Euphio Question." In *CCH*.

"Go Back to Your Precious Wife and Son." *Ladies' Home Journal*, 79 (July 1962), 54–55, 108, 110.
"Deer in the Works." In *CCH*.
"The Lie." *Saturday Evening Post*, 235 (February 24, 1962), 46–47, 51, 56.
"Unready to Wear." In *CCH*.
"The Kid Nobody Could Handle." *Saturday Evening Post*, 228 (September 24, 1955), 37, 136–137.
"The Manned Missiles." In *CCH*.
"Epicac." *Collier's*, 126 (November 25, 1950), 36–37.
"Adam." *Cosmopolitan*, 136 (April 1954), 34–39.
"Tomorrow and Tomorrow and Tomorrow." In *CCH*.

III. PUBLISHED PLAYS

Between Time and Timbuktu, or Prometheus-5. New York: Delacorte Press/Seymour Lawrence, 1972. New York: Delta/Dell, 1972.
"Fortitude." *Playboy*, 15 (September 1968), 99–100, 102, 106, 217–218.
Happy Birthday, Wanda June. New York: Delacorte Press/Seymour Lawrence, 1971. New York: Delta/Dell, 1971. London: Jonathan Cape, 1972. Tallinn, Estonia: Loomingu, 1976.
"The Very First Christmas Morning." *Better Homes and Gardens*, 40 (December 1962), 14, 19–20, 24.

IV. UNCOLLECTED STORIES

"Ambitious Sophomore." *Saturday Evening Post*, 226 (May 1, 1954), 31, 88, 92, 94.
"Any Reasonable Offer." *Collier's*, 129 (January 19, 1952), 32, 46–47.
"Bagombo Snuff Box." *Cosmopolitan*, 137 (October 1954), 34–39.
"The Big Space Fuck." In Harlan Ellison, ed., *Again Dangerous Visions*. Garden City, N.Y.: Doubleday, 1972, pp. 246–250.

"The Boy Who Hated Girls." *Saturday Evening Post*, 228 (March 31, 1956), 28–29, 58, 60, 62.
"Custom-Made Bride." *Saturday Evening Post*, 226 (March 27, 1954), 30, 81–82, 86–87.
"Find Me a Dream." *Cosmopolitan*, 150 (February 1961), 108–111.
"Hole Beautiful: Prospectus for a Magazine of Shelteredness." *Monocle*, 5, #1 (1962), 45–51. With Karla Kuskin.
"Lovers Anonymous." *Redbook*, 121 (October 1963), 70–71, 146–148.
"Mnemonics." *Collier's*, 127 (April 28, 1951), 38.
"A Night for Love." *Saturday Evening Post*, 230 (November 23, 1957), 40–41, 73, 76–77, 80–81, 84.
"The No-Talent Kid." *Saturday Evening Post*, 225 (October 25, 1952), 28, 109–110, 112, 114.
"The Package." *Collier's*, 130 (July 26, 1952), 48–53.
"Poor Little Rich Town." *Collier's*, 130 (October 25, 1952), 90–95.
"The Powder Blue Dragon." *Cosmopolitan*, 137 (November 1954), 46–48, 50–53.
"A Present for Big Nick." *Argosy*, December 1954, pp. 42–45, 72–73.
"Runaways." *Saturday Evening Post*, 234 (April 15, 1961), 26–27, 52, 54, 56.
"Souvenir." *Argosy*, December 1952, pp. 28, 76–79.
"Thanasphere." *Collier's*, 126 (September 2, 1950), 18–19, 60, 62.
"This Son of Mine . . ." *Saturday Evening Post*, 229 (August 18, 1956), 24, 74, 76–78.
"2BR02B." *Worlds of If*, January, 1962, pp. 59–65.
"Unpaid Consultant." *Cosmopolitan*, 138 (March 1955), 52–57.

V. POETRY

"Carols for Christmas 1969: Tonight If I Will Let Me." *New York Times Magazine*, December 21, 1969, p. 5.

VI. COLLECTION OF ESSAYS

Wampeters, Foma, & Granfalloons: Opinions

New York: Delacorte Press/Seymour Lawrence, 1974.
New York: Delta/Dell, 1975.
New York: Dell, 1976.
London: Jonathan Cape, 1975.

Contents and where originally published:

"Preface." Not previously published.

"Science Fiction." *New York Times Book Review*, September 5, 1965, p. 2.

"Brief Encounters on the Inland Waterway." *Venture–Traveler's World*, 3 (October-November, 1966), 135–138, 140, 142.

"Hello, Star Vega" (review of *Intelligent Life in the Universe* by S. I. Shklovskii and Carl Sagan). *Life*, 61 (December 9, 1966), R3 (Regional).

"Teaching the Unteachable." *New York Times Book Review*, August 6, 1967, pp. 1, 20.

"Yes, We Have No Nirvanas." *Esquire*, 69 (June 1968), 78–79, 176, 178–179, 182.

"Fortitude." *Playboy*, 15 (September 1968), 99–100, 102, 106, 217–218.

" 'There's a Maniac Loose Out There.' " *Life*, 67 (July 25, 1969), 53–56.

"Excelsior! We're Going to the Moon! Excelsior!" *New York Times Magazine*, July 13, 1969, pp. 9–11.

"Address to the American Physical Society." *Chicago Tribune Magazine*, June 22, 1969, pp. 44, 48–50, 52, 56 (as "Physicist, Purge Thyself").

"Good Missiles, Good Manners, Good Night." *New York Times*, September 13, 1969, p. 26.

"Why They Read Hesse." *Horizon*, 12 (Spring 1970), 28–31.

"Oversexed in Indianapolis" (review of *Going All the Way* by Dan Wakefield). *Life*, 69 (July 17, 1970), 10.

"The Mysterious Madame Blavatsky." *McCalls*, 97 (March 1970), 66–67, 142–144.

"Biafra: A People Betrayed." *McCalls*, 97 (April 1970), 68–69, 134–138.

"Address to Graduating Class at Bennington College, 1970." *Vogue*, 156 (August 1, 1970), 54, 144–145 (as "Up Is Better Than Down").

"Torture and Blubber." *New York Times*, June 30, 1971, p. 41.

"Address to the National Institute of Arts and Letters, 1971" (published in *Proceedings* as "The Happiest Day in the Life of My Father"). *Vogue*, 160 (August 15, 1972), 56–57, 93 (as "What Women Really Want Is . . .").

"Reflections on My Own Death." *Rotarian*, May 1972, p. 24.

"In a Manner That Must Shame God Himself." *Harper's*, 245 (November 1972), 60–68.

"Thinking Unthinkable, Speaking Unspeakable." *New York Times*, January 13, 1973, p. 31.

"Address at Rededication of Wheaton College Library." *Vogue*, 162 (July 1973), 62–64 (as "America: What's Good, What's Bad?").

"Invite Rita Rait to America!" *New York Times Book Review*, January 28, 1973, p. 47.

"Address to P.E.N. Conference in Stockholm, 1973." Not previously published.

"A Political Disease" (review of *Fear and Loathing on the Campaign Trail '72* by Hunter S. Thompson). *Harper's*, 246 (July 1973), 92, 94.

"Playboy Interview." *Playboy*, 20 (July 1973), 57–60, 62, 66, 68, 70, 72, 74, 214, 216.

VII. UNCOLLECTED ARTICLES AND REVIEWS

"Closed Season on the Kids" (review of *Don't Shoot—We Are Your Children* by J. Anthony Lukas). *Life*, 70 (April 9, 1971), 14.

"Deadhead among the Diplomats" (review of *The Triumph* by J. Kenneth Galbraith). *Life*, 64 (May 3, 1968), 14.

"Der Arme Dolmetscher." *Atlantic Monthly*, 196 (July 1955), 86–88.

"Don't Take It Too Seriously" (review of *Prize Stories 1966: The O. Henry Awards*, ed. Richard Poirier and William Abrahams). *New York Times Book Review*, March 20, 1966, pp. 1, 39.
"Everything Goes Like Clockwork" (review of *Once a Greek . . .* by Friedrich Dürrenmatt). *New York Times Book Review*, June 13, 1964, p. 4.
"The Fall of a Climber" (review of *Any God Will Do* by Richard Condon). *New York Times Book Review*, September 25, 1966, pp. 5, 42.
"Foreword." *Transformations* by Anne Sexton. Boston: Houghton Mifflin, 1971, pp. vii–x.
"Foreword." *Write If You Get Work: The Best of Bob & Ray* by Bob Elliott and Ray Goulding. New York: Random House, 1975, pp. v–vii.
"Headshrinker's Hoyle on Games We Play" (review of *Games People Play* by Eric Berne). *Life*, 58 (June 11, 1965), 15, 17.
"He Comes to Us One by One and Asks What the Rules Are." *Chicago Tribune Book World*, July 15, 1973, p. 3.
"The High Cost of Fame." *Playboy*, 18 (January 1971), 124.
"Infarcted! Tabescent!" (review of *The Kandy-Colored Tangerine-Flake Streamline Baby* by Tom Wolfe). *New York Times Book Review*, June 27, 1965, p. 4.
"Introduction." *Our Time Is Now: Notes from the High School Underground*, ed. John Birmingham. New York: Praeger, 1970, pp. vii–x (expanded from "Times Change," below).
"Introduction." *Rigadoon* by Louis-Ferdinand Céline. New York: Penguin Books, 1975, pp. xiii–xx.
"Joseph Heller's Extraordinary Novel About an Ordinary Man" (review of *Something Happened* by Joseph Heller). *New York Times Book Review*, October 6, 1974, pp. 1–2.
"Let the Killing Stop" (speech at Barnstable High School on Cape Cod). *The Register* (Yarmouth Port, Mass.), October 23, 1969.
"Money Talks to the New Man" (review of *The Boss* by Goffredo Parise). *New York Times Book Review*, October 2, 1966, p. 4.
"Nashville." *Vogue*, 166 (June 1975), 103.
"New York: Who Needs It." *Harper's*, 257 (August 1975), 3.

"Nixon's the One." *Earth Day—The Beginning.* New York: Bantam, 1970, pp. 64–65.

"The Noodle Factory." *Connecticut College Alumni Magazine,* 54 (Fall 1976), 3–5, 42–43.

"Reading Your Own." *New York Times Book Review,* June 4, 1967, p. 6.

"The Scientific Goblins Are Gonna Git Us" (review of *Unless Peace Comes,* ed. Nigel Calder). *Life,* 65 (July 16, 1968), 8.

"Second Thoughts on Teacher's Scrapbook" (review of *Up the Down Staircase* by Bel Kaufman). *Life,* 59 (September 3, 1965), 9–10.

"Times Change." *Esquire,* 73 (February 1970), 60.

"Tom Wicker Signifying" (review of *A Time to Die* by Tom Wicker). *New York Times Book Review,* March 9, 1975, pp. 2–3.

"The Unsaid Says Much" (review of *Absent Without Leave* by Heinrich Böll). *New York Times Book Review,* September 12, 1965, pp. 4, 54.

"Vonnegut on Trout." *Fantasy and Science Fiction,* 48 (April 1975), 158.

"War as a Series of Collisions" (review of *Bomber* by Len Deighton). *Life,* 69 (October 2, 1970), 10.

"Well All Right" (two samples of Vonnegut's student writing). *Cornell Daily Sun,* November 4, 1971, p. 4.

"Writers, Vonnegut, and the USSR." *P.E.N.-Newsletter* #17 (November 1974), pp. 1–2.

VIII. INTERVIEWS AND RECORDED REMARKS

Abramson, Marcia. "Vonnegut: Humor with Suffering." *The Michigan Daily* (Ann Arbor), January 22, 1969, p. 2.

Banks, Ann. "Symposium Sidelights." *Novel: A Forum on Fiction,* 3, #3 (Spring 1970), 208–211.

Bellamy, Joe David, and John Casey. "Kurt Vonnegut, Jr." in Joe David Bellamy, ed., *The New Fiction: Interviews with Innovative*

American Writers. Urbana: University of Illinois Press, 1974, pp. 194–207 (incorporates Casey's interview below).

Blumenfeld, Ralph. "Novelist into Playwright." *New York Post*, November 11, 1970, p. 38.

Bosworth, Patricia. "To Vonnegut, the Hero Is the Man Who Refuses to Kill." *New York Times*, October 25, 1970, Sec. 2, p. 5.

Bryan, C. D. B. "Kurt Vonnegut, Head Bokononist." *New York Times Book Review*, April 6, 1969, pp. 2, 25.

"Can Merlin Save the Whales?" *Boston Sunday Herald Traveler Book Guide*, March 29, 1970, pp. 9–10.

Casey, John. "Kurt Vonnegut, Jr.: A Subterranean Conversation." *Confluence*, 2 (Spring 1969), 3–5. In Bellamy and Casey, above.

Clancy, L. J. "Running Experiments Off: An Interview." *Meanjin Quarterly*, 30 (Autumn 1971), 46–54.

"Commencement Speaker Vonnegut Joins College's 'Extended Family.' " *The Pulteney St. Survey* (Hobart and Smith College), June 1974, p. 1.

"The Conscience of the Writer." *Publishers Weekly*, March 22, 1971, pp. 26–27.

Dunlap, Frank. "God and Kurt Vonnegut, Jr., at Iowa City." *Chicago Tribune Magazine*, May 7, 1967, pp. 48, 84, 86, 88.

Engle, Paul. "A Point That Must Be Raised: The Equalization of Fiction." *Chicago Tribune Book World*, June 10, 1973, p. 1.

Freund, Betsy L. "Who's on Top?" *Harper's Bazaar*, 105 (July 1972), 52–53.

Friedenreich, Kenneth. "Kurt Vonnegut: The PR Man Turned Novelist." *Newsday*, August 11, 1975, magazine section, p. 12.

Friedrich, Otto. "Ultra Vonnegut." *Time*, May 7, 1973, pp. 65–69.

Gerasimov, Genadii. "Vstrecha nad planetoi Zemlia: Dialog sovetskogo i amerikanskogo pistelei—Chingiz Aitmatov, Kurt Vonnegut [A Meeting Above the Planet Earth: A Dialogue between a Soviet and an American Writer . . .]." *Literaturnaia gazeta*, July 23, 1975, p. 2.

Gussow, Mel. "Vonnegut Is Having Fun Doing a Play." *New York Times*, October 6, 1970, p. 56.

Heffernan, Harold. "Vonnegut Likes a Change of Scenery." *Star-Ledger* (Trenton, N.J.), June 8, 1971, p. 26.

Henkle, Roger. "Wrestling (American Style) with Proteus." *Novel: A Forum on Fiction*, 3, #3 (Spring 1970), 197–207.

Hickey, Neil. " 'Between Time and Timbuktu.' " *TV Guide*, 20 (March 11, 1972), 24–26.

"In Vonnegut's View, Life is Absurd But Not Worth Leaving." *Chicago Tribune*, June 14, 1976, p. 5.

Johnson, A. "Authors and Editors." *Publishers Weekly*, 195 (April 21, 1969), 20–21.

Kramer, Carol. "Kurt's College Cult Adopts Him as Literary Guru at 48." *Chicago Tribune*, November 15, 1970, Sec. 5, p. 1.

McCabe, Loretta. "An Exclusive Interview with Kurt Vonnegut, Jr." *Writers Yearbook*—1970, pp. 92–95, 100–101, 103–105.

McLaughlin, Frank. "An Interview with Kurt Vonnegut, Jr." *Media & Methods*, May 1973, pp. 38–41, 45–46.

Mahoney, Lawrence. " 'Poison Their Minds with Humanity.' " *Tropic: The Miami Herald Sunday Magazine*, January 24, 1971, pp. 8–10, 13, 44.

Mitchell, Greg. "Meeting My Maker: A Visit with Kurt Vonnegut, Jr., by Kilgore Trout." *Crawdaddy*, April 1, 1974, pp. 42–51.

Navasky, Victor. "In Cold Print: Copyrights." *New York Times Book Review*, July 20, 1975, p. 22.

Noble, William T. "Unstuck in Time . . . a Real Kurt Vonnegut: The Reluctant Guru of Searching Youth." *Detroit Sunday News Magazine*, June 18, 1972, pp. 14–15, 18, 20, 22–24.

Okrent, Daniel. "A Very New Kind of WIR." *The Michigan Daily* (Ann Arbor), January 21, 1969, pp. 1–2.

———. "The Short, Sad Stay of Kurt Vonnegut, Jr." *The Michigan Daily* (Ann Arbor), January 25, 1969, p. 2.

"People." *Sports Illustrated*, February 19, 1973, p. 52.

Reasoner, Harry. "60 Minutes," 3 (September 15, 1970), CBS News transcript, 14–17.

Reilly, Charles. "An Interview With Kurt Vonnegut, Jr." *dlr* (University of Delaware student magazine), Spring 1976, pp. 20–27.

Reinhold, Robert. "Vonnegut Has 15 Nuggets of Talent in Harvard Class." *New York Times*, November 18, 1970, pp. 49, 77.

Robertson, Nan. "The Vonneguts: Dialogue on a Son's Insanity." *New York Times*, October 23, 1975, p. 45.

Saal, Rollene W. "Pick of the Paperbacks." *Saturday Review*, 53 (March 28, 1970), 34.

Schenker, Israel. "Kurt Vonnegut, Jr., Lights Comic Path of Despair." *New York Times*, March 21, 1969, Sec. 1, p. 41.

Scholes, Robert. "A Talk with Kurt Vonnegut, Jr." In Jerome Klinkowitz and John Somer, eds., *The Vonnegut Statement*. New York: Delacorte Press/Seymour Lawrence, 1973, pp. 90–118.

Sheed, Wilfrid. "The Now Generation Knew Him When." *Life*, 67 (September 12, 1969), 64–66, 69.

———. "The Good Word: Writer as Something Else." *New York Times Book Review*, March 4, 1973, p. 2.

Standish, David. "*Playboy* Interview." *Playboy*, 20 (July 1973), 57–60, 62, 66, 68, 70, 72, 74, 214, 216.

Taylor, Robert. "Kurt Vonnegut." *Boston Globe Sunday Magazine*, July 20, 1969, pp. 10–12, 14–15.

Thomas, Phil. "Growing Sales Puzzle Writer." *Ann Arbor News*, December 12, 1971, p. 41.

Todd, Richard. "The Masks of Kurt Vonnegut, Jr." *New York Times Magazine*, January 24, 1971, pp. 16–17, 19, 22, 24, 26, 30–31.

Troy, Carol. "Carol Troy Interviews Kurt Vonnegut." *Rags*, March 1971, pp. 24–26.

Unger, Art. "Kurt Vonnegut, Jr.: Class of 71." *Ingenue*, December 1971, pp. 14–18.

"Vonnegut's Gospel." *Time*, 95 (June 29, 1970), 8.

"We Talk to . . . Kurt Vonnegut." *Mademoiselle*, August 1970, p. 296.

Wolf, William. "Kurt Vonnegut: Still Dreaming of Imaginary Worlds." *Insight: Sunday Magazine of the Milwaukee Journal*, February 27, 1972, pp. 15–18.

IX. SPECIAL VONNEGUT NUMBERS OF SCHOLARLY JOURNALS

"Kurt Vonnegut, Jr.: A Symposium," *Summary*, 1 (#2, 1971); pictorial and critical essays by Jill Krementz, Robert Scholes, Robert Kiely, David Hayman, Armin Paul Frank, Brian W. Aldiss, Tony Hillman, and "An Ancient Friend of His Family" (individually cited below).

"Vonnegut," *Critique*, 12 (#3, 1971); essays and bibliography by Max Schulz, Leonard Leff, Jerome Klinkowitz, and Stanley Schatt (individually cited below).

X. CRITICAL ESSAYS AND BOOKS ABOUT VONNEGUT

Abádi-Nagy, Zoltán. " 'The Skillful Seducer': Of Vonnegut's Brand of Comedy." *Hungarian Studies in English*, 8 (1974), 45–56.

"An Account of the Ancestry of Kurt Vonnegut, Jr., by an Ancient Friend of the Family." *Summary*, 1 (#2, 1971), 76–118.

Adams, Marion. "You've Come a Long Way Since Shortridge High, Kurt Vonnegut, Jr." *Indianapolis*, October 1976, pp. 27–33.

Bell, Pearl K. "American Fiction: Forgetting Ordinary Truths." *Dissent*, Winter 1973, pp. 26–34.

Bellamy, Joe David. "Kurt Vonnegut for President: The Making of an Academic Reputation." In Jerome Klinkowitz and John Somer, eds., *The Vonnegut Statement*. New York: Delacorte Press/Seymour Lawrence, 1973, pp. 71–89.

Benfey, Theodor. "Seeds and the Vonneguts." *Chemistry*, 45 (November 1972), 2.

Bestuzhev-Lada, I. "Kogda lishim stanovitsya chelovechestvo [When Mankind Becomes Superfluous]," Foreword to *Utopiia 14* (*Utopia 14* trans. by M. Bruhnov from the retitled Bantam edition of *Player Piano*). Moscow: Molodaia gvardiia, 1967, pp. 5–24.

Bodtke, Richard. "Great Sorrows, Small Joys: The World of Kurt Vonnegut, Jr." *Cross Currents*, 20 (Winter 1970), 120–125.

Boni, John. "Analogous Form: Black Comedy and Some Jacobean Plays." *Western Humanities Review*, Summer 1974, pp. 201–215.

"Book Ends." *New York Times Book Review*, August 15, 1976, p. 29.

Borshchagovsky, Aleksandr. "Take dela [Such goings-on]." *Literaturnaia gazeta*, July 15, 1970, p. 13.

Bourjaily, Vance. "What Vonnegut Is and Isn't." *New York Times Book Review*, August 13, 1972, pp. 3, 10.

Bryan, C. D. B. "Kurt Vonnegut on Target." *New Republic*, 155 (October 8, 1966), 21–22, 24–26.

Bryant, Jerry H. *The Open Decision*, New York: Free Press, 1970, pp. 303–324.

Buck, Lynn. "Vonnegut's World of Comic Futility." *Studies in American Fiction*, 3 (Autumn 1975), 181–198.

Burhans, Clinton S., Jr. "Hemingway and Vonnegut: Diminishing Vision in a Dying Age." *Modern Fiction Studies*, 21 (Summer 1975), 173–191.

Carson, Ronald. "Kurt Vonnegut: Matter-of-Fact Moralist." *Listening*, 6 (Autumn 1971), 182–195.

Ciardi, John. "Manner of Speaking." *Saturday Review*, 50 (September 30, 1967), 16, 18.

Clancy, L. J. " 'If the Accident Will': The Novels of Kurt Vonnegut." *Meanjin Quarterly*, 30 (Autumn 1971), 37–45.

Cook, Bruce. "When Kurt Vonnegut Talks—and He Does—the Young All Tune In." *National Observer*, October 12, 1970, p. 21.

DeMott, Benjamin. "Vonnegut's Otherworldly Laughter." *Saturday Review*, 54 (May 1, 1971), 29–32, 38.

Dickstein, Morris. "Black Humor and History: Fiction in the Sixties." *Partisan Review*, 43 (#2, 1976), 185–211.

Diehl, Digby. "And Now the Movies." *Showcase/Chicago Sun-Times*, February 28, 1971, p. 2.

Edelstein, Arnold. "*Slaughterhouse-Five*: Time Out of Joint." *College Literature*, 1 (1974), 128–139.

El'sberg, Iakov. "V Bitve za cheloveka [In Battle for Man]." *Literaturnaia gazeta* (January 1, 1972), p. 4.

Engel, David. "On the Question of Foma: A Study of the Novels of Kurt Vonnegut, Jr." *Riverside Quarterly*, 5 (February 1972), 119–128.

Fiedler, Leslie A. "The Divine Stupidity of Kurt Vonnegut, Jr." *Esquire*, 74 (September 1970), 195–197, 199–200, 202–204.

Fiene, Donald. "Vonnegut's *The Sirens of Titan*." *Explicator*, 34 (December 1975), Item 27.

"Forty-Six and Trusted." *Newsweek*, March 3, 1969, p. 79.

Frank, Armin Paul. "Where Laughing Is the Only Way to Stop It From *Hurting*." *Summary*, 1 (#2, 1971), 51–62.

Fussell, Paul. *The Great War and Modern Memory*. New York: Oxford University Press, 1975, pp. 143–144, 246.

Godshalk, William L. "Kurt Vonnegut's Renaissance Hero." *Clifton: Magazine of the University of Cincinnati*, 1 (1973), 41–45.

———. "The Recurring Characters of Kurt Vonnegut, Jr." *Notes on Contemporary Literature*, 3 (#1, 1973), 2–3.

———. "Vonnegut and Shakespeare: Rosewater at Elsinore." *Critique*, 15 (#2, 1973), 37–48.

Goldsmith, David. *Kurt Vonnegut: Fantasist of Fire and Ice* (Popular Writers Series Pamphlet #2). Bowling Green, Ohio: Bowling Green University Popular Press, 1972.

Goss, Gary L. "The Selfless Billy Pilgrim." *Buffalo Spree*, 5 (Fall 1971), 34–35, 44–45, 47, 52–53, 60–61.

Greiner, Donald J. "Vonnegut's *Slaughterhouse-Five* and the Fiction of Atrocity." *Critique*, 14 (#3, 1973), 38–51.

Grossman, Edward. "Vonnegut and His Audience." *Commentary*, 58 (July 19, 1976), 40–46.

Gubko, N. "Antivoennyi roman Vonneguta [Vonnegut's Antiwar Novel]." *Zvezda*, 6 (1971), 220–222.

Haan, Kalju. "Dramateater alustab hooaega [Drama Theatre Opens for the New Season]." *Sirp ja Vasar*, 36 (September 3, 1976).

Haden-Guest, Anthony. "Out Here in the Hamptons: Snapshots of the Literary Life." *New York*, September 1, 1975, pp. 43–47.

Hansen, Arlen J. "The Celebration of Solipsism: A New Trend in

American Fiction." *Modern Fiction Studies*, 19 (Spring 1973), 5–15.

Harris, Charles B. *Contemporary American Novelists of the Absurd*. New Haven: College & University Press, 1971, pp. 51–75.

Haskell, John D., Jr. "Addendum to Pieratt and Klinkowitz: *Kurt Vonnegut, Jr.*" *Papers of the Bibliographical Society of America*, 70 (1st Quarter 1976), 122.

Hassan, Ihab. "Fiction and Future: An Extravaganza for Voice and Tape." *Liberations*. Middletown, Conn.: Wesleyan University Press, 1971, pp. 193–194. (Reprinted in *Paracriticisms*. Urbana: University of Illinois Press, 1975.)

Hauck, Richard Boyd. *A Cheerful Nihilism*. Bloomington, Ind.: Indiana University Press, 1971, pp. 193–194.

Hayman, David. "The Jolly Mix: Notes on Techniques, Style and Decorum in *Slaughterhouse-Five*." *Summary*, 1, (#2 1971), 44–50.

Hendin, Josephine. "The Writer as Culture Hero, The Father as Son." *Harper's*, 249 (July 1974), 82–87.

Hildebrand, Tim. "Two or Three Things I Know about Kurt Vonnegut's Imagination." In Jerome Klinkowitz and John Somer, eds., *The Vonnegut Statement*. New York: Delacorte Press/Seymour Lawrence, 1973, pp. 121–132.

Hillegas, Mark. "Dystopian Science Fiction: New Index to the Human Situation." *New Mexico Quarterly*, 31 (1961), 238–249.

Hillman, Tony. "Hooked." *Summary*, 1 (#2, 1971), 69–72.

Ileshin, B. "Za politseiskimi bar'erami: Roman 'Boinia nomer piat' i amerikanskaia deistvitel'nost' [Behind the Police Barriers: The Novel *Slaughterhouse-Five* and American Reality]." *Izvestiia*, November 28, 1970.

Isaacs, Neil D. "Unstuck in Time: *Clockwork Orange* and *Slaughterhouse-Five*." *Literature/Film Quarterly*, 1 (1973), 122–131.

Iwamoto, Iwao. "A Clown's Say—A Study of Kurt Vonnegut's, Jr.'s *Slaughterhouse-Five*." *Studies in English Literature* (Tokyo), English Number, 1975, pp. 21–23.

Jones, Peter G. *War and the Novelist*. Columbia: University of Missouri Press, 1976.

Kael, Pauline. "Current Cinema." *New Yorker*, 46 (January 23, 1971), 76–78.

Kateb, George. *Utopia and Its Enemies*. Glencoe, Ill.: Free Press, 1963, pp. 187–188.

Kazin, Alfred. "The War Novel: From Mailer to Vonnegut." *Saturday Review*, 54 (February 6, 1971), 13–15, 36.

Kenedy, R. C. "Kurt Vonnegut, Jr." *Art International*, 15 (May 1971), 20–25.

Keogh, J. G., and Edward Kislaitis, "SF and the Future of Science Fiction." *Media & Methods*, January 1971, pp. 38–39, 48.

Ketterer, David. *New Worlds for Old: The Apocalyptic Imagination, Science Fiction, and American Literature*. Bloomington: Indiana University Press, 1974, pp. 296–333.

Khmel'nitskaia, Tamara. "Slozhnyi put' k prosteishim istinam [A Complicated Path to the Simplest Truths]." *Novyi Mir*, 4 (1971), 245–250.

Kiely, Robert. "Satire as Fantasy." *Summary*, 1 (#2, 1971), 41–43.

Klawans, Stuart. "Vonnegut, Bradbury, and the Fantastic Company They Keep." *Chicago Tribune Book World*, May 19, 1974, p. 4

Klinkowitz, Jerome. "The Dramatization of Kurt Vonnegut, Jr." *Players*, 50 (February–March, 1975), 62–64.

———. "Kurt Vonnegut, Jr." *Literary Disruptions/The Making of a Post-Contemporary American Fiction*. Urbana: University of Illinois Press, 1975, pp. 33–61.

———. "Kurt Vonnegut, Jr." *The Life of Fiction*. Urbana: University of Illinois Press, 1977, pp. 101–122.

———. "Kurt Vonnegut Jr.'s SuperFiction." *Revue Française d'Études Américaines* (Sorbonne) #1 (April 1976), pp. 115–124.

———. "Kurt Vonnegut, Jr.: The Canary in a Cathouse"; "*Mother Night, Cat's Cradle*, and the Crimes of Our Time"; "Why They Read Vonnegut." In Jerome Klinkowitz and John Somer, eds., *The Vonnegut Statement*. New York: Delacorte Press/Seymour Lawrence, 1973, pp. 7–17, 18–30, 158–177.

———. "The Literary Career of Kurt Vonnegut, Jr." *Modern Fiction Studies*, 19 (Spring 1973), 57–67.

———. "Lost in the Cat House." *The Falcon*, #5 (December 1972), 110–113.

———, and John Somer. "The Vonnegut Statement." In Jerome Klinkowitz and John Somer, eds., *The Vonnegut Statement*. New York: Delacorte Press/Seymour Lawrence, 1973, pp. 1–3.

Knight, Damon. *In Search of Wonder*. Chicago: Advent Publishers, 1967, pp. 166–167, 236–237.

Krementz, Jill. "Pictorial." *Summary*, 1 (#2, 1971), between pp. 34 and 35.

Kuz'menko, P. "A kto ubil Billi? [Who really killed Billy?]." *Moskovskii komsomolets*, February 8, 1976.

Lawing, John V., Jr. "Kurt Vonnegut: Charming Nihilist." *Christianity Today*, 19 (February 14, 1975), 17–20, 22.

Lawrence, Seymour. "A Publisher's Dream." *Summary*, 1 (#2, 1971), 73–75.

Le Clair, Thomas. "Death and Black Humor." *Critique*, 17 (#1, 1975), 5–46.

Leff, Leonard. "Science and Destruction in Vonnegut's *Cat's Cradle*." *Rectangle* (Sigma Tau Delta), 46 (Spring 1971), 28–32.

———. "Utopia Reconstructed: Alienation in Vonnegut's *God Bless You, Mr. Rosewater*." *Critique*, 12 (#3, 1971), 29–37.

Leonard, John. "Why Vonnegut Smiles." New York Times Service, syndicated May 9, 1976.

Lessing, Doris. "Vonnegut's Responsibility." *New York Times Book Review*, February 4, 1973, p. 35.

Leverence, W. John. "*Cat's Cradle* and Traditional American Humor." *Journal of Popular Culture*, 5 (1972), 955–963.

Lewis, Flora. "A Writer Of and For the Times." *Chicago Sun-Times*, January 5, 1971, p. 22.

Lifton, Robert Jay. "Kurt Vonnegut: Duty-Dance with Death." *American Poetry Review*, 1 (January–February 1973), 41.

Lundquist, James. *Kurt Vonnegut, Jr.* New York: Frederick Ungar, 1976.

Maksimova, V. "Billi Pilgrim puteschestvuet y proshloe [Billy Pilgrim Travels into the Past]." *Vecherniaia Moskva*, February 9–10, 1976.

May, John R. "Vonnegut's Humor and the Limits of Hope." *Twentieth Century Literature*, 18 (January, 1972), 25–36. Reprinted in *Toward a New Earth*. Notre Dame: Notre Dame University Press, 1972, pp. 191–200.

McGinnis, Wayne. "The Arbitrary Cycle of *Slaughterhouse-Five*: A Relation of Form to Theme." *Critique*, 17 (#1, 1975), 55–68.

———. "Names in Vonnegut's Fiction." *Notes on Contemporary Literature*, 3 (#2, 1973), 7–9.

McNelly, Willis E. "Science Fiction: The Modern Mythology." *America*, September 5, 1970, pp. 125–127.

Meades, Jonathan. "Kurt Vonnegut: Fantasist." *Books and Bookmen*, February 1973, pp. 34–37.

Meeter, Glenn. "Vonnegut's Formal and Moral Otherworldiness: *Cat's Cradle* and *Slaughterhouse-Five*." In Jerome Klinkowitz and John Somer, eds., *The Vonnegut Statement*. New York: Delacorte Press/Seymour Lawrence, 1973, pp. 204–220.

Mellard, James J. "The Modes of Vonnegut's Fiction: Or, *Player Piano* Ousts *Mechanical Bride* and *The Sirens of Titan* invade *The Gutenberg Galaxy*." In Jerome Klinkowitz and John Somer, eds., *The Vonnegut Statement*. New York: Delacorte Press/Seymour Lawrence, 1973, pp. 178–203.

Mendel'son, M. O. *Amerikanskaia satiricheskaia proza XX veka* [*American Satirical Prose of the Twentieth Century*]. Moscow: Nauka, 1972, pp. 306–324.

———. "Kakim vidit mir Kurt Vonnegut? [How Does Kurt Vonnegut View the World?]." *SShA: Ekonomika, politika, ideologiia*, 12 (1974), 79–84.

———. "Amerikanskii roman posle Khemingueia, Folknera, Steinbeka [The American Novel after Hemingway, Faulkner, Steinbeck]." *Novyi Mir*, 8 (1975), 246–263.

Meredith, William. "Meredith on Vonnegut." *Connecticut College Alumni Magazine*, 54 (Fall 1976), 2.

Merrill, Robert. "Vonnegut's *Breakfast of Champions:* The Conversion of Heliogabalus." *Critique*, 18 (#3, 1977), 99–108.

Messent, Peter B. "*Breakfast of Champions:* The Direction of Vonnegut's Fiction." *Journal of American Studies*, 8 (1st Quarter 1974), 101–114.

Nelson, Joyce. "*Slaughterhouse-Five:* Novel and Film." *Literature/Film Quarterly*, 1 (1973), 149–153.

———. "Vonnegut and 'Bugs in Amber.' " *Journal of Popular Culture*, 7 (1973), 551–558.

"New Creative Writers." *Library Journal*, June 1, 1952, p. 1007.

O'Connor, Gerald W. "The Function of Time Travel in Vonnegut's *Slaughterhouse-Five.*" *Riverside Quarterly*, 5 (1972), 206–207.

Olderman, Raymond M. *Beyond the Waste Land.* New Haven: Yale University Press, 1972, pp. 187–219.

Orlova, R. "O romane Kurta Vonneguta [On Kurt Vonnegut's Novel]," Afterword to *Boinya nomer pyat', ili krestovyi pokhod detei*, trans. by Rita Rait-Kovalëva from *Slaughterhouse-Five. Novyi Mir*, 4 (1970), 179–180.

Pagetti, Carlo. "Kurt Vonnegut, tra fantascienza e utopia." *Studi Americani* (Roma), 12 (1966), 301–322.

Palmer, Raymond C. "Vonnegut's Major Concerns," *Iowa English Yearbook* #14 (Fall 1969), 3–10.

"Paper Back Talk." *New York Times Book Review*, July 18, 1976, p. 35, and August 29, 1976, p. 27.

"Playboy Adviser." *Playboy*, 22 (December 1975), 56–57.

Prioli, Carmine A. "Kurt Vonnegut's Duty-Dance." *Essays in English Literature*, 1 (#3, 1973), 44–50.

Pütz, Manfred. "Who Am I This Time: Die Romane von Kurt Vonnegut." *Jahrbuch fur Amerikanstudien*, 19 (1974), 111–125.

Rait-Kovalëva, Rita. "Kanareika v shakhte [Canary in a Coal Mine]." *Rovesnik*, 1 (1974), 16–19.

Ranley, Ernest W. "What Are People For?" *Commonweal*, 94 (May 7, 1971), 207–211.

Reed, Peter. *Writers for the Seventies: Kurt Vonnegut, Jr.* New York: Paperback Library, 1972.

Rice, Susan. "*Slaughterhouse-Five*/A Viewer's Guide." *Media & Methods*, October, 1972, pp. 27–33.

Ritter, Jess. "Teaching Kurt Vonnegut on the Firing Line." In Jerome Klinkowitz and John Somer, eds., *The Vonnegut Statement.* New York: Delacorte Press/Seymour Lawrence, 1973, pp. 31–42.

Samuels, Charles Thomas. "Age of Vonnegut." *New Republic*, 164 (June 12, 1971), 30–32.

Schatt, Stanley. *Kurt Vonnegut, Jr.* New York: Twayne, 1977.

———. "The Whale and the Cross: Vonnegut's Jonah and Christ Figures." *Southwest Quarterly*, Winter 1971, pp. 29–42.

———. "The World of Kurt Vonnegut, Jr." Critique, 12 (#3, 1971), 54–69.

Scholes, Robert. "Afterword." In R. H. W. Dillard et al., *The Sounder Few*. Athens, Ga.: University of Georgia Press, 1971, pp. 186–191.

———. "Chasing a Lone Eagle." *Summary*, 1, (#2, 1971), 35–40. Reprinted in Jerome Klinkowitz and John Somer, eds., *The Vonnegut Statement*. New York: Delacorte Press/Seymour Lawrence, 1973, pp. 45–54.

———. "Fabulation and Satire." In *The Fabulators*. New York: Oxford University Press, 1967, pp. 35–55.

———. " 'Mithridates, He Died Old': Black Humor and Kurt Vonnegut, Jr." *Hollins Critic*, 3 (October, 1966), 1–12. Reprinted in R. H. W. Dillard et al., *The Sounder Few*. Athens, Ga.: University of Georgia Press, 1971, pp. 173–185.

Scholl, Peter A. "Vonnegut's Attack upon Christendom." *Newsletter of the Conference on Christianity and Literature*, 22 (Fall 1972), 5–11.

Schriber, Mary Sue. "You've Come a Long Way, Babbit! From Zenith to Ilium." *Twentieth Century Literature*, 17 (April 1971), 101–106.

Schulz, Max. "The Unconfirmed Thesis: Kurt Vonnegut, Black Humor, and Contemporary Art." *Critique*, 12 (#3, 1971), 5–28.

Schwartz, Sheila. "Science Fiction: Bridge Between the Two Cultures." *English Journal*, 60 (November 1971), 1043–1051.

Scully, Malcolm G. "Books." *Chronicle of Higher Education*, 7 (December 18, 1972), 5.

Seelye, John. "What the Kids Are Reading." *New Republic*, 163 (October 17, 1970), 23–26.

Shipler, David K. "Vonnegut's *Slaughterhouse-Five* Staged in Moscow." *New York Times*, January 13, 1976, p. 40.

Shperlin, K. A. "O zhanre romanov Kurta Vonneguta [On the

Genre of Kurt Vonnegut's Novels]." *Problemy teorii romana i rasskaza.* Riga: Latviiskii gosudarstvennyi universitet im. Stuchki, 1972, pp. 119–134.

Simukov, V. "Stranstviia Billi Pilgrim." *Trud,* 58 (March 10, 1976), 4.

Skorodenko, V. "O bezumnom mire; pozitsii khudozhnika [On the Irrational World and the Position of the Artist]," Afterword to *Kulybel' dyla Koshki,* trans. by Rita Rait-Kovalëva from *Cat's Cradle.* Moscow: Molodaia gvardiia, 1970, pp. 212–233.

Somer, John. "Geodesic Vonnegut: Or, If Buckminister Fuller Wrote Novels." In Jerome Klinkowitz and John Somer, eds., *The Vonnegut Statement.* New York: Delacorte Press/Seymour Lawrence, 1973, pp. 221–253.

Springer, Mary Doyle. *Forms of the Modern Novella.* Chicago: University of Chicago Press, 1976, pp. 12, 78–81, 84, 89, 91–92.

Stelzmann, Rainulf A. "Die verlorene Utopie: Das Werk Vonneguts und die Amerikanische Jugend." *Naus Hochland,* 66 (1974), 271–280.

Tanner, Tony. "The Uncertain Messenger: A Study of the Novels of Kurt Vonnegut, Jr." *Critical Quarterly,* 11 (Winter 1969), 297–315. Reprinted in *City of Words.* New York: Harper & Row, 1971, pp. 181–201.

Trachentenberg, Stanley. "Vonnegut's Cradle: The Erosion of Comedy." *Michigan Quarterly Review,* 12 (1973), 66–71.

Tunnell, James. "Kesey and Vonnegut: Preachers of Redemption." *Christian Century,* 89 (November 22, 1972), 1180–1183.

Turner, Susan M. "Life Is Sure Funny Sometimes . . . and Sometimes It Isn't . . . A Guide to Understanding Kurt Vonnegut, Jr., *or* The Fool's Guide to Confusion *or* A Shot in the Dark *or* What Vonnegut Means to Me (This Week Anyway)." *The Thoroughbred* (University of Louisville), 2 (Spring 1971), 43–46.

Uphaus, Robert W. "Expected Meaning in Vonnegut's Dead-End Fiction." *Novel,* 8 (Winter 1975), 164–174.

Vasbinder, Sam. "The Meaning of Foma in *Cat's Cradle.*" *Riverside Quarterly,* 5 (1973), 300–302.

Vinograde, Ann C. "A Soviet Translation of *Slaughterhouse-Five.*" *Russian Language Journal*, 93 (1972), 14–18.

Vitiello, Greg. "Time and Timbuktu." *Image*, 9 (March 1972), 6–9.

Wakefield, Dan. "In Vonnegut's *Karass.*" In Jerome Klinkowitz and John Somer, eds., *The Vonnegut Statement*. New York: Delacorte Press/Seymour Lawrence, 1973, pp. 55–70.

Walsh, Chad. *From Utopia to Nightmare*. New York: Harper & Row, 1962, pp. 85–88.

Weales, Gerald. "What Ever Happened to Tugboat Annie?" *The Reporter*, 35 (December 1, 1966), 50, 52–56.

Wolfe, G. K. "Vonnegut and the Metaphor of Science Fiction." *Journal of Popular Culture*, 5 (1972), 964–969.

Wolheim, David. *The Universe Makers*. New York: Harper & Row, 1971, pp. 70–71.

Wood, Karen, and Charles Wood. "The Vonnegut Effect: Science Fiction and Beyond." In Jerome Klinkowitz and John Somer, eds., *The Vonnegut Statement*. New York: Delacorte Press/Seymour Lawrence, 1973, pp. 133–157.

Zatonsky, D. V. *Iskusstvo romana i XX vek* [*The Art of the Novel and the Twentieth Century*]. Moscow: Khudozhestvennaia literatura, 1973, pp. 7, 407–437, 441.

Zverev, A. "*De profundis* Kurta Vonneguta [Kurt Vonnegut's *De Profundis*]." *Inostrannaia literatura*, 8 (1970), 265–268.

———. "Skazki tekhnicheskogo veka [Tales of the Technological Age]." *Voprosy literatury*, 2 (1975), 32–66.

XI. DOCTORAL DISSERTATIONS

Austin, Marvin Fraley, Jr. "The Novels of Kurt Vonnegut, Jr.: A Confrontation with the Modern World." University of Tennessee, 1975.

Camara, George C. "War and the Literary Extremist: The American War Novel, 1945–1970." University of Massachusetts, 1974.

Fitzgerald, Sister Ellen. "World War II in the American Novel:

Hawkes, Heller, Kosinski, and Vonnegut." Notre Dame University, 1974.

Goldsmith, David Hirsch. "The Novels of Kurt Vonnegut, Jr." Bowling Green State University, 1970.

Goshorn, James William. "The Queasy World of Kurt Vonnegut, Jr.: Satire in the Novels." University of New Mexico, 1971.

LeClair, Thomas Edmund. "Final Words: Death and Comedy in the Fiction of Donleavy, Hawkes, Barth, Vonnegut, and Percy." Duke University, 1972.

Lonie, Charles Anthony. "Accumulations of Silence: Survivor Psychology in Vonnegut, Twain, and Hemingway." University of Minnesota, 1974.

McGinnis, Wayne Douglas. "Kurt Vonnegut, Jr.'s Confrontation with Meaninglessness." University of Arkansas, 1974.

Olderman, Raymond Michael. "Beyond the Waste Land: A Study of the American Novel in the Nineteen-Sixties." Indiana University, 1969.

Rice, Elaine Fritz. "The Satire of John Barth and Kurt Vonnegut, Jr.: The Menippean Tradition in the 1960's in America." Arizona State University, 1974.

Schatt, Stanley. "The World Picture of Kurt Vonnegut, Jr." University of Southern California, 1970.

Shaw, William Gary. "Comic Absurdity and the Novels of Kurt Vonnegut, Jr." Oklahoma State University, 1975.

Shor, Ira Neil. "Vonnegut's Art of Inquiry." University of Wisconsin, 1971.

Somer, John. "Quick-Stasis: The Rite of Initiation in the Novels of Kurt Vonnegut, Jr." Northern Illinois University, 1971.

St. Germain, Amos Joseph. "Religious Interpretation and Contemporary Literature: Kurt Vonnegut, Jr., Robert Coover, and John Barth." University of Iowa, 1974.

Weinstein, Sharon Rosenbaum. "Comedy and Nightmare: The Fiction of John Hawkes, Kurt Vonnegut, Jr., Jerzy Kosinski, and Ralph Ellison." University of Utah, 1971.

XII. BIBLIOGRAPHIES

Burns, Mildred Blair. "Books by Kurt Vonnegut." *Hollins Critic*, 3 (October, 1966), 7. Updated in R. H. W. Dillard et al., *The Sounder Few: Selected Essays from The Hollins Critic*. Athens, Ga.: University of Georgia Press, 1971, pp. 192–193.

Hudgens, Betty L. *Kurt Vonnegut, Jr.*: *A Checklist*. Detroit: Gale, 1972.

Klinkowitz, Jerome. *Literary Disruptions/The Making of a Post-Contemporary American Fiction*. Urbana: University of Illinois Press, 1975, pp. 197–211.

———, and Asa B. Pieratt, Jr. *Kurt Vonnegut, Jr.*: *A Descriptive Bibliography and Annotated Secondary Checklist*. Hamden, Conn.: Shoe String Press/Archon Books, 1974.

———, and Stanley Schatt. "The Vonnegut Bibliography." In Jerome Klinkowitz and John Somers, eds., *The Vonnegut Statement*. New York: Delacorte Press/Seymour Lawrence, 1973, pp. 255–277.

Schatt, Stanley, and Jerome Klinkowitz. "A Kurt Vonnegut Checklist." *Critique*, 12 (#3, 1971), 70–76.

XIII. REVIEWS

Player Piano

Armstrong, Louise. *Saturday Review*, 49 (May 14, 1966), 44.

Booklist, 49 (September 1, 1952), 15.

Fabun, Don. *San Francisco Chronicle*, August 29, 1952, p. 15.

Fleischer, Leonore. *Publishers Weekly*, 191 (January 30, 1967), 113.

Franklin, H. Bruce. *Southern Review*, 3 (n.s.) (Autumn 1967), 1036–1049.

Goldknopf, David. *New Republic*, 127 (August 18, 1952), 19.

Hall, Elizabeth. *Psychology Today*, 8 (August 1974), 20.
Henderson, Robert W. *Library Journal*, 77 (August 1952), 1303.
Hicks, Granville. *New York Times*, August 17, 1952, p. 5.
Hilton, James. *New York Herald Tribune Book Review*, August 17, 1952, p. 5.
Kirkus, June 1, 1952, p. 330.
Korman, Seymour. *Chicago Sunday Tribune*, August 24, 1952, p. 2.
Lee, Charles. *Saturday Review*, 35 (August 30, 1952), 11.
Merril, J. *Fantasy and Science Fiction*, November 1966, p. 62.
National Observer, 5 (May 23, 1966), 23.
New Yorker, 28 (August 16, 1952), 88.
Petersen, Clarence. *Books Today*, 4 (March 26, 1967), 9.
Pickrel, Paul. *Yale Review*, 42 (Autumn 1952), 20.
Sheppard, R. Z. *Life*, 60 (April 8, 1966), 15.
Sturgeon, Theodore. *National Review*, 18 (May 17, 1966), 478.

The Sirens of Titan

Observer, November 2, 1975, p. 29.
Petersen, Clarence. *Books Today*, 3 (December 4, 1966), 34.
———. *Books Today*, 4 (January 15, 1967), 9.
———. *Books Today*, 4 (May 7, 1967), 9.
Times (London) *Literary Supplement*, June 15, 1967, p. 543.

Mother Night

Armstrong, Louise. *Saturday Review*, 49 (May 14, 1966), 44.
Bannon, Barbara. *Publishers Weekly*, 182 (February 28, 1966), 94.
Choice, 3 (September 1966), 524.
Clark, J. J. *Best Sellers*, 26 (May 15, 1966), 79.
Fleischer, Leonore. *Publishers Weekly*, 191 (March 6, 1967), 78.
Goran, L. *Books Today*, 3 (July 31, 1966), 6.
Grant, Mary Kent. *Library Journal*, 91 (June 1, 1966), 2882.
Greenburg, J. *Denver Quarterly*, 1 (Summer 1966), 119–120.
Kirkus, February 1966, p. 207.
National Observer, 5 (May 1966), 23.
Petersen, Clarence. *Books Today*, 4 (April 23, 1966), 10.

Schickel, Richard. *Harper's*, 232 (May 1966), 103.
Smith, William James. *Commonweal*, 84 (September 16, 1966), 592–594.
Sturgeon, Theodore. *National Review*, 18 (May 17, 1966), 478.
Virginia Quarterly Review, 42 (Summer 1966), xc.

Cat's Cradle

Best Sellers, 25 (October 1, 1965), 274.
Brien, Alan. *Spectator*, 211 (August 2, 1963), 158–159.
Laski, M. *Observer*, August 22, 1965, p. 21.
Southern, Terry. *New York Times Book Review*, June 2, 1963, p. 20.

God Bless You, Mr. Rosewater

Allsop, Kenneth. *Spectator*, 215 (October 29, 1965), 554.
Booklist, 61 (July 15, 1965), 1057.
Coleman, J. *Observer*, October 24, 1965, p. 28.
Dolbier, M. *New York Herald Tribune*, April 5, 1965, p. 21.
Duchene, A. *Manchester Guardian*, November 25, 1965, p. 11.
Fremont-Smith, Eliot. *New York Times*, April 9, 1965, p. 35M.
Grady, R. F. *Best Sellers*, 25 (May 1, 1965), 68.
Hicks, Granville. *Saturday Review*, 48 (April 3, 1965), 19.
Kilpatrick, Clayton E. *Library Journal*, 90 (April 15, 1965), 1935.
Kirkus, February 1, 1965, p. 128.
Knickerbocker, Conrad. *Life*, 58 (April 9, 1965), 6, 10.
Levin, Martin. *New York Times Book Review*, April 25, 1965, p. 41.
Maddocks, Melvin. *Christian Science Monitor*, May 6, 1965, p. B9.
Merril, J. *Fantasy and Science Fiction*, 27 (July 1965), 78–83.
Morgan, Edwin. *New Statesman*, 70 (October 29, 1965), 658.
New Yorker, 41 (May 15, 1965), 216.
Petersen, Clarence. *Books Today*, 4 (May 7, 1967), 9.
Price, R. G. G. *Punch*, 249 (November 17, 1965), 741.
Sheed, Wilfrid. *Commonweal*, 91 (December 5, 1969), 319.
Talbot, Daniel. *New York Sunday Herald Tribune Book Week*, April 11, 1965, p. 6.

Time, 85 (May 7, 1965), 112–114.
Times (London) *Literary Supplement*, November 11, 1965, p. 1007.

Welcome to the Monkey House

Blackburn, Sara. *Nation*, 207 (September 23, 1968), 286.
Christian Science Monitor, 61 (December 5, 1968), 23.
Fleischer, Leonore. *Publishers Weekly*, 196 (November 10, 1969), 51.
Hackett, Alice P. *Publishers Weekly*, 193 (June 3, 1968), 127.
King, Larry L. *New York Times Book Review*, September 1, 1968, p. 4.
Kirkus, June 1968, p. 664.
Levitas, Mitchel. *New York Times*, August 19, 1968, p. 35.
Listener, 81 (May 22, 1969), 732.
Maddocks, Melvin. *Life*, 65 (August 1968), 8.
Nicol, Charles. *Atlantic*, 222 (September 1968), 123.
Observer, June 8, 1969, p. 28, and September 3, 1972, p. 33.
Publishers Weekly, 193 (June 1968), 127, and 196 (November 10, 1969), 51.
Reedy, Gerard. *America*, 119 (September 14, 1968), 190.
Rhodes, Richard. *Book World*, 2 (August 18, 1968), 4.
Sokolov, Raymond A. *Newsweek*, 72 (August 19, 1968), 84–85.
Time, 92 (August 30, 1968), 68.
Times (London) *Literary Supplement*, July 17, 1969, p. 769.

Slaughterhouse-Five

Adams, Phoebe. *Atlantic*, 223 (April 1969), 146.
American Libraries, 1 (March 1970), 227.
Books & Bookmen, 15 (May 1970), 22.
Book World, 4 (April 12, 1970), 17.
Best Sellers, 29 (April 15, 1969), 31.
Borg, Mary. *New Statesman*, 79 (March 20, 1970), 418.
Cain, Seymour. *Christian Century*, 86 (August 13, 1969), 1069.
Coffey, Warren. *Commonweal*, 90 (June 6, 1969), 347.
Crichton, J. Michael. *New Republic*, 160 (April 26, 1969), 33–35.
Crist, Judith. *New York*, 6 (January 1, 1973), 50–53.

Davidson, Eugene. *Modern Age*, 13 (Summer 1969), 324–327.
Deyver, David J. *Catholic World*, 209 (September 1969), 283–284.
Fleischer, Leonore. *Publishers Weekly*, 197 (February 2, 1970), 91.
Greenfield, Josh. *Commonweal*, December 5, 1969, 315.
Guardian Weekly, 102 (March 28, 1970), 18.
Harper, Howard M., Jr. *Contemporary Literature*, 12 (Spring 1971), 332–336.
Hicks, Granville. *Saturday Review*, 52 (March 29, 1969), 25.
Howard, Maureen. *Partisan Review*, 38 (#1, 1970), 132–133.
Johnson, Albert. *Publishers Weekly*, 195 (January 6, 1969), 53.
Kirkus, 37 (January 15, 1969), 69–70.
Lardner, Susan. *New Yorker*, 45 (May 17, 1969), 25.
Lehmann-Haupt, Christopher. *New York Times*, March 31, 1969, p. 35.
Listener, 83 (March 19, 1970), 382.
Martinetti, Ronald. *Wall Street Journal*, June 24, 1969, p. 769.
Menken, Nancy. *Library Journal*, 94 (December 15, 1969), 4624.
National Observer, 8 (June 30, 1969), 17.
Oates, Joyce Carol. *Hudson Review*, 22 (Fall 1969), 535–536.
O'Connell, Shaun. *American Scholar*, 38 (Autumn 1969), 718–722.
Reed, John. *Christian Science Monitor*, April 17, 1969, p. 15.
Richardson, Jack. *New York Review of Books*, 15 (July 2, 1970), 7–8.
Robinson, William C. *Library Journal*, 94 (March 1, 1969), 1021.
Rowley, Peter. *Nation*, 208 (June 9, 1969), 736.
Scholes, Robert. *New York Times Book Review*, April 6, 1969, pp. 1, 23.
Schwartz, Joseph. *Milwaukee Journal*, May 4, 1969, Sec. 5, p. 4.
Sheed, Wilfrid. *Commonweal*, 91 (December 5, 1969), 319.
———. *Life*, 66 (March 21, 1969), 9.
Sokolov, Raymond A. *Newsweek*, 73 (April 14, 1969), 122, 124.
Stern, Daniel. *Book World*, April 13, 1969, p. 7.
Time, 93 (April 11, 1969), 106.
Times (London) *Literary Supplement*, March 26, 1970, p. 329.
Tube, Henry. *Spectator*, 224 (March 21, 1970), 387.

Vanderbilt, Kermit. *Nation*, 209 (December 17, 1969), 663.
Wolff, Geoffrey, *Newsweek*, 74 (December 22, 1969), 98.

Happy Birthday, Wanda June

Adams, Phoebe. *Atlantic*, 228 (October 1971), 136.
Best Sellers, 31 (March 1, 1972), 547.
Booklist, 68 (January 1, 1972), 378, and 68 (January 15, 1972), 431.
Buck, Richard M. *Library Journal*, 96 (October 1, 1973), 3155.
Canby, Vincent. *New York Times*, December 10, 1971, p. 45.
Choice, 9 (July–August 1972), 667.
Clurman, Harold. *Nation*, 211 (October 26, 1970), 414.
Dun's Review, Fall 1973, p. 81.
Kauffmann, Stanley. *New Republic*, 163 (November 7, 1970), 33.
Kerr, Walter. *New York Times*, October 18, 1970, Sec. 2, pp. 1, 18.
Kroll, Jack. *Newsweek*, 76 (October 19, 1973), 123.
Novick, Julius. *Village Voice*, October 15, 1970, pp. 52, 54.
Observer, July 15, 1973, p. 33.
Oliver, Edith. *New Yorker*, 46 (October 17, 1970), 143–144.
Rendle, Adrian. *Drama*, Fall 1973, pp. 84–85.
Sainer, Arthur. *Village Voice*, October 15, 1970, pp. 53, 63.
Time, 96 (October 19, 1970), 74.
Times (London) *Literary Supplement*, July 20, 1973, p. 825.
Weales, Gerald. *Commonweal*, 93 (November 27, 1970), 221–222.

Between Time and Timbuktu

Book World, 7 (April 29, 1973), 14.
Choice, 10 (September 1973), 964.
"Cyclops" (John Leonard). *Life*, 72 (March 17, 1972), 16.
Wood, Michael. *New York Review of Books*, 20 (May 31, 1973), 23–25.
Psychology Today, 7 (June 1973), 102.

Breakfast of Champions

Ahrold, Robbin. *Library Journal*, 98 (April 15, 1973), 1311.
Bannon, Barbara. *Publishers Weekly*, 203 (March 19, 1973), 60.

Bishop, Mary B. *Connecticut Magazine*, July–August 1973, p. 10.
Booklist, 69 (April 15, 1973), 792.
Books & Bookmen, 19 (November 1973), 104.
Book World, June 2, 1974, p. 4.
Burns, Martin. *Critic*, 32 (September 1973), 74–76.
Christian Century, 92 (May 14, 1975), 502.
Choice, 10 (November 1973), 1391.
Commonweal, 99 (December 7, 1973), 272.
Economist, 248 (July 28, 1973), 106–107.
Ellison, Harlan. *Fantasy and Science Fiction*, January 1974, pp. 35–41.
Fuller, Edmund. *Wall Street Journal*, 181 (June 12, 1973), 26.
Gitlin, Todd. *Psychology Today*, 7 (September 1973), 22, 24.
Hand, Judson. *New York Daily News/Leisure*, April 29, 1973, p. 20.
Heath, Susan. *World*, 2 (June 19, 1973), 42.
Hill, Will B. *America*, 129 (November 17, 1973), 382.
Horwitz, Carey. *Library Journal*, 98 (February 1, 1973), 445.
Jordan, Clive. *New Statesman*, 86 (July 13, 1973), 56.
Kirkus, 41 (March 1, 1973), 274.
Klinkowitz, Jerome. *North American Review*, 258 (Fall 1973), 69–73.
Kosek, Steven. *Chicago Sun-Times Book Week*, May 13, 1973, p. 1.
Lehmann-Haupt, Christopher. *New York Times*, May 2, 1973, p. 43.
Library Journal, 98 (February 1, 1973), 445.
Listener, 90 (July 26, 1973), 125.
McInerney, J. M. *Best Sellers*, 33 (July 15, 1973), 193.
Mudrick, Marvin. *Hudson Review*, 26 (Fall 1973), 545–547.
National Observer, 12 (May 26, 1973), 21.
New York Times Book Review, December 2, 1973, p. 76, and May 12, 1974, p. 34.
New Yorker, 49 (May 26, 1973), 146.
Oberdeck, S. K. *Book World*, May 13, 1973, p. 2.
Observer, July 15, 1973, p. 33.

O'Hara, J. D. *New Republic*, 168 (May 12, 1973), 26–28.
Palmer, Tony. *Spectator*, 231 (July 21, 1973), 85–86.
Playboy, 20 (June 1973), 24.
Prescott, Peter S. *Newsweek*, 81 (May 14, 1973), 114, 118.
Sayre, Nora. *New York Times Book Review*, May 13, 1973, pp. 3–4.
Stade, George. *Harper's*, 246 (May 1973), 86–90, 94–95.
Stevick, Philip. *Partisan Review*, 41 (Summer 1974), 302–304.
Stinnett, Caskie. *Travel & Leisure*, 3 (June–July 1973), 17.
Times (London) *Literary Supplement*, July 20, 1973, p. 825.
Wood, Michael. *New York Review of Books*, 20 (May 31, 1973), 23–25.

Wampeters, Foma & Granfalloons

Balakian, Nona. *New York Times Book Review*, August 23, 1974, p. 27.
Best Sellers, 34 (July 1, 1974), 176.
Booklist, 70 (July 1, 1974), 1176.
Book World, December 8, 1974, p. 5, and June 29, 1975, p. 4.
Christian Science Monitor, July 24, 1974, p. 10.
Cosgrave, Mary Silva. *Horn Book*, 50 (October 1974), 160.
Hendin, Josephine. *Harper's*, 249 (July 1974), 83–87.
Hills, Rust. *Esquire*, November 1974, p. 19.
Kosek, Steven. *National Review*, 26 (July 5, 1974), 771.
Lhamon, W. T., Jr. *New Republic*, 170 (June 1, 1974), 27–28.
Library Journal, 99 (September 15, 1974), 2310.
National Observer, 13 (June 29, 1974), 19.
Observer, April 6, 1975, p. 30.
Psychology Today, 8 (October 1974), 144.
Publishers Weekly, 205 (March 25, 1974), 54.
Skow, John. *Time*, 103 (June 3, 1974), 77.
Stuttaford, Genevieve. *Publishers Weekly*, 207 (February 17, 1975), 82.
Theroux, Paul. *New Statesman*, 89 (April 4, 1975), 452–453.
Times (London) *Literary Supplement*, April 11, 1975, p. 387.
Wilson Library Bulletin, 49 (September 1974), 81.

Slapstick

Auchincloss, Eve. *Book World*, August 29, 1976, p. 1.

Bannon, Barbara. *Publishers Weekly*, 210 (July 26, 1976), 69.

Book World, August 29, 1976, p. 1.

Clemons, Walter. *Newsweek*, 88 (October 4, 1976), 93–94.

Epstein, Seymour. *Chicago Tribune Book World*, October 10, 1976, p. 1.

Kirkus, 44 (August 1, 1976), 858, and 44 (August 15, 1976), 912.

Klinkowitz, Jerome. *New Republic*, 175 (September 25, 1976), 40–41.

Kurz, Ron. *Harper's Bookletter*, 3 (October 11, 1976), 8–9.

LeClair, Thomas. *Saturday Review*, 59 (October 16, 1976), 28.

Mason, Michael. *Times* (London) *Literary Supplement*, November 5, 1976, p. 1385.

Publishers Weekly, 210 (July 26, 1976), 69.

Rackstraw, Loree. *North American Review*, 261 (Winter 1976), 63–64.

Sale, Roger. *New York Times Book Review*, October 3, 1976, pp. 3, 20.

Sheppard, R. Z. *Time*, 105 (October 25, 1976), 84.

Updike, John. *New Yorker*, 52 (October 25, 1976), 182–190.

APPENDIX

VONNEGUT ABROAD

Jerome Klinkowitz

A Note on Vonnegut in Europe

Kurt Vonnegut published his first novel outside of the United States in 1953: the British Macmillan edition of *Player Piano*. Macmillan is an old, well-established, and generally conservative house, just like Vonnegut's American publisher at the time, Charles Scribner's Sons, and each seems an unlikely place for an innovative writer to begin his career. Research by Asa Pieratt has shown that these first editions of *Player Piano* met similar fortunes: Each had relatively small printings (3,000 in England, 7,600 in the U.S.), neither sold well (at least 1,000 of the British edition were returned and pulped), and today the Macmillan company cannot locate a copy of their 1953 edition, "not even in the British Museum." Looking back on his first publishing experience, Vonnegut has remarked that *Player Piano* "sold well only in

Schenectady," the town he had parodied into "Ilium, New York." In England there were even fewer reviews than in the U.S., a much smaller paperback edition, and no reputation to build on for subsequent novels. The Italian, Russian, and German editions of Vonnegut's first novel did not appear until the mid-1960s, when his American popular reputation had already been established. So in 1953, for all practical purposes, Vonnegut's international reputation had not yet begun.

It is an irony of Vonnegut's career, however, that the nature of his foreign publication may have influenced his ultimate critical reception at home. For one, Britain and the European countries offered no mass market ready to turn such early efforts as *Player Piano, The Sirens of Titan,* and *Mother Night* into science fiction or grossly exploitative paperbacks. Moreover, European readers were not seeing Vonnegut support himself as a writer of formula fiction for the slick magazines and occasional science-fiction journals. His foreign reputation may have been long in coming, but when it did, it was on the basis of his several novels, making Kurt Vonnegut a far less controversial entrant into the mainstream of major writers.

Today Vonnegut is published in every European language. Most of his novels have been translated into Japanese, and in 1970 his work was pirated in a Hong Kong edition, the dubious international honor which signals that an American author has arrived. Graduate theses on his fiction have been written in European universities from Paris to Moscow, and Vonnegut remains especially popular among academic circles in Hungary, Czechoslovakia, and Poland. In a thesis presented to the Uniwersytet Marii Curie-Skłowskiej in Lublin, Jerzy Kutnik suggests that Vonnegut's critical acceptance in Europe actually predated his similar success at home, and that "it may have been his international fame which made further neglect impossible." Major essays on Vonnegut appeared in Italy (1966), Russia (1967), and England (1969), all predating the surge of American academic criticism, which did not begin until 1971. A British journal, *Summary*, was the first to devote extended treatment to Vonnegut's fiction.

In simple appearance, the foreign editions of Vonnegut's novels are more handsome and respectable than the shabby paperback originals one finds of *The Sirens of Titan*, *Canary in a Cat House*, and *Mother Night*. In England Vonnegut is now published by the highly prestigious firm of Jonathan Cape, a corporate descendant of the British-American partnership which published William Faulkner in the 1930s. The Danish first edition of *Cat's Cradle* totaled 8,000 copies—2,000 more than the American edition, and in a much smaller country. The Polish series which includes *Slaughterhouse-Five* lists Vonnegut as its only American author, sharing company with Borges, Mishima, and Giraudoux. The Czech edition of this same novel places it in the tradition of works by Remarque, Aldington, and Anouilh. Only the Hungarian publishers put Vonnegut in the company of such contemporaries as Roth, Kesey, and Malamud. The others list his works among the classics.

Donald M. Fiene

Kurt Vonnegut as an American Dissident: His Popularity in the Soviet Union and His Affinities with Russian Literature

The appearance in 1970 of Vonnegut's *Slaughterhouse-Five* and *Cat's Cradle* in Russian translation was a major literary event in the Soviet Union. Virtually overnight, Vonnegut became the most popular contemporary American writer in the USSR, and thousands of Russians became convinced that they were members of Vonnegut's karass—a karass being one of the many special teams, according to Bokonon, the religious sage of *Cat's Cradle*, into which all humanity is organized. These teams "do God's will without ever discovering what they are doing," says Bokonon, adding that "if you find your life tangled up with somebody else's life for no very logical reason, that person may be a member of your karass." A karass ignores national, institutional, occupational, familial, and class boundaries. "It is as free-form as an amoeba." As Bokonon's "Fifty-Third Calypso" has it:

Oh, a sleeping drunkard
Up in Central Park,
And a lion-hunter
In the jungle dark,
And a Chinese dentist,
And a British queen—
All fit together
In the same machine.
Nice, nice, very nice;
Nice, nice, very nice;
Nice, nice, very nice—
So many different people
In the same device. [CC, page 14][1]

On a trip to the Soviet Union in December of 1975, I found that almost every educated Russian I met was a Vonnegut fan, and all were quite beguiled by Vonnegut's idea of the karass. One journalist in his thirties solemnly assured me that he just *knew* he and Vonnegut were in the same karass. He dreamed of the time he might meet the author and inform him of this fact. On another occasion, a young woman instructor from Moscow University suggested meeting her for lunch at the Saturn tea shop in downtown Moscow because it suggested the setting of *The Sirens of Titan* and was thus an appropriate meeting place for those, like herself, who aspired to membership in Vonnegut's karass. Also during that December, everyone was seeking tickets for the opening at the Soviet Army Theater of *Stranstviia Billi Piligrima (The Wanderings of Billy Pilgrim)*—a new play based on the translation of *Slaughterhouse-Five* and itself destined to be one of the important cultural events of the 1976 season.[2]

Actually, Vonnegut had been published in the Soviet

Union as early as 1967, when a mediocre translation of *Player Piano* attracting little critical attention (for all its 200,000 copies) appeared in a science-fiction series.[3] *Cat's Cradle* and *Slaughterhouse-Five*, however, enjoyed the advantage of having been translated by Raisa Rait-Kovalëva—one of the Soviet Union's most experienced translators. Mme. Rait-Kovalëva, or Rita Rait, as she is known to friends, was already seventy years old when she first read Vonnegut, "fell in love with him," in her words, and gave him her full attention as a translator. Ten years earlier she had awarded J. D. Salinger instant popularity in the USSR with her superb translation of *The Catcher in the Rye*. Her skill at finding vivid Russian equivalents for the colorful cursing and slangy dialogue of contemporary American fiction is all the more remarkable considering that she has never visited the United States. She once told me in a letter that she had learned most of her American English from U.S. merchant marines and sailors in a hospital in Murmansk, where she had worked as a medical assistant during the war. Her adventurous life had included a period of doing research on physiology with Dr. Ivan Pavlov, giving German lessons to Vladimir Mayakovsky, and falling in love with the young poet Boris Pasternak. Eventually settling on literary translation as her primary vocation, she translated Mark Twain, Sinclair Lewis, Ernest Hemingway, John Galsworthy, Graham Greene, and dozens of other writers into Russian. She was the first to translate Faulkner into Russian—and the first to translate Kafka. Also from the German, she translated Heinrich Böll. And from the French, Nathalie Sarraute. In short, she is a master translator. Certainly she has played an important role in establishing Vonnegut's popularity in the Soviet Union.

Vonnegut himself has acknowledged her role—chiefly by making her one of his closest friends. They met in 1972, after Vonnegut had accepted Mme. Rait's invitation to visit her in Paris, where she was engaged for several weeks doing research on a book. He had sent her a gallant telegram, offering to meet her in any country she cared to name[4]—thereby following his own invented Bokononist philosophy of "agreeing gaily to go anywhere" that anyone suggests, because "peculiar travel suggestions are dancing lessons from God" (CC, page 59). The meeting took place on October 28, 1972. Writer and translator became friends. It was after that meeting that Vonnegut published his open letter in the *New York Times Book Review* entitled "Invite Rita Rait to America!"[5] In October of 1974 he went to the Soviet Union for a week, entirely on his own initiative, chiefly with the aim of visiting Rita Rait and meeting her friends, among them many writers and editors.[6] During my own visit to Moscow in 1975, Mme. Rait showed me a copy of *Cat's Cradle* that Vonnegut had autographed for her. "For Rita Rait," he had written, "the only person I have ever admitted was a member of my karass."

Vonnegut had occasion to defend Mme. Rait in 1976, when a Moscow correspondent for the *New York Times*, David Shipler, complained that the Russian dramatization of *Slaughterhouse-Five* was excessively critical of the Vietnam War. Asked about this in New York, Vonnegut was quoted by the *Times* as saying: "One of my closest friends, Rita Rait, . . . translated my novel. She then worked closely with the authors and director [of the play]. I have trust in her judgment in this matter and continue to do so. She is one of my favorite translators." Vonnegut went on to observe: "I would say that what's remarkable about this production is that its theme deals with pacifism. The Soviet [Union] has been reluctant to put on such plays, which makes the occasion most noteworthy."[7] He might have added or explained that it was especially its sympathy for *German* victims of the war that made the play's appearance in the Soviet Union—in particular, in the Soviet Army Theater—not only noteworthy but unique.

In an article on Vonnegut published in 1974, Mme. Rait declared that her work in translating *Slaughterhouse-Five* and *Cat's Cradle* was one of the most memorable experiences of her long life of literary labor.[8] She did not stop with these two works, however, but went on to translate *Breakfast of Champions* and a half dozen or so of the stories from *Welcome to the Monkey House.* She is now (at the age of seventy-nine) engaged in translating *God Bless You, Mr. Rosewater* for a one-volume edition (scheduled for publication in 1978) of four Vonnegut novels translated by her. For such a book to appear in the Soviet Union is an extraordinary, almost unheard-of, tribute to a contemporary foreign author. In September of 1976 Mme. Rait's translation of the "Prologue" to *Slapstick* was published in the journal *Literaturnaia gazeta*; she will probably translate the entire novel as soon as copyright negotiations with the American publisher are completed.

Until recently, Mme. Rait had few competitors in translating Vonnegut, except for the stories in *Welcome to the Monkey House*. Altogether, a dozen of these have been translated, some more than once, by five or six different translators—including Mme. Rait's daughter, Margarita Kovalëva. Vonnegut has quite a number of science-fiction fans in the Soviet Union who like these stories better than the novels. Early in 1976 a translation of *God Bless You, Mr. Rosewater* by Irina Razumovskaia and Svetlana Samostrelova (not altogether successful, in Mme. Rait's opinion) was published in the journal *Avrora*. Later in the year, *Happy Birthday, Wanda June* was published in an Estonian translation by Valda V. Raud, who had also translated *Slaughterhouse-Five* into Estonian in 1971. (*Cat's Cradle* appeared in a Latvian edition in 1973 and has no doubt by now appeared in other Soviet languages as well.) In November of 1976 *Happy Birthday, Wanda June* had its premiere performance on the stage of the Tallinn Drama Theater in Estonia. It has been a great success. Just now a Russian version of that play in Mme. Rait's translation is being read by the distinguished Leningrad theater director G. Tovstonogov. One may hope that he will produce the play. *Wanda June* has not yet been published in Russian, nor have the novels *Mother Night* and *The Sirens of Titan*—though these seem to have been fairly widely read in English.

Vonnegut's reception in the Soviet Union by reviewers and literary critics, most of whom make a special point of mentioning Mme. Rait's skill as a translator, has been uniformly positive. None dissent from the view that Vonnegut is a master novelist—at the very least, the best contemporary writer of satire in America. This is remarkable, since ordinarily there is a rather sharp disparity in the views of the most conservative and most liberal Soviet critics, especially where the touchy problem of American literature is concerned. Vonnegut's Soviet critics are also united in recognizing the author's genuinely savage attack on Western capitalism and the American way of life. The most conservative critics, such as Iakov El'sberg, do not see very far past this conclusion and are quick to categorize Vonnegut as a critical realist, who, in seeking a better future based on the realization of humanistic ideals, is "objectively influenced by socialist ideas and the principles of socialist realism."[9] The more liberal critics emphasize the moral rather than the political basis for Vonnegut's satire, and even mention that Vonnegut is not a committed socialist. But all see clearly what many American critics have not bothered to examine closely, in their quickness to categorize Vonnegut (not necessarily maliciously) as a universal nihilist or black humorist—classifications, incidentally, that no Soviet critic subscribes to. What the Soviet critics all see is Vonnegut's contempt for specifically *American* values, epitomized in the following vivid denunciation in the opening chapter of *God Bless You, Mr. Rosewater* and quoted by M. O. Mendel'son in his book *Amerikanskaia satiricheskaia proza XX veka* (*American Satirical Prose of the Twentieth Century*) (1972), page 317:

> Thus did a handful of rapacious citizens come to control all that was worth controlling in America. Thus was the savage and stupid and entirely inappropriate and unnecessary and humorless American class system created. Honest, industrious, peaceful citizens were classed as bloodsuckers, if they asked to be paid a living wage. And they saw that praise was reserved henceforth for those who devised means of getting paid enormously for committing crimes against which no laws had been passed. Thus the American dream turned belly up, turned green, bobbed to the scummy surface of cupidity unlimited, filled with gas, went *bang* in the noonday sun. [*GB*, page 21]

Vonnegut is even more sardonic with his hailstorm of anti-American gibes in the opening chapter of *Breakfast of Champions*. For instance: "There were one quardrillion nations in the Universe, but the nation Dwayne Hoover and Kilgore Trout belonged to was the only one with a national anthem which was gibberish sprinkled with question marks" (page 8). Of more interest to Soviet critics was the following passage from *Breakfast of Champions:*

> A lot of people on the wrecked planet were *Communists*. They had a theory that what was left of the planet should be shared more or less equally among all the people, who hadn't asked to come to a wrecked planet in the first place. Meanwhile, more babies were arriving all the time—kicking and screaming, yelling for milk.

In some places people would actually try to eat mud or suck on gravel while babies were being born just a few feet away.

And so on.

Dwayne Hoover's and Kilgore Trout's country, where there was still plenty of everything, was opposed to Communism. It didn't think that Earthlings who had a lot should share it with others unless they really wanted to, and most of them didn't want to.

So they didn't have to.

Everybody in America was supposed to grab whatever he could and hold on to it. Some Americans were very good at grabbing and holding, were fabulously well-to-do. Others couldn't get their hands on doodley-squat. [*BC*, pages 12–13]

(M. O. Mendel'son refers to this passage in an article in *Novyi Mir* in August of 1975.)

Statements such as these in the author's own voice, coupled with not-infrequent negative reviews in the American press, provide considerable justification for the classification of Vonnegut by several of his Soviet reviewers as a genuine dissident writer. A Soviet critic named Aleksandr Borshchagovsky, reviewing *Slaughterhouse-Five* (in translation), took sharp issue with Jack Richardson's review of the same book in the *New York Review of Books* for July 2, 1970. Richardson was not merely critical of Vonnegut in that review, but contemptuous. "*Slaughterhouse-Five*," he wrote, "remains, when all its wearisome inventiveness is done, one of the most unsurprisingly self-indulgent little books ever to work so hard at being selfless and memorable." The reviewer's almost willful indifference to the moral issues raised in the novel could well have seemed to the Soviet critic a perfect example of that American indifference to suffering that characterized the dogged pursuit of the war in Vietnam and has been the principal target of Vonnegut's satire as well. This sort of thing combined with Vonnegut's inadvertent role as a kind of underground cult author during the first two decades of his writing career allows him to be seen as the closest thing to an American counterpart to Solzhenitsyn.

In an interview broadcast in Russian over Voice of America radio in January of 1976, Vonnegut tried to explain to his Soviet listeners why it was mostly the dissident writers from the USSR who were read by Americans.[10] After all, he said, the Soviet Union pays the most attention to our dissidents—among whom he was proud to number himself. At least, he said, he hardly regarded himself as a captive of the CIA, and he had certainly said terrible things about his government.[11] Anyway, he concluded, there's nothing strange in this phenomenon at all: Dissident writers are *always* more interesting. In an interview in 1970, incidentally, he made the offhand remark that he thought Alexander Solzhenitsyn was the greatest living writer.[12] In general, despite his knowledge of his popularity in the Soviet Union, he has continued to take a firm stand against Soviet treatment of dissident writers and other intellectuals. Both as a member of the international writers' society, P.E.N. (the American center of which he has been a vice-president since 1972), and as a private person, Vonnegut has sent a half dozen or more letters and cables to the Writers' Union in Moscow since 1970, protesting the harassment of Solzhenitsyn and other dissident writers. He had sent one such cable, asking that the rights of Andrei Amalrik be protected, during the period when the play based on *Slaughterhouse-Five* was in rehearsal in Moscow. Later he was gloomily convinced that his action had caused the production to be canceled.[13] When it was finally staged anyway—and in the Soviet Army Theater besides—he was understandably elated. In his congratulatory telegram to the director and cast, he wrote: "Nothing has made me so happy and proud. Place a chair in the wings for my soul on opening night—my body must remain here. The Soviet Army saved my life in 1945, now they give me a theater. If I could enlist I would. Much love to you, my brothers and sisters in the arts. [Signed] Private Vonnegut, formerly U.S. Infantry, serial number 12102964."[14] An astonishing telegram in view of the pacifist, antimilitarist theme of *Slaughterhouse-Five*—yet altogether understandable and delightful.

What all this means, of course, is that Vonnegut is ambivalent in his attitude toward that complex entity known as the Soviet Union—as must be any thoughtful person. Even the persecution of dissident writers in the USSR, while reprehensible, still has something to be said for it; at least writers are taken seriously there. As Vonnegut ruefully remarked at a P.E.N. conference in Sweden in 1973, American journalists and teachers may be jailed for their views, but never novelists: "Fiction is harmless in the U.S."[15] Vonnegut has often expressed his frustration at not being taken seriously as a writer in America, and he takes a very Russian view of what the role of a writer should be. In answer to an interviewer's question, "Why do you write?" he replied (in 1973): "My motives are political. I agree with Stalin and Hitler and Mussolini that the writer should serve his society. I differ with dictators as to *how* writers should serve. Mainly, I think they should be—and biologically *have* to be—agents of change. For the better, we hope" (*WFG*, page 237). Later in that same interview, when asked if he considered himself a radical in any sense, Vonnegut answered: "No, because everything I believe I was taught in junior civics during the Great Depression . . . I simply never unlearned junior civics. I still believe in it. I got a very good grade" (*WFG*, pages 274–275). And in Vonnegut's novel *Mother Night*, the narrator, when asked accusingly, "You hate America, don't you?" replies: "That would be as silly as loving it . . . It's impossible for me to get emotional about it, because real estate doesn't interest me. It's no doubt a great flaw in my personality, but I can't think in terms of boundaries" (*MN*, page 100).

The sum of all these views is that while Vonnegut may not be a true political radical, he is very much a radical humanist. And the values he expresses in his novels are deeply felt by him. On this point, too, virtually all of Vonnegut's Soviet critics are in agreement. Again and again they refer to his *humanity*, to his genuine compassion for the insulted and injured, the destitute, the ignorant, and the unemployed—for the unlovable and bewildered souls who can only cry out absurdly, "What are people for?" They love to quote his aphorisms: "People can use all the uncritical love they can get" (*GB*, page 213); "God damn it, you've got to be kind" (*GB*, page 110); "Pretend to be good always, and even God will be fooled" (*GB*, page 203). Vonnegut's laughter they see as laughter through tears (as they see Gogol's), and behind his most cynical sarcasm they hear a cry of anguish. They see him as a writer who has suffered in the Russian kenotic tradition. "*De profundis*," writes A. Zverev in his review of *Boinia nomer piat'* (*Slaughterhouse-Five*), "—a cry carried up from the depths of hell—that is the sensation remaining after reading Vonnegut's book" (page 267).

While Soviet critics are united with Vonnegut in condemning war for all societies everywhere, they are inclined to view the bulk of his social satire as applying especially to America. And the satire in *Player Piano*, insists Bestuzhev-Lada in his foreword to the translation, is directed *only* at the United States; he thus conveniently ignores the fact, or is oblivious of it, that Soviet Marxism is no less appalled at man's sinful incompetence, no less dedicated to the Promethean idea of man's perfectibility—Vonnegut's primary target in that novel—than American industrial capitalism. Most Soviet critics, too, are loath to find in San Lorenzo, the island dictatorship of *Cat's Cradle,* anything other than a satire on capitalist exploitation. This attitude does not always lead to shallow, propagandistic commentary, however. For instance, V. Skordenko concludes his afterword to the translation of *Cat's Cradle* as follows: "Kurt Vonnegut has shown us the world in which he lives and which he knows well. He has done this with the courage of a genuine patriot of a great country, with the dignity of a human being—an inhabitant of our rather small planet, and with the straightforwardness of a true artist."

The only Russian critic who seems to me to be truly sensitive to Vonnegut's real point of view in *Cat's Cradle,* however, is A. Zverev—in a thirty-five page article devoted exclusively to Vonnegut's novels, in the February 1975 issue of *Voprosy literatury.* When he first mentions *Cat's Cradle* (page 33), he finds it instructive to quote the "Fourteenth Book" of Bokonon, which is entitled: "What Can a Thoughtful Man Hope for Mankind on Earth, Given the Experience of the Past Million Years?" The book consists of only one word: "Nothing" (CC page 199). Zverev subsequently shows (pages 46 ff.) that Vonnegut's philosophy does not entail striving after some perfect kingdom for mankind where only good prevails. Zverev cites Bokonon's theory of "Dynamic Tension": "his sense of a priceless equilibrium between good and evil. . . . It was the belief of Bokonon that good [that is, workable] societies could be built only by pitting good against evil, and by keeping the tension between the two high at all times" (CC page 90). It is precisely this "dynamic tension" (a term Vonnegut borrowed from Charles Atlas) that is the basis for the author's world view, concludes Zverev, and he goes on to show that it is the informing principle of all of Vonnegut's major fiction. Although Zverev refrains from applying Vonnegut's insight to the Soviet Union, it is clear that he sees Bokononism as a philosophy suited to all human societies, and that however ironic the pronouncements of Bokonon seem to be at times, they nevertheless constitute a real rather than a merely parodistic expression of Vonnegut's understanding of humanity. Zverev is thus able to demonstrate that the failure of the Luddite uprising in *Player Piano* and the cessation of Eliot Rosewater's attempt to love the unlovable are not necessarily pessimistic, but instead fulfill "Vonnegut's artistic requirement, that in the ocean of soulless rationalism there must be found at least one lonely island of true humanity" (page 49). It is the effort, however short-lived, to battle evil that counts, rather than the establishment of a realm of ultimate Good—which is impossible by definition anyway.

Although Zverev does not, for instance, comment on how the arbitrary outlawing of Bokononism in San Lorenzo resembles the attitude of Stalin toward the Russian Orthodox Church, surely he perceives the ironic connection—as must virtually every sensitive and intelligent Soviet citizen who reads *Cat's Cradle.* One reason for Vonnegut's popularity in the Soviet Union is that the average reader there is able to identify with Vonnegut's fictional victims of manipulative rulers and heartless, ubiquitous bureaucracies—and to feel that Vonnegut is his spokesman.[16] He feels that Vonnegut does not merely advocate a kind of Dostoevskian charity, but is in some sense a suffering victim himself. In fact, it is my impression that Vonnegut must seem to Russian readers to be almost a Russian writer, that they recognize in his prose many of the familiar features of classical Russian literature, and that this, too, helps account for his extraordinary popularity in the USSR.

Vonnegut's Russian critics do not explore this feature of his work systematically, but they do mention him with Saltykov-Shchedrin as a master satirist and refer to a few of the more obvious parallels with Gogol.[17] N. Gubko notes a connection between Dostoevsky's "Dream of a Queer Fellow" (in which the narrator dreams of a visit to another planet) and Billy Pilgrim's time-tripping to Tralfamadore, in that the point of departure for both is a rejection of unjust life on Earth.[18] Vonnegut himself acknowledges the Russian source of *Player Piano:* "I cheerfully ripped off the plot of *Brave New World,* whose plot had been cheerfully ripped off from Eugene Zamiatin's *We*" (*WFG*, page 261). S. Vishnevsky, in his commentary on *Breakfast of Champions,* notes Vonnegut's technique in that novel of "making strange" the common objects he draws and describes. That is, he describes a revolver, for instance, as though it were unfamiliar to the reader, calling it "a tool whose only purpose was to make holes in human beings" (*BC*, page 49). Though Vishnevsky does not use the term *ostraenie,* it is clear that he has in mind that very literary term applied by the formalist Viktor Shklovsky especially to the literary style of L. N. Tolstoy. "Tolstoy's works, Shklovsky observed astutely, abound in passages where the author 'refuses to recognize' . . . familiar objects and describes them as if they were seen for the first time. Thus, while describing in *War and Peace* an opera performance, he refers to the setting as 'pieces of painted cardboard' . . ."[19] Because Vonnegut uses *ostranenie* as a vehicle for social criticism, just as Tolstoy did, he may be said in that respect to have a recognizable link with that author. (He is not, however, a "fox," in Isaiah Berlin's use of that term, but rather more of a hedgehog, like Dostoevsky.) In a quite different way, a Vonnegut novel such as *God Bless You, Mr. Rosewater* may be seen as a thematic counterpart to Gorky's "Lower Depths," wherein Eliot Rosewater and Luka both feel a humanistic need to tell compassionate lies to souls in distress—to try "to love people who have no use" (*GB* page 210). And in both works there exists a kind of "dynamic tension" between that laudable aim and the equally human necessity of speaking the truth, whatever the cost. (A similar tension around this theme is to be found in *The Sirens of Titan* with respect to "Unk" or Malachi Constant.) Vonnegut's penchant for inventing new religions might also be regarded as a tentative counterpart to Gorky's *bogostroitel'stvo* or "God-building." Aside from all this, Vonnegut is a man possessed by the messianic, the apocalyptic, the eschatological, and the chiliastic—preoccupations so obviously "Russian" in character, if we think of the course of Russian political and religious history, themes in nineteenth-century literature, and the response of early-twentieth-century Russian authors to the Revolution, that there is really no need here to cite parallels. As to why modern Russians in the USSR should feel drawn to the old-fashioned, Russian-style religious stewings of a half-demented American, I think it is almost a commonplace by now to speak of the current Russophilic spiritual revival now taking place in the USSR. In any case, Hedrick Smith, in his book *The Russians* (1976), frequently comments on this phenomenon. (And I believe that I found evidence of it myself in my own brief tour of Moscow, Leningrad, and Kiev at the end of 1975.)

So far as the question of literary influence is concerned, I somehow doubt that a genuine Russian influence can be proved in Vonnegut's case. At least, he almost never speaks of Russian authors when the question of influence comes up in interviews and the like. He has mentioned in this connection Conrad, Mark Twain, Orwell, John O'Hara, R. L. Stevenson, F. Scott Fitzgerald, H. G. Wells, H. L. Mencken, Karel Čapek, Edgar Lee Masters (his favorite American author, he once said), Céline, the radio comedians Bob Elliott and Ray Goulding, and the movie comedians Laurel and Hardy (to whom he dedicated his last novel, *Slapstick*).[20] But he has not, so far as I know, even mentioned Dostoevsky as an influence—the one Russian author who at least appears by name in several of his novels. By now, of course, in this discussion, it should be obvious that it is Fëdor Dostoevsky, of all Russian writers, with whom Vonnegut has the greatest affinity. (And this, too, may be said to have special meaning now for modern Russians, since there has been a renewed interest in this writer as the centenary of his date of death approaches, and as the new Soviet edition of his collected works appears fresh from the printing presses, volume by volume.)

Vonnegut's most memorable reference to Dostoevsky is that in *Slaughterhouse-Five,* when Eliot Rosewater says to Billy Pilgrim in the mental hospital: "[E]verything there [is] to know about life [is] in *The Brothers Karamazov* . . . But that isn't *enough* any more . . ." (*SF*, 87). This passage, together with brief quotations from Dostoevsky in *Breakfast of Champions* and *Slapstick*, indicates that Vonnegut is perhaps not so much influenced by Dostoevsky as in some way in contention with him or complementary to him.[21] That Vonnegut has at least read *The Brothers Karamazov* I ascertained by querying him in a letter, to which he courteously replied as follows: "About *The Brothers Karamazov*: it was the first book I read after becoming a civilian after WW II. My new wife (nee Jane Cox, a Phi Beta Kappa from Swarthmore) made me read it on our honeymoon in Culver, Indiana. Culver is on Lake Maxincuckee. The cottage in which we stayed had belonged to my family for three generations. It had just been sold. The new owner let us honeymoon there because he was a sentimentalist. I also painted my first picture there. It was of a chair. It was really pretty good. I have no idea what became of it."[22]

As I have already mentioned in passing, Vonnegut's writings and attitudes display certain similarities to those of Dostoevsky, regardless of any provable direct influence. For instance, to add to the list, there is the matter of Vonnegut's occasional sentimentality, so often condescendingly criticized by American book reviewers, and so often observed in Dostoevsky by a host of commentators. Second, there is the matter of Vonnegut's preoccupation with psychosis. Although Soviet critics, to a man, abhor all effort on the part of American critics to classify Vonnegut's writing as "schizophrenic," the fact remains that insanity, suicide, and despair make up a substantial element in most of Vonnegut's fiction, beginning especially with the early novel *Mother Night*.[23] And there is also that widely quoted Vonnegut aphorism from an early interview: "A writer is a person who makes his living from his mental disease." Dostoevsky might have said the same in a rare jocular moment. That Dostoevsky was so seldom jocular and Vonnegut so frequently so might seem to be a fair refutation of my effort to draw parallels between the two writers.[24] But few of Vonnegut's critics, American or Russian, fail to recognize that much of Vonnegut's humor is only a way of coping with horror. Vonnegut is no less serious than Dostoevsky in his quest of ultimate reality, but the discovery of cosmic absurdity by Vonnegut (in dynamic tension with "universal meaning") might perhaps be regarded by him as an effort (however halting) to transcend the limits of Dostoevsky's vision. (But if that should be judged impossible by those who worship Dostoevsky, then one need only point to *Notes from Underground* as an archetypal recognition of existentialist absurdity and a potential source for Vonnegut's lesser forays in that field.)

Another tentative similarity between Vonnegut and Dostoevsky is the tendency of both to dramatize in a single work of fiction one major idea, often exaggerating it to an extreme limit. Noting in addition the continual concern of each for basic moral questions in human relationships allows one to classify both writers as essentially philosophical novelists. Several Russians I talked with casually about Vonnegut and

Dostoevsky mentioned this similarity first of all. Perhaps the two are also alike in that neither has created many irredeemable villains. Neither can imagine a character so dark that he can't find something in common with him.

It is *The Brothers Karamazov*, however, that provides the most meaningful basis for comparing and contrasting Vonnegut and Dostoevsky. First, something more must be said about Vonnegut's assertion that everything there is to know about life is in *The Brothers Karamazov*—"but that isn't *enough* any more." Perhaps what Vonnegut has in mind here is his own sense of the new perspective of the twenty-first century, in relation to Dostoevsky's prescient vision of the twentieth. Dostoevsky's prophetic genius was sufficient for him to be able to perceive in Lobachevsky's non-Euclidean "pangeometry" the possibility of a new reality—even a reality of more than three dimensions, as Ivan Karamazov complains in his conversation with Alësha just before he narrates his "poem" about the Grand Inquisitor.[25] Ivan's rejection, "with his infinitely small Euclidean mind," of God's world is thus based not only on his revulsion at the apparent necessity of torturing children in order for ultimate harmony to be achieved, but on his dimly felt intuition of the forlornness and alienation to be experienced by Euclidean twentieth-century man—in a world where Einstein's relativistic space-time continuum is not merely a theoretical possibility, but a proven actuality with the explosion of the atom bomb over Hiroshima. Vonnegut's literary heroes look toward the twenty-first century with the same sort of trepidation (or awe) that Ivan felt in looking toward the twentieth. Vonnegut, it may be said, with his extensive education in twentieth-century science, is more or less at ease in a pseudo-spherical Lobachevskian universe where an infinite number of parallels to a line may be drawn through a point not on that line—and where the geometry of a given locality is a function of gravity. To Vonnegut, the four-dimensional space-time continuum is duck soup. What gives *him* anxiety are five-dimensional time funnels, or "chrono-synclastic infundibula," as he calls them in *The Sirens of Titan:* "places . . . where all the different kinds of truths fit together as nicely as the parts in your Daddy's solar watch" (*ST*, page 14). When Winston Niles Rumfoord runs his private space ship into the heart of an uncharted time funnel between Earth and Mars, he is transformed into a wave phenomenon pulsing in a distorted spiral with its origin in the Sun and its terminal in Betelgeuse. Whenever sun spots flare up, he gives off electrical discharges; he is finally blasted out of Vonnegut's novel by a solar explosion.

Meanwhile, the injustices that Ivan Karamazov found so unbearable still exist in God's world a century later—only now on so colossal a scale that not even Dostoevsky would have dared to predict them: not merely a few battered children now, but whole concentration camps full of them, and man-made firestorms that reduce peaceful metropolises to ashes in a matter of hours or even minutes. Like Dostoevsky's Ivan, Vonnegut has felt compelled to invent compassionate Grand Inquisitors, such as Winston Niles Rumfoord, who possess the necessary ingredients for creating spurious earthly harmony: "showmanship, a genial willingness to shed other people's blood, and a plausible new religion to introduce during the brief period of repentance and horror that usually follows bloodshed" (*ST*, page 174). Rumfoord's new Church of God the Utterly Indifferent has all the Dostoevskian requirements of miracle, mystery, and authority, and there seems little doubt that Vonnegut was aware here that he was composing a variation on Dostoevsky's original theme. He even adds the ironic touch of making Rumfoord the manipulated victim of an even higher dimensional order—the Tralfamadorian robots.

Perhaps the most crucial thing separating Dostoevsky from Vonnegut is that the essentially traditional God in which Dostoevsky himself believed is now, in a historical sense, deceased. And Vonnegut himself, moreover, was raised in his family's tradition of atheistic humanism, agnosticism—at best, Unitarianism (see *WFG*, page 240). In addition, Vonnegut's most usual tone is irreverence, as opposed to Dostoevsky's pervasive reverence, even in the midst of rebellion. Vonnegut, for instance, may give us a picture of Jesus in heaven "as just another guy playing shuffleboard"—with Adolf Hitler or anyone else up in heaven who happens to want a game (*HB*, page 136). He wears a blue-and-gold warm-up jacket with *Pontius Pilate Athletic Club* written on the back. Nevertheless, despite this rampant demythologization of Christianity, it is impossible to say that Vonnegut is truly irreligious. At any rate, as the narrator of *Cat's Cradle* warns his readers: "Anyone unable to understand how a useful religion can be founded on lies will not understand this book either" (*CC*, page 16). Those who think they understand Vonnegut find him to be religious. Looking at Vonnegut in relationship to Dostoevsky, we may say that Dostoevsky was a believer who was able to feel in the depths of his being the despair of the atheist, while Vonnegut is a despairing atheist who is able to feel in the depths of his soul the life-saving faith of the believer. The difference is significant, yet the "dynamic tension" remains much the same, so that Vonnegut has a "Dostoevskian feel" without being a mere imitator of Dostoevsky. The reason the difference is significant, though, is that Vonnegut's religion without God must confront Ivan Karamazov's conclusion that "if God does not exist, then all is lawful." Vonnegut's literary inventions represent a continuous effort to prove Dostoevsky wrong—to prove that moral good can exist without God. Vonnegut the moralist seeks in all his works to instruct his readers in love for the least of men and for all men. He uses twenty-first-century parables to teach Americans, Russians, and Germans that we are all responsible to all for all. But in that message he is *exactly* like Dostoevsky.

By way of concluding this survey of Vonnegut's affinities with Russian literature and the Soviet Union, I would like to mention an interesting coincidence. Fëdor Dostoevsky was born on October 30, 1821, old style; corrected for calendar error, that date becomes November 11, 1821. Kurt Vonnegut was also born on November 11, exactly one century and one year later, in 1922. I hasten to add that I discovered this coincidence only after I had supposed a Dostoevskian influence on Vonnegut.[26] And Vonnegut himself was unaware of it until 1972 or thereabouts.[27] So obviously this accident can have no rational significance. Vonnegut himself teaches us as much in Rumfoord's religion of God the Utterly Indifferent. Yet what a temptation to see in these dates the possibility of a Buddhistic reincarnation—or at the very least a Bokononist proof that Dostoevsky and Vonnegut are in the same karass. But we must resist that temptation and be content just to experience the resulting dynamic tension.

However, there is nothing to keep us from whispering, "Busy, busy, busy."

"*Busy, busy, busy* is what we Bokononists whisper whenever we think of how complicated and unpredictable the machinery of life really is" (CC, page 61).

NOTES

1. The titles of Vonnegut's books will be abbreviated in notes as follows: BC: *Breakfast of Champions*; CC: *Cat's Cradle*; GB: *God Bless You, Mr. Rosewater*; HB: *Happy Birthday, Wanda June*; MN: *Mother Night*; PP: *Player Piano*; SF: *Slaughterhouse-Five*; SS: *Slapstick*; ST: *The Sirens of Titan*; WFG:

Wampeters, Foma & Granfalloons; *WMH*: *Welcome to the Monkey House.*

2. After one year the play has had fifty performances and is still going strong.
3. For full information about translations of Vonnegut published in the Soviet Union, see the Annotated Bibliography below.
4. Quoted in Russian in R. Rait-Kovalëva, "Kanareika v shakhte," *Rovesnik*, 1 (1974), 16–19.
5. *New York Times Book Review*, January 28, 1973, page 47. Reprinted in *WFG*. Several universities responded to Vonnegut's suggestion to invite Rita Rait to America, but Mme. Rait was unable to obtain an exit visa. At the present writing (February 1977) Mme. Rait has accepted an invitation from the University of Tennessee to visit the United States in April 1977; it is not yet known whether she will receive official permission to make the trip.
6. This was Vonnegut's second trip to the Soviet Union, the first having been in 1967—a brief visit to Leningrad when Vonnegut was traveling (on a Guggenheim grant) in Eastern Europe with his friend Bernard V. O'Hare, primarily to see Dresden again. (See *SF*, pages 1 and 17.) Vonnegut published a brief report on his 1974 trip in *P.E.N.-Newsletter*, # 17 (November 1974), 1–2: "Writers, Vonnegut and the USSR." Also in that report is the text of a letter Vonnegut wrote at that time to Nikolai T. Fedorenko, editor of *Inostrannaia literatura* (*Foreign Literature*), suggesting that a scholarship fund be established to enable young American writers of modest means to travel to the Soviet Union. Vonnegut suggested that "the moneys for the fund could come from unclaimed rubles apportioned for works by American authors published in the USSR before the Soviet accession to the International Copyright Convention."
7. David Shipler, "Vonnegut's 'Slaughterhouse-Five' Staged in Moscow," *New York Times*, January 13, 1976.
8. "Kanareika v shakhte," *Rovesnik*, 1 (1974), 17.
9. See El'sberg's 1972 article in Part II of the Annotated Bibliography below.

10. See Part III of Annotated Bibliography for further information about this broadcast.
11. An interesting example of Vonnegut's political criticism outside of his novels is the following letter he wrote to the *New York Times*, published February 1, 1974: "The most serious objection to Richard M. Nixon's remaining in office is the bad example he sets for children. He is the most visible and instructive father figure we have, our most impressive teacher. What does he teach our children? To give almost nothing to charity, to cheat in money matters at every opportunity, to lie, to reject all criticism, to be indifferent to the needs of strangers, to treat laws disrespectfully, to love only close friends and relatives and sports on television, and to carpet bomb at Christmas."
12. See Bruce Cook, "When Kurt Vonnegut Talks—And He Does—The Young All Tune In," *National Observer*, October 12, 1970, p. 21.
13. Information given in a letter to me dated November 3, 1975. To offset such criticism, however, there had also been Vonnegut's friendly remarks in the spirit of U.S.-Soviet détente on the Apollo-Soyuz linkup the previous July. A reporter for *Literaturnaia gazeta* had interviewed both Vonnegut and Soviet writer Chingiz Aitmatov together in New York on that occasion. (See Gerasimov in Part II of the Annotated Bibliography.)
14. Quoted in full in Shipler's review of the play. The full text of the telegram also appears in *Moscow News*, 11 (1976), in a caption under a photograph of a scene from the play.
15. "P.E.N. Power," *Sweden Now*, 7 (3, 1973), 6–8.
16. This, of course, accounts for his popularity in the soulless bureaucratic society of America as well.
17. For instance, with the mood of the narrator at the end of Gogol's "The Story of How Ivan Ivanovich Quarreled with Ivan Nikiforovich": "Skuchno na ètom svete, gospoda [It is tedious in this world, gentlemen]."
18. Another connection between Vonnegut and Dostoevsky's "queer fellow" lies in a tentative gesture by both authors to

identify themselves with Jesus Christ. Thus, the narrator of "Dream," who may be seen as a spokesman for Dostoevsky, says at the end of his tale of how he had corrupted the paradisiacal planet—that other Earth: "I implored them to crucify me on the cross. I taught them how to make a cross. I could not kill myself, I had not the power, but I wanted to submit to torture from them, I yearned for torments, I longed that in those torments my last drop of blood should be spilled. But they only laughed at me, and at last began to think me mad" (Dostoevsky, *The Dream of a Queer Fellow and the Pushkin Speech* [London: Unwin, 1961], page 28). Vonnegut's inclination to see himself at times as a Christ figure may be deduced from his actual identification of Kilgore Trout (his confessed alter ego) as a "Jesus figure" in *God Bless You, Mr. Rosewater* ("Think of the sacrilege of a Jesus figure redeeming stamps" [page 212]). More interesting, however, is Vonnegut's drawing of his own eye with one tear hanging from its lower lid (followed by a drawing of his own face in profile, showing the eye and tear again) in the concluding pages of *Breakfast of Champions*—a self-portrait that we recognize at once in *Slapstick* when the narrator describes a leaflet of the Church of Jesus Christ the Kidnapped: "At the very top of the leaflet was a primitive picture of Jesus, standing with His Body facing forward, but with His Face in profile—like a one-eyed jack in a deck of playing cards.

"He was gagged. He was handcuffed. One ankle was shackled and chained to a ring fixed to the floor. There was a single perfect tear dangling from the lower lid of His Eye" (*SS*, page 185).

19. Victor Erlich, *Russian Formalism* (The Hague: Mouton, 1965), p. 177.
20. In addition, critics and dissertation writers have sought influences and parallels in Voltaire, Swift, Anatole France, Ring Lardner, Sinclair Lewis, Norman Mailer, William Golding, Joseph Heller, Jack London, Ray Bradbury, Isaac Asimov, Shirley Jackson, Richard Brautigan, J. P. Donleavy, John Hawkes, John Barth, Walker Percy, Ken Kesey, Stanley Elkin,

Thomas Pynchon, Peter S. Beagle, Jerzy Kosinski, Ralph Ellison, Robbe-Grillet, Jorge Luis Borges, and Gunther Grass. Such contemporaries and friends of Vonnegut's as Donald Barthelme, J. D. Salinger, John Updike, Vance Bourjaily, Hunter Thompson, and Dan Wakefield should also be mentioned. Somebody also ought to add Kafka to this list. Finally, we should not forget the references to Shakespeare in *Breakfast of Champions* and *Slapstick* and the elaborate commentary on Shakespearean parallels in Vonnegut's novels by John Updike in his long review of *Slapstick* in the *New Yorker*, October 25, 1976, pp. 182–190.

Note: Much of the information for such sweeping surveys as the above in this paper comes from *The Vonnegut Statement*, edited by Jerome Klinkowitz and John Somer (New York: Delacorte Press/Seymour Lawrence, 1973) and *Kurt Vonnegut, Jr.: A Descriptive Bibliography and Annotated Secondary Checklist*, compiled by Asa B. Pieratt and Jerome Klinkowitz (Hamden, Conn.: Archon, 1974). These books are indispensable to anyone doing research on Vonnegut. A number of Soviet critics, I have noticed, make frequent use of *The Vonnegut Statement* (not always with acknowledgment).

21. The quotation from Dostoevsky in *Breakfast of Champions* is on p. 228 (with Vonnegut narrating in his own voice): " 'It's all like an ocean!' cried Dostoevski. I say it's all like cellophane." (*The Brothers Karamazov*, Book VI, Chapter III, Section g.)

The quotation in *Slapstick* is on p. 90 (with Wilbur Swain, a spokesman for Vonnegut, narrating): "Fëdor Mikhailovich Dostoevski, the Russian novelist, said one time [in the last chapter of *The Brothers Karamazov*] that, 'One sacred memory from childhood is perhaps the best education.' I can think of another quickie education for a child, which, in its way, is almost as salutary: Meeting a human being who is tremendously respected by the adult world, and realizing that that person is actually a malicious lunatic." Swain adds a footnote two paragraphs later: "I have an Encyclopaedia Britannica here in the lobby of the Empire State Building, which is the reason I am able to give Dostoevski his middle name" (p. 91).

22. Letter to me of July 2, 1975. Vonnegut was married September 1, 1945.
23. See Michael Wood's perceptive comments on *Mother Night* in this respect in his article "Dancing in the Dark," *New York Review of Books*, May 31, 1973, p. 23. Another brief but excellent treatment of *Mother Night* is Doris Lessing's "Vonnegut's Responsibility," *New York Times Book Review*, February 4, 1973, p. 34, which explores Vonnegut's recognition of mutual responsibility for holocausts—thereby calling to mind Father Zosima's ineluctable perception: "Vsiaki pred vsemi za vsekh vinovat [We are all responsible to all for all]."
24. This is not to say that Dostoevsky is utterly lacking in humor, of course; one immediately thinks of "Another Man's Wife or the Husband Under the Bed," "The Friend of the Family" ["Selo Stepanchikovo i ego obitateli"], "Crocodile," and *Notes from Underground*, for that matter. This list is hardly exhaustive.
25. See Modern Library edition of *The Brothers Karamazov*, p. 279. Ivan's statement on the same page that the new geometers "even dare to dream that two parallel lines, which according to Euclid can never meet on earth, may meet somewhere in infinity" is in fact only a restatement of the definition of parallel lines based on Euclid's fifth postulate. It is difficult to tell here whether Dostoevsky is trying to describe the proposition of Lobachevsky or Riemann (or both); I have arbitrarily selected the Russian mathematician as the basis for my remarks on non-Euclideanism. What is important here in any case is not Dostoevsky's mathematics but his intuition of a new kind of alienation appropriate to the twentieth century.
26. Other biographical parallels between the two writers are that both grew up in a secure, middle-class environment, Dostoevsky's father having been a doctor and Vonnegut's an architect; both were educated as engineers and served in the army; both spent time in a labor camp; and the mothers of both died when their sons were still young (Dostoevsky was fifteen, Vonnegut twenty-one).
27. Mentioned in conversation with me, December 26, 1974.

Kurt Vonnegut and the Soviet Union: An Annotated Bibliography

Note: Language of entries is Russian unless otherwise specified. This list is probably complete for Russian translations (through autumn of 1976), except that some printings of some of the stories and a few recent translations of stories were undoubtedly missed; information about translations into Soviet languages other than Russian is known to be incomplete, especially with regard to stories. Information on criticism in the Russian language is more or less complete as far as consultation of standard reference works (through the early months of 1976) is concerned. However, since information about a number of the items in this category was not obtained from standard indexes, this means that many more such articles (or references in books of criticism, theses, and the like) have been overlooked. For assistance in assembling this bibliography and obtaining copies of most items listed, the compiler is grateful to Raisa Rait-Kovalëva, Moscow; Yuri Kuznetsov, Leningrad; Ursula Põks and Valda Raud of Tallinn, Estonian SSR; George Kolodziej of Columbus, Ohio; Alvin Kapusta of Silver Springs, Md.; Jerome Klinkowitz of Cedar Falls, Iowa; Martin Tucker, editor of *P.E.N.-Newsletter*, New York; and Ruth Walter, Public Information Office, Voice of America, Washington, D.C.

I. TRANSLATIONS PUBLISHED IN THE SOVIET UNION

Player Piano (1952)

1. *Utopiia* 14, tr. M. Brukhnov. M: Molodaia gvardiia, 1967. 398 pp. With foreword by I. Bestuzhev-Lada (see entry 28). Title is that of Bantam edition of *Player Piano*, 1954: *Utopia* 14.

Slaughterhouse-Five (1969)

2. "Boinia nomer piat', ili Krestovyi pokhod detei," tr. R. Rait-Kovalëva. *Novyi Mir*, 3 (1970), 78–132, and 4 (1970), 148–178. With afterword by R. Orlova (see entry 45).
3. *Tapamaja, korpus viis, ekh Laste ristisõda*, tr. Valda Raud. Tallinn: Eesti Raamat, 1971. 165 pp. With translator's afterword (see entry 48). Estonian.
4. *Stranstviia Billi Piligrima (The Wanderings of Billy Pilgrim)*, play based on *Slaughterhouse-Five*, written by Mark Rozovsky and Yuli Mikhailov, with the assistance of the original translator, R. Rait-Kovalëva. Directed by Mikhail Levitin. Official premiere at Central Academic Theater of the Soviet Army, Moscow, on December 25, 1975.

Cat's Cradle (1963)

5. *Kolybel' dlia koshki*, tr. R. Rait-Kovalëva. M: Molodaia gvardiia, 1970. 211 pp. With afterword by V. Skorodenko (see entry 52).
6. *Kaka šūpulis*, tr. A. Bauga. Riga: Liesma, 1973. 225 pp. With translation of Skorodenko's afterword (see entry 5).

Welcome to the Monkey House (1968)

Collection of stories and short articles published between 1950 and 1968; includes all the stories published in an earlier collection, *Canary in a Cat House* (1961). These stories have not appeared in collected form in the Soviet Union, nor have all the stories in the collection been translated; they have appeared singly as follows:

Author's "Preface," *WMH* (Delacorte Press/Seymour Lawrence), pp. xiii-xv

7. "Kurt Vonnegut o sebe (predislovie k sborniku rasskazov) [Kurt Vonnegut on Himself (Foreword to a Collection of Stories)]," *Sovetskaia molodezh'* (Riga), January 1972; reprinted: *Prostor*, 5 (1972), 114–115. Tr. R. Rait-Kovalëva.

"Harrison Bergeron" (*WMH*, pp. 7–13)

8. "Garison Berzheron," *Nedelia*, 33 (16–22 VIII 1976), 10–11. Tr. M. Zagot.

"Who Am I This Time?" (*WMH*, pp. 14–26)

9. "Kem ia budu v ètot raz?" *Literaturnaia Rossiia* (4 I 1974), 22–23. Tr. M. Zagot.
10. "A kto my teper'?" *Rovesnik*, 6 (1974). Tr. M. N. Kovalëva.
"Long Walk to Forever" (*WMH*, pp. 46–52)
11. "Dolgaia progulka—navsegda," *Literaturnaia gazeta* (11 X 1972), 16. Tr. R. Rait-Kovalëva.
"The Foster Portfolio" (*WMH*, pp. 53–66)
12. "Nasledstvo Fostera," *Prostor*, 5 (1972), 115–120. Tr. R. Rait-Kovalëva.
"Miss Temptation," (*WMH*, pp. 67–79)
13. "Iskusitel'nitsa," *Prostor*, 5 (1972), 120–124; repr. under title "Soblazitel'nitsa," pp. 150–163 in collection *Gon spozaranku*. M: Progress, 1975. Tr. R. Rait-Kovalëva.
"Tom Edison's Shaggy Dog" (*WMH*, pp. 99–105)
14. "Lokhmatyi pës Toma Edisona," *Literaturnaia gazeta* (2 II 1972), 16. Tr. M. N. Kovalëva.
"D. P." (*WMH*, pp. 146–155)
15. "Peremeshchennoe litso [Displaced Person]," *Sem'ia i shkola*, 9 (1974), 52–55. Tr. È. Kravchuk.
"Report on the Barnhouse Effect" (*WMH*, pp. 156–170)
16. "Doklad ob èffekte Barnkhauza," *Znanie-sila*, 11 (1970); repr. in anthology *Fantasticheskie izobreteniia*. M: 1971. Information on translator lacking.
17. "Èffekt Barnkhauza," in anthology *Biblioteka fantastiki*. M: Molodaia gvardiia, 1973. Tr. M. N. Kovalëva.
"The Euphio Question" (*WMH*, pp. 171–186)
18. "Kak byt' s 'Èifi'," in anthology *Prakticheskoe izobretenie*. M: 1974. Information on translator lacking.
"The Lie" (*WMH*, pp. 215–228)
19. "Lozh'," in anthology *Segodnia i vchera*. M: Detskaia literatura, 1973. Tr. R. Rait-Kovalëva.
20. "Lozh'," pp. 135–149 in anthology *Gon spozaranku*. M: Progress, 1975. Tr. I. Gurova.
"Unready to Wear" (*WMH*, pp. 229–243)
21. "Liudi bez tel [People without Bodies]," *Literaturnaia Rossiia*, 13 (26 III 1976), 22–23. Tr. M. Zagot. With brief unsigned introductory note by translator (see entry 56).

"Epicac" (*WMH*, pp. 268–275)

22. "Liubov' i smert' Èpikaka [The Love and Death of Epicac]," *Literaturnaia gazeta* (1 I 1973), 13; reprinted in anthology *Biblioteka fantastiki*. M: Molodaia gvardiia, 1973. Tr. M. N. Kovalëva.

Breakfast of Champions (1973)

23. "Zavtrak dlia chempinov," tr. R. Rait-Kovalëva. *Literaturnaia gazeta* (1 I 1974), 15. Excerpt.
24. "Zavtrak dlia chempioov," tr. R. Rait-Kovalëva. *Inostrannaia literatura*, 1 (1975), 154–200, and 2 (1975), 148–209. With afterword by S. Vishnevsky (see entry 55).

God Bless You, Mr. Rosewater (1965)

25. "Da blagoslavit bog, mister Rouzuoter," tr. Irina Razumovskaia and Svetlana Samostrelova. *Avrora*, 3 and 4 (1976).

Happy Birthday, Wanda June (1970)

26. *Õnne sünni päevaks, Wanda June*, tr. Valda Raud. Tallinn: Loomingu, 1976. 91 pp. With foreword by translator (see entry 49). Estonian. Note: The play (same title) premiered in Tallinn Drama Theater, November 27, 1976, directed by Mikk Mikiver.

Slapstick (1976)

27. "Siuzhet dlia skazki s prizraniiami," tr. R. Rait-Kovalëva. *Literaturnaia gazeta*, 38 (22 IX 1976), 15. [Subject for a Tale with Apparitions]: translation of author's "Prologue" to *Slapstick*, the Russian equivalent of which is: *Balagan ili Konets odinochestvu*; includes unsigned note by translator (see entry 47).

II. CRITICISM PUBLISHED IN THE SOVIET UNION

28. Bestuzhev-Lada, I. "Kogda lishnim stanovitsia chelovechestvo [When Mankind Becomes Superfluous]," pp. 5–24 (foreword)

in trans. of *PP* (see entry 1). Sociopolitical commentary on novel and its portrayal of Western capitalism; author is historian and sociologist.

29. Borshchagovsky, Aleksandr. "Takie dela . . . [Such goings-on]," *Literaturnaia gazeta* (15 VII 1970), 13. Review of trans. of *SF*; *takie dela* is Russian version of "so it goes."
30. Chernichenko, Liudmila. Dissertation for candidate degree on American authors of "black humor" school, including Vonnegut. Moscow University, 1975. (Information incomplete.)
31. El'sberg, Iakov. "V bitve za cheloveka [In Battle for Man]," *Literaturnaia gazeta* (1 I 1972), 4. Compares *SF* with Viktor Astaf'ev's war novel *Pastukh i pastushka* [*Shepherd and Shepherdess*]; says V. is critical realist who objectively exhibits influence of socialist ideas and socialist realism.
32. ———. "Sovetskaia literatura i sovremennoe literaturnoe razvitie [Soviet Literature and Contemporary Literary Development]," *Znamia*, 5 (1973), 208–221. Discusses *SF* on pp. 220–221; essentially repeats earlier article.
33. Gerasimov, Genadii. "Vstrecha nad planetoi Zemlia: Dialog sovetskogo i amerikanskogo pisatelei—Chingiz Aitmatov, Kurt Vonnegut [A Meeting above the Planet Earth: A Dialogue between a Soviet and an American Writer . . .], *Literaturnaia gazeta* (23 VII 1975), 2. On occasion of Soyuz-Apollo linkup; V. affirms that there is no enmity between Russians and Americans; recalls meeting at Elbe River, 1945; warns against romanticizing war.
34. Gubko, N. "Antivoennyi roman Vonneguta [V.'s Antiwar Novel]," *Zvezda*, 6 (1971), 220–222. On *SF*, applies Tolstoy's standards of art, finds basic moral stance in V.; also on CC, notes certain similarities between V. and Gogol, Dostoevsky.
35. Haan, Kalju. "Dramateater alustab hooaega [The (Tallinn) Drama Theater Opens for the New Season]," *Sirp ja Vasar*, 36 (3 IX 1976). Mentions coming Estonian premiere of *HB* (see entry 26); refers to V. as "outstanding humorist of our time."
36. Ileshin, B. "Za politseiskimi bar' erami: Roman 'Boinia nomer piat' ' i amerikanskaia deistvitel'nost' [Behind the Police Bar-

riers: The Novel *Slaughterhouse-Five* and American reality],” *Izvestiia* (28 XI 1970). Brief review of *SF*.

37. Khmel'nitskaia, Tamara. “Slozhnyi put' k prosteishim istinam [A Complicated Path to the Simplest Truths],” *Novyi Mir*, 4 (1971), 245–250. On *CC*, places V. in tradition of Voltaire, Anatole France, Karel Čapek.
38. Kuz'menko, P. “A kto ubil Billi? [Who Really Killed Billy?],” *Moskovskii komsomolets* (8 II 1976). Brief review of dramatization of *SF* (see entry 4).
39. Maksimova, V. “Billi Piligrim puteshestvuet v proshloe [Billy Pilgrim Travels into the Past],” *Vecherniaia Moskva* (9/10 II 1976). Brief review of dramatization of *SF* (see entry 4).
40. Mendel'son, M. O. *Amerikanskaia satiricheskaia proza XX veka* [*American Satirical Prose of the Twentieth Century*]. M: Nauka, 1972. In a chapter devoted to “Kurt Vonnegut—mladshii [Jr.],” pp. 306–324, discusses *PP*, *CC*, *GB*, *MN*, *SF*. See also pp. 7, 23, 64, 73, 74, 284, 294, 325, 332, 344, 345, 359.
41. ———. “Dukhovnyi krizis burzhuaznogo obschchestva i khudozhestvennogo proza (Kriticheskii realizm v romane i novelle) [The Spiritual Crisis in Bourgeois Society and in Its Prose Fiction (Critical Realism in the Novel and Novella)],” Chapter III, pp. 96–182, in *Osnovnye tendentsii razvitiia sovremennoi literatury SShA* [*Basic Tendencies in the Development of Contemporary Literature in the U.S.A.*], ed. M. O. Mendel'son et al. M: Nauka, 1973. See pp. 151–153, on *SF*, with references to *CC* and *GB*. There are other brief references to V. in this anthology of articles, on pp. 20, 38, 39, 171, 181.
42. ———. “Kakim vidit mir Kurt Vonnegut? [How Does K. V. View the World?],” *SShA: Ekonomika, politika, ideologiia*, 12 (1974), 79–84. On *BC*.
43. ———. “Amerikanskii roman posle Khemingueia, Folknera, Steinbeka [The American Novel after Hemingway, Faulkner, Steinbeck],” *Novyi Mir*,. 8 (1975), 246–263. Praises *BC*, pp. 257–259, as satire on American avarice and greed.
44. *Moscow News*, 11 (1976). Has photograph by A. Okhmakevich

of scene from *The Wanderings of Billy Pilgrim* (see entry 4), with caption (in English) noting that play has attracted a good deal of attention; includes text of V.'s telegram (December 30, 1975) to cast of play.

45. Orlova, Raisa. "O romane Kurta Vonneguta [On K. V.'s Novel]," *Novyi Mir*, 4 (1970), 179–180. Afterword to trans. of *SF* (see entry 2).
46. Rait-Kovalëva, R. "Kanareika v shakhte [Canary in a (Coal) Mine]," *Rovesnik*, 1 (1974), 16–19. (Also translated into Estonian, pub. in journal *Noorte Hääl* [1974]; information incomplete.) Portrait of V. based on meeting with him in Paris, October 28, 1972, with the addition of some biographical material taken from *Vonnegut Statement* (1973), ed. J. Klinkowitz and J. Somer. Includes Russ. tr. of V.'s telegram to R. of October 11, 1972.
47. Rait-Kovalëva, R. Brief unsigned prefatory note to trans. of introd. to *Slapstick* (1976) in *Literaturnaia gazeta*, 38 (22 IX 1976), 15. (See entry 27.)
48. R[aud], V[alda]. "Saateks" (translator's afterword to Estonian tr. of *SF*, 1971), pp. 166–167. (See entry 3.)
49. ———. "Saateks" (translator's foreword to Estonian tr. of *HB*, 1976), pp. 5–8. (See entry 26.) Includes part of author's foreword as well.
50. Shperlin, K. A. "O zhanre romanov Kurta Vonneguta [On the Genre of K. V.'s Novels]," pp. 119–134, in *Problemy teorii romana i rasskaza: Sbornik nauchnykh statei aspirantov kafedry zarubezhnyx literatur Latviiskogo universiteta* [*Problems of the Theory of the Novel and the Short Story: A Collection of Investigative Articles by Graduate Students in the Department of Foreign Literatures, Latvian State University*]. Riga: Latviiskii gosudarstvennyi universitet im. Stuchki, 1972. On antiutopian aspects of *PP*, *CC*, and *SF*; sees V. in tradition of Jack London's *Iron Heel*, K. Čapek's *War with the Newts*, R. Bradbury's *Fahrenheit 451*, Isaac Asimov's *The End of Eternity;* and *Trudno byt' bogom* [*It Is Difficult to Be God*] by the brothers A. & B. Strugatsky.

51. Simukov, V. "Stranstviia Billi Piligrima," *Trud*, 58 (10 III 1976), 4. Brief review of play (very positive); see entry 4.

52. Skorodenko, V. "O bezumnom mire i pozitsii khudozhnika (Roman K. Vonnegata 'Kolybl' dlia koshki') [On the Insane World and the Position of the Artist (K. V.'s Novel *Cat's Cradle*)]," afterword, pp. 212–224 to tr. of *CC*, 1970. (See entry 5.) Very favorable discussion.

53. Task, Sergei. "K voprosu ob uslovno-metaforicheskoi forme b sovremennom romane SShA [On the Question of Conventional-Metaphorical Form in the U.S. Novel]," diploma thesis, Moscow University, 1974. (Have not seen this; includes discussion of V.)

54. Turovsky, V. "Liudi i teni [People and Shadows]," *Komsomol'skaia pravda* (6 II 1976), 2. Brief review of play (see entry 4).

55. Vishnevsky, S. "Kogda real 'nost' absurdna . . . [When Reality Is Absurd]," *Inostrannaia literatura*, 2 (1975), 209–213. Afterword to trans. of *BC* (see entry 24).

56. Zagot, M. Unsigned, untitled translator's note, 1976 (see entry 21). Notes similarity of V.'s story "Unready to Wear" to Jack London's *Star Rover*.

57. Zatonsky, D. V. *Iskusstvo romana i XX vek [The Art of the Novel and the Twentieth Century]*. M: Khudozhestvennaia literatura, 1973. Analysis of form and style in *SF*, in chapter titled "Ideia i vremia [Idea and Time]," pp. 407–437. See also pp. 7, 413–419, 421–422, 441.

58. Zverev, A. "*De profundis* Kurta Vonneguta [K. V.'s *De Profundis*]," *Inostrannaia literatura*, 8 (1970), 265–268. Review of trans. of *SF*.

59. ———. "Skazki tekhnicheskogo veka [Tales of the Technological Age]," *Voprosy literatury*, 2 (1975), 32–66. Detailed, insightful discussion of *PP*, *CC*, *SF*, *GB*; also mentions *BC*.

III. ARTICLES IN ENGLISH AND MISCELLANEOUS ITEMS

60. Anon. "Writers, Vonnegut and the USSR." *American P.E.N.-Newsletter* (November 17, 1974), 1–2. Includes report of V. on trip to USSR, October 1974, and letter of V. to Nikolai D. Fedorenko, editor of *Inostrannaia literatura*, suggesting that a scholarship fund be established, the money coming from unclaimed royalty money in rubles of American authors, to enable young American writers of modest means to travel to the Soviet Union.
61. Cook, Bruce. "When Kurt Vonnegut Talks—And He Does—The Young All Tune In," *National Observer* (October 12, 1970), 21. Reports on press conference given by V. for sixty student editors in New York City area. The only item relevant to this bibliography is the following exchange: "Do you read?" "Yes. I think the greatest living writer is Solzhenitsyn."
62. Shipler, David K. "Vonnegut's 'Slaughterhouse-Five' Staged in Moscow," *New York Times* (January 13, 1976). Reviews play (see entry 4); includes text of telegram sent by V. to cast of play ca. December 30, 1975, and quotes brief interview with V. on subject of play and his Russian translator, Raisa Rait-Kovalëva.
63. Vinograde, Ann C. "A Soviet Translation of *Slaughterhouse-Five*," *Russian Language Journal*, XXVI, 93 (Winter 1972), 14–18. On discrepancies between translation and original text.
64. Vonnegut, Kurt. "Invite Rita Rait to America!" *New York Times Book Review*, January 28, 1973, p. 47; reprinted: pp. 221–224 in *Wampeters, Foma & Granfalloons*. New York: Delacorte Press/Seymour Lawrence, 1974. Brief biographical sketch of Raisa Rait-Kovalëva; defends her as a translator; does not mention that she translated his own books.
65. ———. Interview broadcast in Russian over Voice of America Radio in two installments, January 22 and 28, 1976, about 25 min. altogether. Tape may be listened to only at VOA archives

in Washington, D.C. The first installment is biographical; the second deals with V.'s new book (*Slapstick*), his two trips to the Soviet Union, his association with Mme. Rait-Kovalëva, his belief that there should be more American-Soviet literary exchanges; discusses American and Soviet dissident writers, including himself (in that context) and Solzhenitsyn.

Note: For other items containing original material by Vonnegut, see entries 33, 44, 46, 60, 61, 62.

Contributors

JEROME KLINKOWITZ is Professor of English at the University of Northern Iowa in Cedar Falls, Iowa, where he also works nightly as a rock and jazz musician. He is the author of *Literary Disruptions* and *The Life of Fiction*, co-author of *The Vonnegut Statement*, compiler of bibliographies of Donald Barthelme and Kurt Vonnegut, and co-editor of *Innovative Fiction*. His essays have appeared in *The New Republic, The Village Voice, Partisan Review*, and elsewhere in the United States, Europe, and Australia.

DONALD L. LAWLER is Associate Professor of English at East Carolina University. He has published extensively on Oscar Wilde and other Victorian writers, and recently completed a critical edition of *The Picture of Dorian Gray*. He has also edited *Approaches to Science Fiction*, and is an active scholar in the area of science fiction and modern fantasy.

WILLIS E. MCNELLY of California State University—Fullerton has been a pioneer in science-fiction studies, having authored *Above the Human Landscape* and *Science Fiction: The Academic Awakening* (College English Association).

WILLIAM VEEDER, Associate Professor of English at the University of Chicago, is the author of books on William Butler Yeats and Henry James.

CONRAD FESTA teaches both Victorian and contemporary literature at Old Dominion University in Virginia. His previous publications include studies of Christina Rossetti and Gerard Manley Hopkins.

PETER REED published the first book-length study of Kurt Vonnegut in 1972. Originally from England (where he served in the Royal Air Force), he now lives and teaches in Minneapolis.

DONALD M. FIENE teaches Russian literature at the University of Tennessee, and has written extensively on Solzhenitsyn and other literary figures. In 1977 he was appointed literary executor for Kurt Vonnegut.

Index

Abádi-Nagy, Zoltán, x
Above the Human Landscape, 191
Absent Without Leave, 29
Alcoholics Anonymous, 171, 179
Aldington, John, 257
Aldiss, Brian, 88, 90–91, 93, 95, 192–193, 214
Allen, Fred, 9–10
Allen, Woody, 91
Amalrik, Andrei, 266
"Ambitious Sophomore," 59
America, 92
American Physical Society, 23
Analog, 208
Anouilh, Jean, 257
Anthropology, 4–5, 13, 30, 55, 189
"Any Reasonable Offer," 55
Apollo XI, 21, 27
Appel, Alfred, Jr., 118
Argosy, 18, 58
Arnold, Matthew, 194
As I Lay Dying, 198
Asimov, Isaac, 88, 93–94
Astounding, 208
Atlas, Charles, 269
Auschwitz, 144–145
Avon Books, 25

"Bagombo Snuff Box," 57
Ballard, J. G., 63
Bantam Books, 4, 20
Barry, Fred, 8
Barth, John, 22, 63, 213–214
Barthelme, Donald, 22, 63, 211, 214

Battle of the Bulge, 3, 12
Beatles, 162
Beckett, Samuel, 98
Benny, Jack, 9–10
Berlin, Isaiah, 271
Bestuzhev-Lada, 268
Better Homes & Gardens, 205
Between Time and Timbuktu, 5, 9, 150, 156, 200, 209
"Biafra: A People Betrayed," 5, 176
The Big Trip Up Yonder," 20
Billion Year Spree, 88, 90
Blake, William, 138, 196
Boaz, 68
Bob & Ray (Bob Elliott and Ray Goulding), 10, 272
Bokonon, 31, 90, 143, 194, 196, 258–259, 261, 269–270, 278
Böll, Heinrich, 29, 260
Booth, Wayne, 128, 197
Borges, Jorge Luis, 257
Borshchagovsky, Aleksandr, 265
Bourjaily, Vance, 25
"The Boy Who Hated Girls," 59
Boyd, John, 193
Bradbury, Ray, 88, 93–95, 193
Brautigan, Richard, 63
Brave New World, 271
Breakfast of Champions, 5, 8–9, 16, 56, 77, 90, 92, 95, 136, 147, 150–169, 170, 184–185, 200–205, 262, 264–265, 271, 273
Breton, André, 63–64
"Brief Encounters on the Inland Waterway," 155
Brontë, Charlotte, 97
The Brothers Karamazov, 92, 273, 275–277
Bryan, C. D. B., 142
Bryant, Jerry H., 138–139
Bunyan, John, 129
Burger, Knox, 16, 19
Burgess, Anthony, 6
Campbell, John W., 191–192, 205, 208
Campbell, Howard W., Jr. 92, 95, 99–132, 143, 198–200, 204–205, 208
Canary in a Cat House, 17, 19, 26, 257
Candide, 84
Cape Cod, 4, 17, 18, 25, 27–28, 33, 57, 60
Čapek, Karel, 272
Carnegie Institute of Technology, 3, 12
Cassill, R. Verlin, 25
The Catcher in the Rye, 260
Cat's Cradle, xii, 5, 20, 24–25, 31, 53, 58, 90, 94–95, 143, 170, 178, 185, 196, 257, 258–263, 269–270, 277–278
CBS News, 21
Céline, Louis Ferdinand, 272
Chaplin, Charlie, 9, 91
Chaucer, Geoffrey, 129
Chicago, 4, 14, 24
Chrono, 68, 74, 80
City University of New York, 6
Clarke, Arthur C., 88, 93–95, 193
Coleridge, Samuel Taylor, 180
Collier's, 4, 14, 16–20, 53–55, 57, 187
A *Connecticut Yankee in King Arthur's Court*, 84
Conrad, Joseph, 21, 272
Constant, Malachi, 68–70, 74, 78–80, 92, 139, 271
Cordiner, Cordelia Swain, 180
Cornell *Sun*, 3, 12, 22
Cornell University, 3, 9, 11–12, 14, 16, 22
Cosmopolitan, 14, 56–59
Costa, Tony, 29
Cox, Jane Marie, 4, 13, 273
"The Critic as Artist," 212

Critique, 211
Cronkite, Walter, xi
Cubism, 14
"Custom-Made Bride," 56
Czechoslovakia, 256–257

Darwin, Charles, 175
Delacorte Press, 5–6, 54
Delaney, Samuel, 191, 214
Dell Publishing Co., 20, 25
Denmark, 257
The Depression, 8–11, 30, 58, 267
De Quincey, Thomas, 91
Derby, Edgar, 143–144
Dick, Philip K., 63, 93–94, 193
Dickens, Charles, 52
Dostoevsky, Feodor, 92, 270–278
Doubleday & Co., 4
"Dream of a Queer Fellow," 271
Dresden, 3–4, 9, 13, 24–26, 28–30, 92–93, 144–145, 151, 185, 203–204

"East Coker," 93, 193
Easy Aces, 9
The Eden Express, 5
Eichmann, Adolf, 119, 204
Einstein, Albert, 275
Eliot, T. S., 93, 193
Ellison, Harlan, 89, 191, 214
El'sberg, Iakov, 263
England, x, 255–257
Ernst, Max, 211
Esquire, 26, 189
Estonia, 263
Euclid, 275
"The Euphio Question," 20, 134
Expressionism, 62–63

The Fabulators, 25
Family Week, 20
Fantasy and Science Fiction, 205
Farlowe, Jean, 116–117
Faulkner, William, 198, 257, 260
Fiedler, Leslie, 152–153
"Find Me a Dream," 59
Finnegans Wake, 214
Finnerty, Ed, 170, 203
Fisher, John, 18
Fisher, Josephine, 18
Fitzgerald, F. Scott, 272
"Fluctuations Between Good and Evil in Simple Tales," 14, 55, 189
Fowles, John, 154
France, x
French New Novel, 154
Frye, Northrop, 135

Galaxy Science Fiction, 20
Galsworthy, John, 260
General Electric Corporation, 4, 15–16, 18–21, 28, 54, 57, 89, 151, 170, 203
Germany, x, 256
Gernsback, Hugo, 70
Gershwin, George, xi
Ghost Dance Society, 14
Giraudoux, Jean, 257
God Bless You, Mr. Rosewater, 5, 23–24, 31, 77, 87–88, 95, 170, 185, 189, 192, 262, 264, 268, 271
Goethe, Johann Wolfgang von, 97–98, 110, 114, 129
Gogol, Nikolai, 268, 270
Goldberg, Rube, 78
Golding, William, 183
Gorky, Maxim, 271–272
Greene, Graham, 260
Gubko, N., 270
Guggenheim Fellowship, 5
Gulliver's Travels, 84, 139, 194–196

Hagstrohm, Edgar Rice Burroughs, 179
"Hal Irwin's Magic Lamp," 58

Happy Birthday, Wanda June, 5, 32, 150–153, 200, 209–210, 262–263, 277
Hardy, Thomas, 142–143
Harper & Row, 26
Harris, Charles B., 138
"Harrison Bergeron," 78, 134
Harvard University, 5
Hassan, Ihab, 211
Hawthorne, Nathaniel, 52
Heinlein, Robert, 89, 93–94, 191–192
Helmholtz, George, 59
"Helter Skelter," 162
Hemingway, Ernest, xi, 202, 209, 260
Hiroshima, 13, 275
Hitler, Adolf, 98, 110, 267, 277
Hoenikker, Angela, 170
Hoenikker, Frank, 170
Hoenikker, Newton, 170
Holt, Rinehart & Winston, 20, 26
Hong Kong, 256
Hoobler, Wayne, 166
Hoover, Bunny, 159
Hoover, Dwayne, 157–163, 166–167, 200, 203, 264
Hopefield School, 4
Hopkins, Gerard Manley, 110
Horace, 148
Huffman, Julie, x
Humbert, Humbert, 99–130
Hungary, x, 256–257
Hurty, Phoebe, 9
Hyannis, MA, 28, 189
"The Hyannis Port Story," 188–189

Indianapolis, 3, 8–9, 11, 28, 33, 171, 175
"Invite Rita Rait to America!", 261
Iowa City, 24–25, 29
Italy, x, 256–257
Iwamoto, Iwao, 151

James, Henry, 197
Japan, 256
Jefferson, Thomas, 168
Jesus Christ, 181, 277
Job, 166
John/Jonah, 170, 277
Johnson, Samuel, 77, 89
Jonathan Cape, 257
Joyce, James, 9, 191, 213, 214
Juvenal, 136

Kafka, Franz, 63, 260
Karabekian, Rabo, 158, 162–166, 168
Kazin, Alfred, 142
Keaton, Buster, 9
Keats, John, 142
Kennedy family, 28, 59, 189
Kennedy, Joseph, 60
Kesey, Ken, 257
Kidder, Harvey, 60
Kiev, 272
King, Martin Luther, 144–145
Klinkowitz, Elaine, x
Knight, Damon, 88, 192
Korean War, 54
Kosinski, Jerzy, 63
Kovalëva, Margarita, 262
Kraft, George, 111–113, 197
Krementz, Jill, x
Kutnik, Jerzy, x, 256

Ladies' Home Journal, 18, 53
Lasher, James J., 31
Latvia, 262–263
Laurel & Hardy, 9, 11, 171, 181, 184, 272
Lawrence, Seymour, 5–6
Lefkowitz, Alan, 213
Leningrad, 263, 272
Le Vot, André, x,
Lewis, C. S., 213
Lewis, Sinclair, 260
Life, 15, 26

The Life of Fiction, 212
Literary Disruptions, 187
Littauer, Kenneth, 16, 19
Lobachevsky, Nikolai, 275
Lolita, 97–132
Lord of the Flies, 183
"Lovers Anonymous," 59
"Lower Depths," 271

McCabe, Earl, 31, 196
McGovern, George, 176
Macmillan, 4, 255
Maharishi Mahesh Yogi, 27
Malamud, Bernard, 257
Manicheanism, 207–208
Manson, Charles, 162, 176, 178
The Marriage of Heaven and Hell, 196
Masters, Edgar Lee, 272
Mayakovsky, Vladimir, 260
Meeter, Glenn, 140
Mencken, H. L, 272
Mendel'son, M. O., 264–265
Menippus, 135, 144, 147
Milford, PA, 87, 192
Miller, Mary Alice, 164
Mishima, Yukio, 257
Modern Times, 91
"A Modest Proposal," 195
Morgan, Henry, 9–10
Moscow, 256, 259, 261, 266, 272
Moscow University, 256, 259
Mother Night, 4–5, 17, 19, 25–26, 33, 95, 97–132, 146, 185, 195–200, 256, 257, 263, 267–268, 274
Murdoch, Iris, 165
Murmansk, 260
Mussolini, Benito, 267
Mylett, Andrew, x

Nabokov, Vladimir, 97–132, 197
Napoleon III, 22
National Educational Television, 5
National Institute of Arts and Letters, 5
New Journalism, 27
New York, 5, 21, 166, 178
New Yorker, 55, 189
New York Review of Books, 265
New York Times, 30, 261
New York Times Book Review, 26–27
New York Times Magazine, 19, 26
New Wave Science Fiction, 214
"A Night for Love," 57
Nixon, Richard, 27, 177
"The No-Talent Kid," 59
"Notes from Underground," 274
Noth, Helga, 99, 107–110
Noth, Resi, 99, 111–113, 197
Now It Can Be Told, 161–164, 200

O'Connor, Flannery, 98, 110
O'Hara, John, 272
Olderman, Raymond, 135
Orwell, George, 271–272
Out of the Silent Planet, 213

"The Package," 57
Paracriticisms, 212
Paris, 22, 256
Partridge, Eric, 81
Pasternak, Boris, 260
Pavlov, Ivan, 260
Pearl Harbor, 144
P.G.N. American Center, 5, 266–267
Penelope, 150, 209
Pieratt, Asa, x, 255
Pilgrim, Billy, 30, 140–141, 145, 158, 271, 273
Playboy, 11, 17, 88–90, 175–176, 179, 181, 184, 190, 196, 205, 208
Player Piano, 4–5, 15, 20–21, 26, 31, 57, 66, 95, 134, 147, 169–170, 173–174, 176, 179, 185, 203, 207, 212, 255–256, 260, 268, 270–271

Players, 209
Poland, x, 256–257
"Poor Little Rich Town," 57
Portnoy's Complaint, 195
"The Powder Blue Dragon," 57
"A Present for Big Nick," 58–59
Proteus, Anita, 173–174
Proteus, Paul, 170, 173–174, 203
Provincetown, MA, 4
Puetz, Manfred, x
Pynchon, Thomas, 22, 63

Rackstraw, Loree, x
Rait-Kovalëva, Raisa (Rita Rait), 260–263
The Random House Dictionary, 27
Raud, Valda V., 262
Ray, John, Jr., 100–102
Razumovskaia, Irina, 262
Reasoner, Harry, 22
Redbook, 18, 59
Reed, Peter, 134
The Relatives, 175
Remarque, Erich Maria, 257
"Report on the Barnhouse Effect," 4, 16, 134
The Return of the Native, 143
Richardson, Jack, 265
The Rime of the Ancient Mariner, 180
Robbe-Grillet, Alain, 98
Rockwell, Norman, xi–xii, 60
Rogers, Buck, 192
Rosewater, Eliot, 30, 87, 92, 140, 192, 204, 270–271, 273
Roth, Philip, 195, 257
Rumfoord, Beatrice, 68–70, 79–80
Rumfoord, Winston Niles, 67, 69–70, 78–80, 139, 191, 276, 278
"Runaways," 59
Russia, 256–293
The Russians, 272

Saab automobiles, 17
Salinger, J. D., 260
Salo, 68, 74, 80, 190
Samostrelova, Svetlana, 262
Santa Claus, 58–59
Sarraute, Nathalie, 260
Saturday Evening Post, xiii, 14, 16–20, 53, 56–57, 59–60, 187–188
Schenectady, 4, 15–16, 21, 57, 151, 170, 203, 256
Scholes, Robert, 10, 25, 89, 93, 95, 136, 141, 145, 193
Schorer, Mark, 98
Science Fiction Book Club, 4
Science Fiction: The Academic Awakening, 191
"Science Fiction: The Modern Mythology," 92
Science Fiction Writers Association, 88, 191–192
Scribner's, 4, 16, 255
Sewell, Amos, 60
Shakespeare, William, 21, 70, 90–91, 97, 110, 198
Sheed, Wilfrid, 11
Shenker, Israel, 23
Shipler, David, 261
Shklovsky, Viktor, 271
Shortridge *Echo*, 3, 12, 22
Shortridge High School, 3, 22
Shriver, Sargent, 131, 176
Silverberg, Robert, 193, 214
The Sirens of Titan, 4, 17, 19–20, 61–86, 95, 131, 134, 170, 89–191, 199, 202, 206–207, 211–213, 256, 257, 259, 263, 271, 276
Skordenko, V., 269
Slapstick, 6, 10, 32, 77, 150–152, 169–185, 262, 272–273
Slaughterhouse-Five, xii, 5, 14, 24–25, 29–30, 53, 59, 70, 73, 77, 88, 90–91, 93, 95, 143–147, 150–156, 164, 167, 170, 184–185, 188–189, 192–193,

196, 200–203, 208, 257, 258–262, 265–268, 273
Sleeper, 91
Smith, Cordwainer, 63
Smith, E. E. "Doc," 94
Smith, Hedrick, 272
Solzhenitsyn, Alexander, 266
Somer, John, x, 140
Soviet Union, 256–293
Stalin, Joseph, 267
Starr, Harrison, 145
Starr, Ringo, 91
Stevenson, Robert Louis, 16, 272
Stewart, Samuel, 20
Stoopnagel & Bud, 9
Stranstviia Billi Piligrima, 259
Strindberg, August, 63
Structural Fabulation, 89
Sturgeon, Theodore, 92, 94
Summary, 257
Surrealism, 61–64, 74–75, 77, 81–82
Swain, Eliza, 172–175, 180, 182
Swain, Sophie Rothschild, 177
Swain, Wilbur, 172–178, 180–184
Swarthmore College, 273
Sweden, 267
Swift, Jonathan, 73, 84, 136–137, 139, 146, 191, 194–196

Tallinn Drama Theatre, 263
Taoism, 207–208
"Thanasphere," 54–55
"This Son of Mine . . .", 59
Thompson, Hunter S., 27
Todd, Richard, 19
Tolstoy, L. N., 271
Tovstonogov, G., 263
Tralfamadore, 65, 67–70, 73, 78, 80, 82, 90, 93, 96, 141, 144, 191, 193, 196, 271, 276
Trilling, Lionel, 107
Trout, Kilgore, 19–20, 31, 92, 94, 96, 140, 157–158, 160–163, 166–167, 169, 176, 193, 200, 203, 264
Twain, Mark, xi, 9, 21, 73, 84, 191, 260, 272

Ulysses, 129
University of Chicago, 4–5, 13, 55, 189
University of Iowa Writers Workshop, 5, 10, 17, 23–24
University of Michigan, 29
University of Tennessee, 3, 12
Uniwersytet Marii Curie-Skłowskiej, 256
"Unpaid Consultant," 56
"Unready to Wear," 20
Upstairs and Downstairs, 8
Utopia-14, 4, 20

Venture: Traveller's World, 19, 28, 59
Venus on the Half-Shell, 140
Victorian Institute Journal, 194
Vietnam, 24, 261, 265
Villavicencio, Carlos Daffodil-11, 177
Vishnevsky, S., 271
Voice of America, 77, 266
Voltaire, 84, 191
Von Peterswald, Melody Oriole-2, 180, 183
Vonnegut, Alex, 171–172, 179
Vonnegut, Alice, 3–4, 171–172, 175
Vonnegut, Bernard, x, 3, 9, 15, 171, 175
Vonnegut, Edith Lieber, 3, 8, 12, 175
Vonnegut, Jane C., 4, 13, 273
Vonnegut, Kurt, Sr., 3–4, 8–9, 11, 175
Vonnegut, Mark, 5–6
Vonnegut, Zachary, 6
The Vonnegut Statement, 10, 187

Wakefield, Dan, 27
Wampeters, Foma & Granfalloons, xii, 6, 23, 26, 66, 131, 150–153, 155–156, 176, 179, 181, 184, 200, 267, 271, 277
War and Peace, 271
Watt, Ian, 211
We, 271
Weinstein, Sharon, 141–142
"Welcome to the Monkey House," 134
Welcome to the Monkey House, 5, 17, 25, 54, 262
Wells, H. G., 21, 272
West Barnstable, MA, 4, 28, 33, 57, 205
West Palm Beach, FL, 28, 59
West Virginia, 166
Western Printing Co., 20
Wilde, Oscar, 212
Wilkinson, Max, 16, 19
Wirtanen, Frank, 28, 60
Wolfe, Tom, 27
Worlds of If, 19

Yeats, William Butler, 191, 197
"Yes, We Have No Nirvanas," 27

Zappa, Vera Chipmunk-5, 178, 181, 183
Zamiatin, Eugene, 271
Zverev, A., 268–270